To David
all our love
Catriona and Kirsteen xxx

(If)

THE BLACK CLOUD

I. D. S. Thomson

D1470675

THE ERNEST PRESS

Published by The Ernest Press 1993
© Copyright I. D. S. Thomson
Typeset by EMS Phototypesetting, Berwick upon Tweed
Printed by St. Edmundsbury Press

A CIPP catalogue record for this book is available from the British Library

ISBN 0-948153-20-2

Acknowledgements

I wish to thank Faber and Faber Ltd for permission to quote from the *Four Quartets* of T. S. Eliot.

The publishers would like to acknowledge the editorial work and supervision of production by Mrs Margot Blyth.

CONTENTS

Time and the bell have buried the day,
The black cloud carries the sun away.

T. S. Eliot: Burnt Norton.

Introduction

This book had its origin at New Year 1989 when my father produced an envelope of newspaper cuttings which had belonged to my late grandfather. They contained accounts of three Cairngorm misadventures of sixty years or so before in the days when such events were sufficiently rare to inspire extensive coverage in the national press. With two of them, there was sufficient material to provide the basis for magazine articles. I approached *The Scots Magazine* with a proposal to produce a piece on one of them, the other having already been the subject of an article in the same magazine some ten years previously.

As I worked with the material which, initially, had seemed more than adequate, there arose questions which could not be answered from the press cuttings or from personal knowledge of the area or from a reasoned interpretation of the evidence. As a way of trying to resolve these problems, but without great hope of success, I wrote a letter to the editor of *The Strathspey Herald* and its publication produced replies from several people with knowledge of the event who were willing to assist. A surprising amount of interesting information came to light and I finished with much more material than I had expected; indeed, far more than could be included in the magazine article. Contact with these correspondents, some of whom I met, expanded the investigation of the accident and suggested that it might be possible to write a book on selected mountain misadventures, based on published material, other extant records and the recollections of witnesses of the events. In this way, a comprehensive account of each incident could be given, which would be as near the truth as it is now possible to reach. It was to be a venture that would absorb much of my free time during the next three years, no little proportion of that time being devoted to the writing of over 600 letters of enquiry whose total length significantly exceeded the length of the book which resulted.

The first stage was to identify those misadventures which would lend themselves to a detailed examination and this was done by sifting through all the reported mountain accidents. The principal source was the Scottish Mountaineering Club Journal (S.M.C.J.) whose sections on mountain accidents are easily located. In the earlier years, there were relatively few reported accidents and this made the task of selection fairly easy, but the number began increasing significantly in the mid 1950s. Inevitably, the vast majority were rejected as being either of minor interest or lacking in available documentation – an essential basis for any detailed investigation. The original manuscript covered eight incidents, but its length required one, the death of Alexander Lawson Henderson on Beinn Achaladair in 1925, to be omitted from this book, moving the starting date to 1928. The three week search for Henderson was made notable by a series of six letters emanating from Boddam, near Peterhead, and purporting to provide information obtained by a medium identifying the exact location of Henderson's body. Not only did the chapter show that this location was 3km distant from the place where the body actually lay, it also cast considerable doubt on the existence of the 'supernatural agency' from which the information was supposed to have come. A decision had to be made on how close to the present day this study of mountain accidents could be brought without injuring the feelings of those who, as survivors, relatives or friends, were involved in the accidents. Thirty years seemed a reasonable space of time and the book would have terminated in 1959 with the loss of five men near Glen Doll, but a letter to Iain Ogilvie, who gave his willing co-operation to a request to include what he called his 'escapade' on An Teallach, allowed the terminal date to be brought forward to 1966.

There is a striking gap in the middle of this span of 38 years: there were no incidents worthy of inclusion between early May 1934 and late December 1951. There are two main reasons for this. Firstly, the six years of World War Two curtailed mountaineering activity in the United Kingdom so that mountain accidents were relatively rare. Secondly, the chief source of information about such accidents was, and often still is, the press. The severe wartime restrictions on newsprint, restrictions which continued into the post-war period, allowed scope for only brief reports on most of the items which were considered newsworthy – and few mountain accidents even fell into the newsworthy category. Three incidents in this period might have supplied material for chapters, one in late November 1945, the second in early March 1946 and the third in July 1946. In the first a nineteen-year-old student from London, Trevor Craine, on holiday on his own in Kinlochleven, went missing for three days, necessitating a large search which eventually located his body near the top of a gully close to the Chancellor Buttress on the Aonach Eagach in Glen Coe. The third concerned a Captain A. J. Maryon, an accountant from Kent, who left the Sligachan

Hotel in Skye to walk in the Cuillin Hills but without leaving word of where he was going. He failed to return to the hotel and an extensive search over three weeks, involving holiday visitors as well as local people, failed to find him. It was not until almost two years later that his skeleton was found in the hills near Loch Coruisk.

It was hoped that the second of these immediately post-war incidents would provide sufficient material for a chapter since the central character was one of the most famous of all mountain explorers, Major H. W. Tilman. As he was descending from the Carn Mor Dearg arête on Ben Nevis towards the C.I.C. Hut where he was staying with some friends, he slipped on ice and slid into Coire Leis. He sustained damage to a leg and an arm but, with characteristic toughness, adamantly refused to evacuate himself to Fort William for treatment on the grounds that the injuries would mend themselves just as well, if not better, where he was. He stuck it out for a week with Donald Duff, the surgeon at Belford Hospital, keeping in distant contact with him. Ultimately, however, he was forced to admit defeat and, somewhat to his embarrassment, a party of A.T.C. cadets from Fort William Secondary School, accompanied by Lord Malcolm Douglas-Hamilton, A.T.C. Commandant for Scotland, made their way to the hut and brought the great man back on a sledge stretcher. It was not an episode of which Tilman was proud and it seems that he made an attempt to conceal his identity from the press, altogether without success, *The Scottish Daily Express* even having the temerity to publish a photograph of Tilman on board the stretcher.

As an amusing postscript to this story, Tilman's niece, Mrs Pamela Davis, recalls her uncle's return after the accident. She says:

I well remember the accident and him coming home to my mother's house in Wallasey. What does stick in my mind about the incident is that my uncle was sent to a specialist in Liverpool in order to have his injured arm attended to. My husband, who was home on leave, drove him there and sat in the waiting room. He became aware of voices getting ever louder in the doctor's sanctum and then the door sprang open and out strode my uncle looking very cross. The specialist went up to my husband and, in an aside, hissed: 'When you take him home drive him to the tunnel by such and such a road. It has cobble stones on it and it will make him jump.' When they were ensconced in the car, my husband enquired what was the matter. 'Stupid fool, that doctor,' replied my uncle. 'If he thinks I am going to wear an aeroplane splint and have my arm waving above my head, he has another think coming.' My husband knew better than to argue, and home they came. The arm rested casually in an ordinary sling for a short time, and was as good as new remarkably quickly.

Another obvious feature of the book is that, although two of the seven misadventures involved people from England, all took place in Scotland. In part this is because Scotland has a much larger area of mountainous country with mountains of considerably greater height than in the other parts of the United Kingdom and a mountain climate which in winter can be polar. Consequently, it has accidents which are both more numerous and more serious and which confront the rescue parties with greater difficulties than elsewhere in the country. Also, living as I do in Scotland, the resources for the Scottish misadventures are fairly readily available, a situation not replicated with accidents occurring outside Scotland.

The main resources used in writing the book were reports in the press and in certain mountaineering club journals, weather charts and other weather data for the period of each of the accidents, Ordnance Survey and Bartholemew maps of the relevant areas and dates, a number of books and magazines, six personal diaries, death certificates and their corrected entries, and the recollections of people who were participants in the events. The newspapers found to be of greatest general value were the *Aberdeen Press and Journal*, *The Courier and Advertiser*, *The Glasgow Herald*, *The Scotsman* and *The Scottish Daily Express*, with somewhat less reference to *The Scottish Daily Mail*, *The Daily Record*, *The Times*, the *Glasgow Evening News*, *The Sunday Post* and the *People's Journal*. *The Strathspey Herald*, the *Forres, Elgin and Nairn Gazette*, *The Northern Scot and Moray and Nairn Express* and the *Badenoch Record* were especially useful for information about the Cairngorm accidents, while the *Glasgow Observer and Scottish Catholic Herald* and the *Glasgow Weekly Herald* supplied much information on a specific misadventure and *The Oban Times* provided details on two.

The mountaineering club journals consulted were those of the Scottish Mountaineering Club (S.M.C.), the Cairngorm Club, the Climbers' Club, the Rucksack Club and the Manchester University Mountaineering Club. Considerable assistance was provided by the following books, magazines and journals: the S.M.C. District Guides to *The Cairngorms* by Adam Watson, *The Central Highlands* by Campbell R. Steven, *The Northern Highlands* by Tom Strang and *The Southern Highlands* by Donald Bennet; *High Altitude Medicine and Physiology* by Michael P. Ward, James S. Milledge and John B. West; *Hypothermia and Cold Stress* by Evan L. Lloyd; *Mountaincraft and Leadership* by Eric Langmuir; *Scotland's Winter Mountains* by Martin Moran; *The Charm of the Hills* by Seton Gordon; *Let's Go Climbing!* by Colin F. Kirkus; *Welsh Rock* by Trevor Jones and Geoff Milburn; *High Drama* by Hamish MacInnes; *The Scots Magazine; Climber and Hillwalker; Mountaineering Journal; Nature;* and the *Glasgow University Magazine.*

Press coverage of all the misadventures in this book, with the exception of the An Teallach accident of 1966, was extensive and comprehensive. In contrast, the accident reports in the mountaineering club journals tended to confine themselves to the essential facts as they had them, with some comment on the reasons for the accidents and the lessons these might have for other hill-walkers and climbers. There are well-known dangers in being overly dependent on newspapers for information as their reports can be erroneous, selective and distorted and there is always the risk that events are being sensationalised. Nevertheless, with careful handling and an awareness of the limitations of the press as purveyors of reliable information, the newspapers, especially the more responsible ones, are of much value. The overall impression is that reporters made commendable efforts to be accurate in circumstances where accuracy was not always easy. In the earlier incidents in particular, they were sometimes to be numbered among the searchers themselves and when this was not the case the newspapers might include an extended interview with, or a written account from, one of those who had been present in the search.

Another noticeable feature of the press reporting is that it was, in general, sympathetic towards the victims of the tragedies, with little adverse comment directed at them. Indeed, more in the way of such criticism came from the police and from the mountaineering club journals who saw it as part of their responsibility to point to mistakes as a way of warning others against repeating them. The attentions of the press were, quite understandably, often unwelcome to the survivors of these misadventures and to the relatives and friends of those who succumbed; and there is evidence of some intrusion of privacy in the post-war reporting. However, it was only through the media's extensive coverage of accidents that there developed public awareness of the dangers which could face even experienced people in the hills. It is probable that in this way the publicity saved lives.

The reports in both the press and the mountaineering club journals have the great advantage of being recorded at the time or shortly afterwards and are fixed in the immutable medium of print. This observation applies to the other sources employed in researching the details of the misadventures with the minor exception of one or two books and magazines and the major exception of most of the personal recollections of those involved in the incidents. If information gleaned from the pages of the press has to be treated with some caution, even scepticism at times, personal memories of events which took place thirty years and more ago, no matter how conscientiously recalled, are more requiring of care. There are various reasons for this. It may be that the memory has become vague without the person realising this and details may be added or changed quite convincingly without any factual basis for them. Assumptions may be made or misconceptions formed at the time of the incident which are later recalled as established facts; in addition, few people, if any, have a complete picture of events and what at the time is a mere impression or information received second-hand later becomes a certainty. Sometimes the memory conflates two or more experiences of a similar nature. There was one correspondent who was involved in the search for Norman MacLeod in 1934 and who clearly recalled that the body was found, not on the slopes of Ben MacDui, but close to the upper bothy in Gleann Einich, the spot where Hugh Barrie was found six years earlier. It seems likely that he was one of the large band of searchers involved in that search and was simply confusing the two incidents. This was an easily detected error; but quite often small errors of recollected detail may be impossible to identify, especially if that detail comes from only one person and it cannot be checked against other evidence.

There is a particular problem in handling the memories of someone who was hypothermic or under severe stress at the time when the recollected events occurred: these conditions can affect the memory, both confusing and distorting it, and making it vague and partial. There is doubt about the effect these conditions may have on the recollection of events in the few hours preceding their onset, partly because it varies from individual to individual; in some cases, indeed, there may be little or no effect. The extent to which memory and cerebral function is affected once a person has become hypothermic is also individual and virtually impossible to measure except under controlled conditions. In two of the misadventures studied in this book, that of May 1934 and December 1951, much of the information about what happened was necessarily derived from the sole survivor of each of these tragedies; in the first case there are grounds for believing that the survivor may have suffered mild hypothermia for a time before he eventually left his companion to seek help, while in the second the survivor was quite seriously hypothermic before reaching safety.

These reservations on the use of the recollections of participants having been expressed, it has to be said that they supply an additional dimension to the description of events and a realism not always provided by the other sources: they come from people who are a direct link with what happened so long ago. They provide details unobtainable elsewhere and can be used to verify information coming, in particular, from the pages of the press.

Normally it is possible to know when the memory is suspect: it may be that it is too much at variance with other evidence, is presented in a rather uncertain manner or is plainly vague. In cases where the memories are of uncertain value, qualified use can still be made of them. More certain ground is found where the recollections are based upon some kind of written record such as a diary, a personal account produced for a local newspaper, or some other memorial still in the person's possession; photographs, too, can be a helpful aid to the memory.

Events in the past cannot be properly comprehended if viewed primarily from the vantage point of the present: understanding and valid judgement demands that past events are considered from the standpoint of their own time. Those who venture into the wilder parts of the country today enjoy greater knowledge, better equipment and better provision of services than was the case in the period covered in this book. All seven accidents treated within these pages happened in winter or in winter conditions and almost all those who lost their lives succumbed to hypothermia, formerly often called exposure. This is a measure of the insidious nature of hypothermia and the much greater danger of the hills in winter than in summer. It is only in recent years that the real nature of hypothermia has been understood, even by medical experts. As a result, there is today a much wider awareness of it, how it can be avoided and how, if it develops, it is best treated. It was, at least in part, the loss of life to this mountain killer in the past that led to the greater and wider knowledge in the present.

Since hypothermia played a role of such significance in the misadventures, it is appropriate to describe it. For the body to function satisfactorily, the temperature of the central core, which houses the vital organs such as the brain, heart, lungs and kidneys, must be between 36°C and 38°C. The core temperature is maintained at this level through a combination of behavioural and physiological changes. The main behavioural changes are the donning and discarding of clothing and the increase or reduction of physical activity. Physiologically, the body has a complex thermostatic mechanism which operates to cool the core if it is becoming too hot and to conserve core heat if it is becoming too cold. The chief cooling processes are sweating and vaso-dilatation which increases blood flow to the cooler surface of the skin, thus causing the skin to flush; the chief heat-conserving processes are increased metabolism which generates more heat and vasoconstriction which limits blood flow to the peripheral shell of the body, thus causing a pallor of the skin. Metabolism depends on fuel in the form of food which is also used to generate other forms of energy, particularly motor energy. If the body has an insufficient supply of food to meet the demands placed upon it, fatigue and then exhaustion will develop and the body will be unable to keep going; moreover, it will not have the resources to maintain the central core temperature and hypothermia will result.

Medically, hypothermia is defined as the lowering of the central core temperature below 35°C. Someone with a core temperature lying between 32°C and 35°C suffers from mild hypothermia. He complains of feeling cold and his sole concern is to get warmer; he may also hallucinate. This condition, of course, must be treated seriously but it should be said that it is possible for a fit person or one experienced in mountaineering to walk out of the condition by generating sufficient heat through physical activity. However, for so many this does not happen. As the cooling continues, the victim becomes uncoordinated, is unable to keep up with the rest of the party and then starts to stumble. Violent attacks of shivering, a physiological process to generate heat, may develop. At core temperatures below 32°C, the person suffers from severe hypothermia in which he is careless about protecting himself from the cold. Thinking becomes slow, decision-making difficult and often wrong, and the memory deteriorates; irrational behaviour, such as the shedding of clothing, can develop and there may be a strong desire for sleep which should be avoided as heat production during sleep is reduced by 9% of its value when awake and at rest. In its final stage, the will to survive collapses with the individual becoming increasingly unresponsive and lapsing into coma. It is easy to think that someone with profound hypothermia has succumbed to the condition since he may have all the signs of death, with the skin ice-cold, the muscles and joints stiff and no measurable respiration or pulse. However, he may not be dead and it is, therefore, important to do everything possible to maintain life. The only certain diagnosis of death is failure to revive when the core temperature has been brought back to normal.

With regard to the action which should be taken when someone becomes hypothermic, it is not possible to give a rule that applies in all cases. If good shelter, such as a refuge hut or a building of some kind, is close to hand, normally it will be wise to try to reach it. The problem lies in deciding if such a shelter is sufficiently close for the attempt to be made and this will depend on the condition of the person, the weather and the difficulties of the terrain ahead. Often a house clearly visible a mere kilometre away will be too far and an endeavour to battle on to it may risk death. There is the question of fitness and experience to consider. In the words of Michael Ward, the surgeon and authority on high altitude medicine:

The more experienced the climber is, the more able and likely is he to 'walk out of the apparently hypothermic state'. But it is a difficult judgement to make in the field.

The general rule, which should be adopted if there is any doubt at all, is that the hypothermic person should be stopped immediately and found shelter from the wind and the precipitation. Every effort should be made to prevent further heat loss and, if possible, he should be changed out of wet or damp clothes into dry ones and placed in a sleeping-bag, insulated from the ground. It is important to keep the head, through which large amounts of heat can be lost, well covered. Warm fluids should be given, if these are available, but never alcohol; nor should his skin be rubbed to try to warm him. Both alcohol and rubbing will encourage further heat loss. It is easy to provide this wisdom from the comfort of the armchair; it requires considerable strength of will to apply when faced with conditions in the field. How much more tempting to try to reach the warmth and security of a house, a bothy, a tent or a youth hostel rather than spend the night, often without proper bivouac equipment, sheltering from a wind which is driving rain, sleet, snow or hail before it, when the party is already wet, cold and perhaps hungry – and fearful that someone may die of the cold if he has to endure the long hours of darkness in the open. How much less likely would be the decision to stop and sit out the storm in the days of lesser knowledge; indeed, in those days, the days of the misadventures in this book, it would have seemed the very worst course of action to take.

If nothing of hypothermia was known to most hill-walkers and climbers in those years, there was an almost equal ignorance of the severe chilling power of the wind. It has been known as wind-chill since 1939 when Siple first used the term. In five of the seven incidents, the single most important factor was the wind, combined with insufficient or inadequate clothing which in every case was almost certainly wet. Conditions do occur in the Scottish hills in which, even clad in today's top quality clothing, human beings simply will not survive. Apart altogether from the exhausting effects of high winds on physical resources and morale, there is the cooling effect it has on the unprotected or poorly protected parts of the body. Wind-chill is a means of correlating the effects of wind speed and temperature and provides an index of the degree of discomfort experienced. It can be quantified by quoting the equivalent still air temperature required to produce the same effect on the body. Even at low wind speeds the wind-chill factor is quite marked; at high wind speeds the chilling effect on the human body is devastating. Thus, for instance, if the ambient air temperature is 0°C and the wind speed

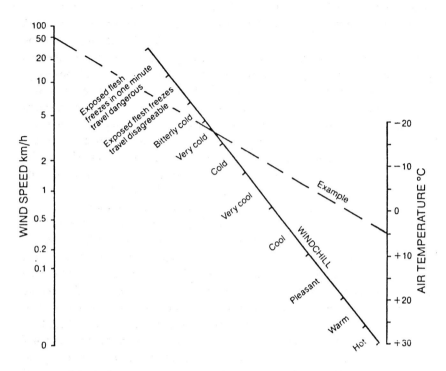

Fig. 18.1 Nomogram showing effect of wind speed and air temperature on windchill

is 10 km/h – only Force Two on the Beaufort Scale – the effect on the skin
is the same as a temperature of about −6°C in still air; at the same air
temperature and with a wind speed of 50 km/h the equivalent still air
temperature is about −20°C. It should perhaps be pointed out that at the
lower wind speeds even a small increase in wind speed can have a great
effect on the degree of cooling; above 25 km/h the factor changes more
slowly and above 50 km/h the factorial increase becomes negligible.
However, it has to be remembered that the greater the wind the more
debilitating its effects on energy and morale.

An understanding of hypothermia is facilitated by having some knowledge
of how heat is exchanged between the body and the environment. Body heat
is lost in five main ways: convection, conduction, evaporation, radiation and
respiration. Convection is the transference of heat by air currents. Warm air

currents generated next to the skin rise and are replaced by cold air which is heated at the expense of body temperature. The rate at which body heat is lost by convection will depend on the amount of skin directly exposed to the environment and the amount of air movement within the clothes, the less windproof the clothing the greater the rate of heat loss through convection for any given wind speed. Conduction is the transference of heat by direct contact and is a factor of importance if the clothes are wet through precipitation or sweat when these clothes conduct heat away from the body. Clothing can lose up to 80% of its insulating value when it becomes wet, a figure that can be increased to 90% when wetness is combined with the effect of wind. Heat transference through evaporation occurs when body heat is used to convert liquid into vapour – in other words, to dry out wet clothes. Much heat is lost in evaporating moisture, in the form of water or sweat, from clothes. The less waterproof the outer shell of clothing or the greater the condensation created by it in the clothes underneath, the greater the loss of body heat by conduction and evaporation. Radiation is less important as a route of heat loss. The smaller the temperature difference between the surface of a person and his immediate environment, the less the heat which will be lost through radiation. The purpose of clothing is to insulate the wearer from his environment, thus reducing radiant heat loss. Furthermore, when the body is cold, vasoconstriction can result in the outer 2.5 centimetres of body tissue having a thermal conductivity equivalent to that of cork. Respiratory heat loss is caused through warming and humidifying the inspired air, the deeper and more rapid the breathing, as it is during exercise, the greater the heat loss through respiration. Normally, the quantity of heat lost through respiration is not excessive and can be readily replaced by an increase in metabolic heat production. However, respiratory heat loss can become important when metabolic heat production is impaired as it is in hypothermia and when the person is becoming exhausted.

Before leaving the matter of hypothermia, two aspects of the condition which have some bearing on the incidents described in the following chapters should be mentioned. Firstly, there is the role of weakened morale in the onset and development of hypothermia. Being essentially psycho-logical, it cannot readily be measured or its effects quantified, but there can be little doubt that it is a factor of significance. It is known that the extreme discomfort caused by low skin temperature has a seriously weakening effect on morale. Apprehension and fear have the physiological effect of increasing the flow of blood to the peripheral parts of the body and cause sweating with the consequent loss of body heat. If this state of mind is sustained, it acts as a drain on the energy resources of the body. Moreover, in situations of stress, lowered morale in one member of a party can quickly spread to others and seriously undermine the will to survive of the party as a whole. It may be that this was a factor of some importance in the tragedies of late 1951 when four men died and of early 1959 when five men perished.

Secondly, subcutaneous fat is the body's most important form of natural insulation, in part because fat has few blood vessels through which heat can be lost. The greater the layer of fat, the greater the degree of insulation. Women, in general, have a thicker layer of subcutaneous fat than men and are, therefore, less susceptible to hypothermia than men, a resistance which may be enhanced by a greater will to survive in women. Incidentally, areas of the body with little or no subcutaneous fat, such as the tips of the fingers, the nose and the ears are more liable to local cold injury, such as frostnip and frostbite; of course, these areas, being more exposed, are also more susceptible to the effects of the wind. Physical size and shape also have a bearing on the susceptibility of individuals to hypothermia: short, heavily built people are considerably more resistant to it than tall, slightly built people.

Today it is possible to venture forth protected by an outer shell which is not only almost impermeable to water and largely windproof, but which also creates minimal condensation because it is permeable to water vapour. Moreover, this outer shell is designed to give a high degree of protection from the elements by the inclusion of such features as anorak hoods which project well beyond the face and have a leading edge held internally by a stiff but malleable wire and by having the shell fit closely at the neck, wrists and ankles so as to maximise the amount of trapped warm air within the shell. The wearer is well shielded from the natural elements with relatively little heat lost through convection, conduction and evaporation. In earlier days, some of the materials used for the vital outer shell may have been intrinsically fairly windproof but the design of the clothing made it rather draughty. If the shell was made of a waterproof material there would be the persistent problem of condensation wetting the clothes underneath and even freezing inside the shell; moreover, the design often allowed water to find its way in through such features as buttonholes and zips. Also today, in contrast with former times, there is a wide range of inner clothing made of synthetic materials which do not retain moisture or which continue to insulate well even when wet. Synthetic undergarments which transfer sweat from the skin to the next layer of clothing and plastic boots, which are light, warm and waterproof, are now commonly worn.

Much of this modern clothing does not come cheaply. However, in the present days of relative affluence, many hill-walkers and mountaineers can afford to buy good protective clothing and, what is more, are able to equip themselves quite adequately before they start taking to the hills or within a short time of doing so. This was simply not the case with the vast majority of people in the period covered in the book. Then, it was a case of using such clothes as they had, often old ones that had seen much better times. It was also a matter of equipping themselves over a period of time as money permitted and this meant, for instance, that waterproof overtrousers were something of a luxury which could be left until later. In this case, something like one third of the surface area of the body, and an area through which a great deal of heat is lost, was quite inadequately protected from rain, sleet, snow and wind; furthermore, capillary attraction, causing the wet to be drawn up from the trousers and underwear into the clothing above, would eventually make the clothing underneath the anorak quite wet, however waterproof the anorak may have been.

In this earlier period the hills were considerably less accessible than they are today. There are three main reasons for this. Firstly, on the whole people today have a good deal more leisure time with free weekends and longer holidays: gone for most of the working population is the era of the five-and-a-half-day or six-day working week; gone, too, is the era of the fortnight's annual holiday entitlement. Secondly, their relative affluence provides them with the financial means to visit the hills regularly and, thanks to the great expansion of mountain activities, facilities have become established in many of the main mountain areas which provide alternative activities if the weather is inclement or, for that matter, if the will is weak.

Thirdly, most people who go to the hills use private transport which allows them to reach their destinations conveniently and quickly; furthermore, they can usually drive themselves close to the area in which they wish to walk or climb. Often, they can leave the decision about whether and where to go until they have obtained a last-minute weather forecast, probably one specifically prepared for hill-walkers and climbers. Today many people leave home in the morning, travel many miles, have a full day in the hills and return home at night, all at modest cost if two or three of them share the expenses. This was not the case in the days when many people, if not most, were dependent on public transport. Then, train and bus timetables played a major role in the organising of expeditions, often causing much inconvenience, long and uncomfortable approach marches to the main-line railway and bus stations, and tiresome journeys to destinations which might be at some distance from the chosen mountain bases which in turn, as often as not, had little to offer if the weather was unsuitable for going into the hills. It is perhaps not without significance that four of the seven misadventures in this book involved parties who had made their way to the hills on public transport.

The relative inaccessibility of the wilder areas of the country in earlier times quite understandably influenced the attitude of those who went there. Being able to visit the hills only occasionally, if they changed their minds and did not go, it might be a considerable time before they would have another opportunity. Once there, if the weather conspired against them, they were faced with the choice of sitting about with a deep sense of wasted time, effort and money or venturing forth when prudence dictated otherwise. It is not difficult to understand that the decision was often made to fulfil the intended plan of activity, even if there was a chance that it might lead the party into trouble. There were occasions when these plans included an expedition to another base, perhaps a bothy or a youth hostel, to meet friends who would be there awaiting the party's arrival. With the poorer communications of those days, it might not be possible to notify those waiting of a change of programme or to advise the police of the change so that there be no concern if they were reported missing by their friends; as a result, the party would feel obliged to fulfil its plans, even against its wiser judgement. It is the case that a rendezvous with friends was a significant factor in at least two of the tragedies that follow.

Since the period covered by this book, mountain search and rescue has become much more efficient through the use of highly trained and relatively well-equipped personnel, through modern technical innovations and, in particular, through the widespread employment of helicopters to airlift rescuers close to those in trouble or to lift the latter directly from where they are waiting. The 1959 Glen Doll tragedy saw the beginnings of this development but earlier search parties were largely dependent on those with local knowledge through their work on the moors and uplands: stalkers, gamekeepers, ghillies and shepherds with their dogs who with remarkable willingness went out, wearing ordinary clothes and footwear, sometimes in the most appalling of weather and at peril to their own lives, to search for an injured or missing mountaineer. The only equipment they carried that might be of assistance in locating the missing person was a stick or a crook and a telescope; their only means of communicating with each other was a shout, a whistle or a wave of a handkerchief; their only means of contacting their base was to dispatch one of their number on foot; and their only means of carrying the injured or dead was a pony or a stretcher, as often as not constructed on the spot from crooks and staves.

It was the responsibility of the local policeman to raise the team and he would normally be among their number, if not their actual leader. If it was considered desirable to have a larger number of searchers than could be provided by those with intimate knowledge of the area, an appeal was made in the surrounding communities for all able-bodied volunteers to report by making their own way to the search area, at their own expense, using whatever transport they could find and dressing in whatever clothing and footwear they possessed which they considered suitable. Indeed, many arrived shod in wellington boots and wearing raincoats. The largest number of volunteers to participate in a day's search was produced by such an appeal: the two hundred and fifty or so who arrived in Glen More on the final day of the search of Cairn Gorm for MacKenzie and Ferrier in early January, 1933. If people with mountaineering skills and equipment were needed, it was often the case that they had to be summoned from the cities, chiefly Edinburgh and Glasgow, by telephone or by telegram with all the consequent delays that this entailed. Members of the S.M.C. sometimes found their services in demand in this way. Of course, by the time they were able to reach the scene of the incident, there was often little they could do other than assist in the recovery of a body.

With the large number of hill-walkers and climbers found nowadays, even in remote places, a party or an individual in difficulty knows that there is a good chance that it will be possible to attract attention within a reasonable length of time. It is, therefore, much easier today to remain in place and await assistance than it was in the time when one could walk all day, even in areas now overrun with people, without seeing a single other person. In those days, individuals or parties who found themselves in trouble were far more dependent on their own resources and this sometimes forced them into fighting their way through weather from which they would have been wiser to have sought some immediate shelter.

Those involved in five of the seven misadventures were caught in violent weather by which they were overcome; in each case, the weather was unexpected by the parties, although not entirely so to the meteorological offices. Today, there is little excuse for hill-walkers and climbers setting out without knowing the weather they are likely to encounter. Weather forecasting has become generally reliable and has permitted the creation of a wide range of weather services easily available to the public, either through radio and television or the telephone service. Among these are weather forecasts designed specifically for the mountaineering fraternity. Moreover, these forecasts offer a real-time source of weather information, unlike those published in newspapers which are likely to have been prepared a considerable time before they are read by the public. Modern technology has produced transistors and printed circuits so that radios can be cheap, small and battery operated and can be carried by those going into wild and remote areas as a means of providing weather information as well as entertainment.

There is no readily available material on the history of weather forecasting but Mr R. J. Ogden, Honorary Secretary of the History Group of the Royal Meteorological Society, has provided the following interesting information about the nature of weather forecasting and its dissemination. He says:

The Met. Office was founded in the mid-19th century primarily to serve maritime interests. From the 1920s onwards, aviation needs began to dominate the Office output, culminating in the massive upsurge of activity by the R.A.F. during the War and by Civil Aviation in the immediate post-war years. Incidentally, current weather information was classified as **secret** throughout the war itself from Sept 1939 to May 1945, so no forecasts of any kind were then available to the public. The multiplicity of public weather services so familiar today did not really start to develop until the mid-1950s; the first public Weather Centre opened in London early in 1959 and the second in Glasgow late that year.

Originally as a spin-off from its primary maritime function, the Met. Office issued brief general weather forecasts for the whole country daily to the Press in London from 1861 to 1866; except during wartime, similar forecasts have been issued regularly ever since 1879. Weather maps were also prepared specially for *The Times* from the late 19th century. Such written forecasts as may have appeared pre-war in the Scottish Press almost certainly originated in London the previous day and were thus already out of date when first seen by the reader. The countrywide Press forecasts are of necessity very succinct and cannot include all the information needed by mountaineers. It is true that during the post-war decade there were a few aviation forecast offices in Scotland which provided local forecasts to the Press, but most services of this kind in Scotland had to await the opening of the Glasgow Weather Centre in December 1959.

The next forecasts to come into the public domain were the Shipping Forecasts which, except during the war, have been broadcast by the B.B.C. since 1920. These . . . for anyone with sufficient background knowledge of meteorology . . . could and still do provide a good framework of weather information of use to those on the hills. But I suspect that the proportion of pre-War climbers with such a background and interest was extremely small. . . . Formal scripted forecasts for the general public have been read on radio by B.B.C. announcers since November 1922. To the best of my recollection, before the war these were broadcast no more than 2 or 3 times per day and were very general forecasts for the whole country; they did however offer a real-time source of weather information in more or less everyday language, but with very little, if any, detail about areas such as the Highlands. Admittedly in the mid-1930s, the all-embracing national text was replaced by a set of forecasts for each B.B.C. Region, but these were still all written by staff in London. It was not until some time after the War that the presentation was again revised to include a short 'National' forecast, written at the Central Forecasting Office at Dunstable (later at Bracknell), normally followed by a 'Regional' forecast prepared by the Main Met. Office responsible for the Region concerned – for Scotland, then the M.M.O. at Pitreavie; and I recall that even in the early 1960s, on Sunday mornings we still had to write all the Regional forecasts at Bracknell . . .

I have no record to hand as to the exact date when the more informal personal presentations on radio by Met. Office staff started; I think it must have been in the late 1950s when staff in London first made experimental broadcasts . . . I am fairly sure that personal presentations were not made by forecasters based in Scotland before 1967. Some extremely crude weather charts were shown experimentally on television in 1936, but the now familiar 'Weathermen' did not appear on screen until January 1954. Satellite cloud pictures were not available in real-time until the late 1960s and it was not technically possible to show these in the television weather broadcasts until the late 1970s.

Prior to the late 1960s when computer predictions became available on a regular basis, weather forecasts were essentially extrapolations from an analysed current weather situation on the basis of physical understanding of atmospheric processes and a great deal of experience. Prior to the outbreak of the war, there were only about a dozen synoptic reporting stations in Scotland, of which, if my memory serves me correctly, only 2 or 3 were well inland, i.e. Dalwhinnie, Eskdalemuir and I believe Huntly. At that time there were only two 24-hour forecasting offices in the whole country, one at the Met. Office H.Q. then in London and the other at Croydon Airport. Knowledge of the actual weather over the Scottish Highlands as the starting point for any forecast was almost non-existent . . . The wartime expansion of met. services certainly improved the observational network considerably and forecasting offices were opened at many R.A.F. and later Civil Aviation stations in Scotland, some of which provided very limited public services. During the early 1960s, following the opening of the Glasgow Weather Centre, the observational network in hilly areas was improved and, for the first time, forecasts were prepared specifically for outdoor activities; these were initially sent to the Ski Centres and to Press and Radio, but later were also shown on Independent Television. . . .

As a postscript, it should be added that *The Glasgow Herald* was publishing daily synoptic weather charts by the end of 1932 but, as Mr Ogden says, these 'almost certainly originated in London the previous day and were thus already out of date when first seen by the reader.' It is quite evident from the information provided by Mr Ogden that, prior to the 1960s, weather forecasting had a very limited value for mountaineers. In those days it was important to be able to read the sky and to know something about local weather patterns. Many would simply not have this skill and knowledge.

In general, as can be seen from the weather maps, there is a relationship between the pressure pattern shown by the isobars (lines joining points of equal pressure, with the observed values corrected to sea level) and the observed mean wind speed and direction. When the isobars are closer together, the wind speed is stronger; also, the wind direction is nearly parallel to the isobars, but somewhat across them from high to low pressure. At a height of about 600 to 800m above the surface the winds correspond closely to the so-called geostrophic wind which can be calculated directly from a pressure map, but at lower levels they are affected by the resistance to air movement caused by the surface. This resistance varies in amount from relatively small effects caused by waves at sea and crops on flat land to larger effects due to buildings and trees and major effects from large topographic features, such as mountains and valleys.

In mountainous areas, both wind speed and direction can vary greatly from that which might be expected from the pressure pattern, especially in the bottoms of the valleys and on the slopes of the mountains. On the higher mountain tops, the mean speed will generally approximate to the geostrophic wind, whereas with certain wind directions a valley may be completely sheltered from the wind, giving little warning of extreme conditions which may prevail at higher levels. Wind directions are also much altered by the topography.

The Beaufort Scale is used to describe the winds and their strengths. Only winds of Gale Force Eight and higher are of special concern in the chapters which follow. The Meteorological Office Observers' Handbook uses two sets of wind descriptions: one for observing and the other for forecasting. They are not identical. It is the descriptions for observing that are employed in the book. This should cause no difficulty for the reader who is familiar with shipping and other forecasts broadcast on radio and television, except with Force Nine which is described as 'Severe Gale' in forecasting, but as 'Strong Gale' in observing. The other wind descriptions used within these pages are identical. They are: Force Eight – Gale; Force Ten – Storm; Force Eleven – Violent Storm; Force Twelve – Hurricane.

Something should be said about the calculation of temperatures at different altitudes. Almost all the temperatures shown on the weather charts and recorded in the Meteorological Office's daily weather reports were made at or close to sea level. Since the Second World War, however, radiosonde data has also been available, radiosondes being soundings of the atmosphere made with equipment carried by balloons, measurements being made of pressure, temperature, humidity and wind speed. From the sea level temperatures, it is possible to calculate the temperatures at higher altitudes, but some care has to be exercised. If a parcel of air is displaced upwards in the atmosphere, it moves into an environment where the pressure is less and consequently it expands, leading to a lowering of its temperature. If no external source of heat is involved, the process is called adiabatic. All air contains moisture in the form of water vapour and the amount of water vapour which the air can hold before some of it starts to condense depends on its temperature. Warm air can hold considerably more water vapour than can cold air. If no condensation takes place, the fall of temperature with height is approximately 1°C per 100m and this is called the dry adiabatic lapse rate.

If the air cools to a temperature (the dew point) at which condensation into water droplets starts to take place, latent heat is released which partially counteracts the fall in temperature. In contrast to the dry adiabatic lapse rate, the saturated (or wet) adiabatic lapse rate is not a constant but varies with the temperature since warm air initially contains much more water vapour than cold air and so more latent heat can be released. The saturated adiabatic lapse rate at a temperature of around 5°C is about 1°C per 165m, while at 15°C it is about 1°C per 200m.

The actual lapse rate in the lower layers of the atmosphere, as measured by a radiosonde carried by a balloon or by an observer climbing a mountain, depends on the past history of the air and may be as great as the dry adiabatic lapse rate (and exceed it close to the surface on a sunny day) or even be negative if there is an inversion. The latter means that the temperature increases with height through part of the atmosphere. Inversions occur most commonly close to the surface on clear, cold nights with little wind. The ground loses heat to space through radiation and the air in contact with the ground is cooled. Air is a very poor conductor of heat so, in the absence of a wind to mix the air, the surface air cools much more than does air at some distance above the ground. Since cold air is denser than warm air, in hilly areas cold air tends to slide into the valleys which may actually be colder than the tops. Under such conditions, the warmest areas around dawn are usually to be found at some intermediate level on the hillside. Once the sun is up and the ground begins to warm, the overnight inversion is usually broken, but in the winter months it may persist throughout the day, particularly in deep valleys. Inversions can also occur at higher levels in the atmosphere, either when there is an anticyclone over the area or when an approaching front brings in warmer air over the colder air at lower levels. In those circumstances, temperatures at the summits of the mountains may be considerably higher than those in the valleys.

On average, the actual lapse rate in the lower layers of the atmosphere is about 1°C per 160m and as a first approximation this is a useful method for estimating the temperature at different altitudes from observations close to sea level, as long as account is taken of the overnight cooling at low level sites on calm, clear nights and heating during the day. The observations which were made at the summit of Ben Nevis from 1883 to 1904[1] showed how little diurnal variation there is in the temperatures at the tops of the mountains when compared with those in inland valleys.

In researching this book, examination was made of the causes of death as shown on the death certificates and their corrected entries. These are held in the General Register Office for Scotland, New Register House, Edinburgh. In the event of an accidental death, the actual cause of death may not be known at the time of completion of the death certificate; in this case, when the cause is determined it is entered in the Register of Corrected Entries which was succeeded by the Register of Corrections Etc. on 1st January, 1966.

A word should also be said about the place-name spellings adopted in the book. Nearly all of the names of the hills, streams, glens, bothies and other mountain features are Gaelic or of Gaelic origin. Very often these are anglicised to facilitate pronunciation for non-Gaelic speakers; thus Coire Odhar becomes Corrour, Braigh Riabhach becomes Braeriach and Beanaidh becomes Bennie. Variations can develop with these anglicisations and they may change from time to time. The spellings employed in the book are those used by the Ordnance Survey, even when this spelling is at variance with local, and even more general, currency. Thus, for instance, 'Glen More' is used instead of the more usual 'Glenmore' and 'Ben MacDui' rather than 'Ben MacDhui'. The exception to this principle is where the word appears in a quotation: in these cases, the spelling of the quotation is retained.

Every effort has been made in the writing of this book to be as accurate as possible. All the evidence was examined critically and it was important that this evidence inspired confidence in its trustworthiness. Where there was conflict over points of detail the prevalent or the more probable account was accepted. In those instances where a decision was not possible the conflicting information is provided; perhaps the reader can make sense where the author has failed. Successful attempts were made to locate many people involved directly in the accidents, either as members of the parties

1   See *Twenty Years on Ben Nevis* by W. T. Kilgour

which met with misfortune or as searchers, and they were able to provide additional information and help to resolve difficulties with the evidence. They also gave valuable assistance in reading the drafts as they were written and suggesting changes and improvements. Many questions arose as the evidence was examined and, although most of these found answers, it was impossible to resolve all of them. In such circumstances either the answers are left open or reasoned interpretations are given. In spite of all the effort to avoid error, there is little doubt that some will exist; that is in the very nature of historical research and is made the more likely in any study which depends to a significant extent on material produced in difficult circumstances and originating in times of emergency.

The chapters in the book do more than give a factual account of the events on those fateful days. Attempts are made both to identify the reasons for the misadventures and to deduce the course of events during the time for which there is little or no evidence. Inevitably this involves a measure of speculation, but it was felt that the book would be incomplete otherwise. The author, having handled so much information on each of the incidents, is in a good position to undertake this task, but sufficient evidence exists within each chapter for the reader to propose alternative interpretations. When reading about the accidents, it is important to appreciate that all made what they considered to be adequate preparations for their journeys and correct decisions on the appropriate courses of action to take, decisions made sometimes in the most exacting of circumstances. That their preparations may not have been sufficient and their judgements not always the wisest emerged only after the ensuing events had tragically overwhelmed them. The central characters in this book had a spirit of adventure which took them out of their carpet slippers and into the hard reality which so many experience only vicariously through the pages of a book. These were the unlucky ones; many others in similar situations have lived to tell the tale.

This book could not have been written without the willing and generous assistance of so many people, too numerous to mention by name. However, there are some whose considerable contribution must be specifically acknowledged. Frank Bennett, who led the team which tried to reach Maurice Linnell on the Castle Buttress of Carn Dearg, Ben Nevis, on Easter Saturday, 1934 and which recovered his body the following day, provided much information about these efforts and assisted in unravelling difficulties with the published accounts of the accident. Alastair Borthwick gave freely with information for the chapter on Kirkus and Linnell, even though criticism is made in this chapter of his own account of the accident in the

Glasgow Weekly Herald. Robert Campbell, who was a member of the small search party which located the bodies of MacKenzie and Ferrier in January 1933, provided both recollections of the search and illustrative matter. Steve Dean supplied valuable material for the Kirkus and Linnell chapter and helped clarify problems with the evidence. Ex-Inspector Thomas Deas of Tayside Police gave extensive help in the writing of the chapter on the Jock's Road tragedy of 1959, both with details of the search which lasted over three months and in resolving some difficulties with the published accounts. Charles Donaldson and James Russell gave useful information about the accident near Corrour Lodge at the end of 1951, including details about the weather and the recovery of the bodies of the four men who died, while Christine Bainbridge supplied the relevant extract from the mountain diary of her late husband, Donald Mill, and other material. John Duff, Charles Smith and Robert Ewan provided details on the Jock's Road misadventure, the two former also supplying illustrations. Ian Gowdie spent a great deal of time producing the cover, the maps and other line drawings for the book to its considerable enhancement; his patience and commitment were remarkable. Affleck Gray, himself an author, who has an unrivalled knowledge of the Cairngorms stretching back over sixty-five years, provided much material and information on the Cairngorm misadventures and gave a great deal of his time answering questions and reading parts of the book; his encouragement was endless.

Peter Hodgkiss and Jack Baines, my publishers, have been most encouraging and patient and have provided valuable additional material. Jim Hyslop was very helpful in the writing of the chapters on MacKenzie and Ferrier and on MacLeod and Lawrie, answering numerous questions which would have tested a much younger memory; he also provided a number of photographs and lent his diary of 1934 which described the search for the missing MacLeod. John Linnell was able to provide information about the Linnell family which led to Bonnie Phipps and unpublished photographs of Maurice Linnell. John Llewellyn, archivist of the Rucksack Club, went to considerable trouble to provide material for the chapter on Kirkus and Linnell and to supply the names of people to contact about the accident. Evan Lloyd, an authority on cold stress and hypothermia, gave very useful information about their effects on the memory. Mae Marshall and her brother, Hamish, gave much general information of assistance in the writing of the Cairngorm incidents and this included access to the diary of Dr Ross and the supply of illustrative matter. James Martin, General Secretary, Scottish Youth Hostels Association, supplied illustrations and details about the youth hostels in Braemar, in Glen Doll and beside Loch Ossian. Douglas Mathieson of the National Library of Scotland willingly and untiringly provided material for all the incidents and was even prepared to undertake a search for some of the material himself. Brock Nethersole-Thompson and his half sister, the late Jessie MacDonald, together with their neighbours, Jock MacKenzie and Jessie Garrow, contributed illustrations and many recollections for the chapter on Baird and Barrie.

Dick Ogden of the Royal Meteorological Society went to a great deal of labour to give detailed information about weather forecasting and its dissemination in the years covered by this book. Iain Ogilvie willingly gave his diary, photographs and illustrations and a great deal of his time and patience to assist in the writing of the account of the accident which befell him and his two companions on An Teallach in 1966 while Carol Francis-Johnston provided copies of the photographs which were in her late father's camera when the accident happened. Marjory Roy, former superintendent of the Edinburgh Meteorological Office, gave invaluable assistance with the meteorological parts of the book, supplying photocopies of the relevant weather maps and daily weather reports, offering comments and providing from the Meteorological Office archives supplementary data which gave insights into some of the accidents; in addition, she undertook some research herself and read all the weather references in the book to check them for accuracy. Douglas Spence, Librarian, D. C. Thomson and Company, went to much trouble to provide archive material on a number of the misadventures and illustrations for the chapter on the Glen Doll tragedy of January 1959.

Anne Tewnion, who survived the dreadful storm which took the lives of her husband and three friends near Corrour Lodge at the end of 1951 and who has since remarried, very kindly provided much information about that tragedy and made valuable comment on the chapter relating the mis-adventure. As a result of her contribution, it has been possible to produce a revision of the existing accounts of the accident. Bill Wallace, former president of the Scottish Mountaineering Club, was tireless in providing a variety of information connected with the S.M.C. and in helping with the illustrations. Michael Ward, a leading authority on high altitude medicine and a mountaineer of note, gave generous and extended assistance with the medical aspects of the book and was kind enough to check the presentation of these, making suggestions for improvements; his contribution is greatly appreciated. Dr Peter Ward, librarian of the Cairngorm Club, supplied information on the accidents of January 1933 and May 1934 and illustrations which included photographs from the Cairngorm Club Journal and photocopies of entries in the Shelter Stone Visitors' Books which are in the custody of his Club. Finally, Noel Williams went to great lengths to assist in resolving the matter of Kirkus's route of reascent after the accident which claimed the life of Maurice Linnell on the Castle in 1934; this included an ascent of the Castle with careful observations made during the climb and the taking of a number of photographs.

A great debt of gratitude is owed not just to those named above, but to all who assisted in the writing of the book. Without their help and time, the book would never have been written. Any errors are entirely the fault of the author.

A Note on Units of Measurement

A decision had to be made on which units of height, distance and temperature to use in the book: metric or imperial; Celsius or Fahrenheit. To provide both on every occasion when measurements are given would regularly interrupt the flow of the narrative and so unitary conversions are not made in the chapters. Most of the quoted material dates from the days of imperial units and Fahrenheit and these units are retained in the quotations. In the rest of the text, metric and Celsius units are used. It is hoped that this will not cause confusion. There is only one Fahrenheit reference in the quoted material. With reference to the weather chart data, it is probably sufficient to know that 0°C = 32°F; each 2°C approximating to 3.5°F. To convert metres into feet the multiplier is 3.28 and to convert feet into metres divide by the same factor. One kilometre (1,000 metres) equals 0.6 mile and one mile equals 1.6 kilometres, while one metre is about one yard three inches.

Km represents kilometre(s) and m represents metres (vertical height). Fractions of a kilometre are generally taken to the nearest whole number. Note: Square brackets are used in quoted passages to indicate information provided for clarification by the author.

Barrie's grave
•Whitewell
Achnagoichan •
Loch an Eilein

Glen More

Route taken by Baird and Barrie _ _ _ _
Baird's route down Gleann Einich _._._.

Windy Corner
Carn Eilrig
742 metres

Gleann Einich

Lower
(Dunc's) Bothy
Beanaidh Bheag

Baird found

Am Beanaidh

Sgoran Dubh Mor
1,111 metres
Old Sluice

Barrie found

Upper Bothy

Pools of Dee

Coire Bogha-cloiche

Braeriach
1,296 metres

Lairig Ghru

Ben MacDui
1,309 me[t]

Coire Dhondail

Einich Cairn
1,237 metres

Loch Einich

Cairn Toul
1,291 metres

Coire Odhar

Corrour Bothy

The Devil's Point
1,004 metres

Monadh Mor
1,113 metres

Thomas Baird and Hugh Barrie:
Cairngorms 28th December, 1927 to 1st January 1928.

Baird and Barrie in Gleann Einich. New Year, 1928

On Wednesday, 28th December, 1927 there arrived in Aviemore by train from Glasgow two young men whose plan was to spend a few days of their Christmas vacation climbing and exploring in the Cairngorms. They were Thomas Baird who, as assistant demonstrator, was one of the junior staff of the Geology Department of the University of Glasgow and secretary of the University's Geological Society; and Hugh Alexander Barrie, a medical student in the same university. Both men were of sound physique, active members of the Officers' Training Corps and fond of the hills. Barrie was a skilled tennis and badminton player and in the latter sport he represented his university. They shared an interest in the writing of verse, some of which had seen publication in the university magazine of which Barrie was assistant editor. In this field, Barrie, in particular, showed potential talent. Their verse reveals a sensitivity to nature and to the rugged remoteness of the Scottish hills.

Baird had a special leaning towards the problems of mountain geology and on excursions would often weigh down his pack with specimens. This visit had, as part of its purpose, a study of the geology of the Cairngorms and it was Baird's intention to collect a few specimens on the barer patches of the hills. This concern would determine to some extent the course taken by the two men during their excursions and may account, at least partially, for the limited number of summits they seem to have visited. Baird, although only twenty-two, had established sufficient a reputation as a field geologist to merit an obituary in the science magazine, 'Nature', in its issue of 21st January, 1928. It was his cherished ambition to explore some of the great Asiatic mountain ranges whose geological structures remained to be unravelled. This expedition to the Cairngorms would provide him with further experience of mountaineering in winter conditions as training for what might lie ahead.

Both men, who were members of the Junior Mountaineering Club of Scotland, were experienced in climbing the Scottish hills. It had been their intention, together with Ronald Burn of the University's Department of Humanity, to found a Glasgow University climbing club at the beginning of the following academic term. Baird's parents lived in Baldernock in Stirlingshire where Mr Baird was the village dominie, while Barrie's father had been headmaster of a school in the village of Sorbie in Wigtownshire. It was to be a sad time for Barrie's only sister, Nancy, a teacher with whom he shared his lodgings in Ballieston, Glasgow. Both parents were dead, her father, James Barrie, having died not much over a year before. He had failed to return home on 25th October, 1926 but, despite all efforts to locate him, no sign of him nor any evidence which would explain his disappearance was found until his body was discovered in a stream in the vicinity of Sorbie. Nancy was now to lose her one brother.

Today Gleann Einich is without bothies but in 1927/8 it boasted two, one known as the upper bothy and standing close to the north-eastern end of Loch Einich, and the other known, appropriately enough, as the lower bothy nearly 3 km north of the upper one and standing beside the confluence of Am Beanaidh, sometimes written in its anglicised form of the Bennie, and Beanaidh Bheag or Little Bennie. The former stream is the outflow of Loch Einich and the latter drains the water from the three great northern corries of Braeriach to the south-east of the bothy. Loch Einich itself lies in dark, brooding confines, imprisoned by steep walls on three sides, at the head of the glen. At the point where Am Beanaidh leaves the loch on its journey to the river Spey, there were and are the remains of a sluice. In the days when logs were floated down Am Beanaidh, there was a dam with sluice gates used to create a sufficient rush of water to float the logs. On the lower reaches of Am Beanaidh, which by then is a little river, the logs were placed along the banks. When the water level at the dam was at the required height, the sluice gates were opened; as the flood reached the spot where the logs were lying, they were rolled into the water and poled downstream. The man who opened the sluice gates was usually sent up to the dam on the night before a timber run. One stormy night of hail and snow, the young man in charge of the gates set off on the 16km trek to the loch. In the morning the water came down as scheduled, but the young man did not return. A search party found him beside the dam where he had sat down to shelter from the storm after opening the gates. He had died from hypothermia.

The bothies of the Cairngorms had been built by the landowners as accommodation for the deer watchers whose tasks were to prevent poaching and to ensure that the deer did not wander on to a neighbouring estate. By the time of the events in this chapter, the Gleann Einich bothies were no longer used for this purpose: the upper bothy lost its original use in the early 1900s and the lower bothy in the mid 1920s. The lower bothy was also known as Dunc's bothy after Duncan Cameron who had been a deer watcher in Gleann Einich in the summer months. Big Dunc had occupied the lower bothy in Gleann Einich for many years. Dunc's bothy was a solid, single-roomed, wooden structure of Rothiemurchus fir with a corrugated iron roof and an attached stable for the deer watcher's horse, together with small piece of greensward adjacent to the bothy for grazing. Only the chimney was constructed in stone. The wooden-floored bothy was furnished with a table, forms and a cupboard, while the walls and ceiling were board-lined with Rothiemurchus fir.

The upper bothy was larger than Dunc's and comprised two living rooms and a stable at the east end. The construction and furniture were similar, but the upper bothy had the additional luxury of iron bedsteads on which a comfortable heather bed could be placed. Both bothies met their ends about 1944, Dunc's being blown down in a storm and the upper bothy being destroyed by fire. Both were the property of the landowner, Major J. P. Grant of Rothiemurchus, known locally as Colonel Bones; they were kept locked, although the attached stables were left open. Sadly, the landowners in the Cairngorm area had been forced to keep their bothies locked as it was not uncommon for casual users to break wood from the huts to provide fuel for a fire. This may have cost Baird and Barrie their lives.

It had been the original intention of the two men to use the lower bothy as the base from which they would climb the neighbouring peaks. The owner had given them permission to use the hut but then asked them to apply also to the shooting lessee for his consent since the purchase of the shooting lease included rights over the huts. It is not clear what then happened. Professor J. W Gregory of the University of Glasgow's Geology Department wrote an article on the accident for the S.M.C.J. (Volume XVIII, April 1928). It was prepared after the body of Baird, but not that of Barrie, had been found. On the eve of publication, the body of Barrie was found. In this article, he said:

They [Baird and Barrie] had intended to use the lower bothy in Glen Eunach as headquarters. The proprietor [of the estate] had kindly given them permission to use the hut, but as he then realized that the application should have been made to the shooting tenant, Baird obtained the further permission by telegraph. The keeper, in the absence of instructions, had no authority to lend the key of the hut, but he kindly recommended them to an empty house beside his parents' home at Achnagoichan, where Baird and Barrie spent the night of Wednesday the 28th. [In common with other place names, Gleann Einich had various spellings.]

In fact, they spent the night at Whitewell half a kilometre to the north-east of Achnagoichan with Mr and Mrs MacKenzie whose son, John, was second stalker on the Rothiemurchus estate and played a major role in the later search for the missing Barrie. It may be that 'the keeper' in Professor Gregory's account was John MacKenzie himself; if so, he probably regretted that he had been unable to give the key of the bothy to the young men. However, the head stalker on the estate was Mr Carr and it is more likely that he it was who had to deny them access to the bothy.

It may be that the professor, a mountaineer and explorer who had been a member of the first party to cross Spitzbergen in 1896 and had been a pioneer in the exploration of Tibet, was correct. He knew Baird well and had a liking for him but he was apparently in London when the news of the tragedy broke and it is not immediately clear how he came by all the details he gives, although some of his information will have come from John MacKenzie and his parents. In the short article from which the quotation is taken, he makes a few errors of fact: for instance, in addition to ascribing the wrong name to the house where the two men spent the night, he states that 'the weather during the three days [when the men stayed in the Corrour bothy] was fine and calm' and this simply was not the case. Since he is erroneous here, it may be that he is not entirely reliable elsewhere in his article.

Rev. R. B. Thomson of Newtonmore, one of the search leaders who knew the Cairngorms well, said in an article, published in *The Glasgow Evening News* on Friday, 13th January, 1928:

Had the lower Eanaich bothy been granted them as a base of operations – and there is no reason within the bounds of right reason and our native humanity why it should not, none but the strictures of the shooting lessee of the glen, out of season – a different tale might have been told of their outing on the Monadh Ruadh [the Cairngorms].

In this, Rev. Thomson implies, if he does not actually state, that the consent sought from the shooting tenant was withheld. But, again, no indication is given of the source of the information and the tenor of the article is hostile to those of wealth who seek to deny access to the land, even to the local population. Whatever the truth – and both accounts may be wrong, such are the perils of historical research – Baird and Barrie were given accommodation on the night of Wednesday, 28th December by Mr and Mrs Alexander (Sandy) MacKenzie at Whitewell, a croft 5km from Aviemore and 6km north of the lower bothy in Gleann Einich. The croft obtained its water from a well beside which, in summer, a profusion of daisies grew; hence its name.

On arriving in Aviemore, Baird and Barrie spent seventeen shillings and sixpence (87 pence) on food for their stay in the hills but it seems fairly clear that they went forth the following day with insufficient food: when their rucksacks were eventually found, the only food they contained was some porridge in a billycan in Barrie's pack and there is no evidence that they left any behind in the Corrour bothy. As their limited supply of food may have played a significant part in their ultimate fate, it is worth giving brief consideration to the factors which may have led them to restrict the amount.

It may be that they were treating the visit as training for more arduous expedition work when they might have to survive on short rations. It could be that their packs were already heavy and they did not wish to overburden themselves with an excess of food. It is also possible that, as they were hoping – perhaps even expecting – to stay in the lower bothy which was within reasonable access of Aviemore, they saw no need to take an excess of food as they should be able to obtain additional supplies if these were needed. However, it is also possible that they were simply unaware of the amount of food needed for an expedition of the nature they had in mind at a time of year when the weather could become the most terrible of enemies.

Affleck Gray makes two interesting comments on the men's food provisions, or the lack of them. He says:

It seems that they did not have such a thing as iron rations and they appear not to have had an onion which is one of the best stimulants one can have on the mountains in winter. I always had a big one in my rucksack in winter and I had reason to prove its value with Edd Davidson [of the Moray Mountaineering Club] after leaving Corrour bothy the following winter when he became ill and turned purple in the face. Just after midday when we left Corrour, his pace began to drag on the way north along the Lairig Ghru but, after feeding him with an onion, I succeeded in cutting steps and hauling him up Coire Ruadh. I managed to get him over the ridge and down Coire Beannaidh to our base at Dunc's Bothy.

Baird and Barrie arrived only to be denied the key for the lower bothy. This presented them with an immediate problem: the lower bothy could easily have been reached that day by using the rough road to Loch Einich but it would be considerably more difficult, if not out of the question, to reach the Corrour bothy. The Corrour bothy lies in the Lairig Ghru on the Braemar side of the pass and below the eastern slopes of Cairn Toul, 16km from Whitewell. The terrain is rough and on that day the footpaths leading to the Lairig Ghru, such as there were, would have been concealed under deep snow. To assist the young men, the MacKenzies offered to

The house at Whitewell where Baird and Barrie stayed.   *Author*

accommodate them that night in an unoccupied house a short distance below their own home. It is not clear if they were willing to allow the men to use it as a base for the duration of their stay, but it was too far from the hills to be of much service to them in this respect.

The small house in which Baird and Barrie spent the night was built of corrugated iron, quite common as a building material in the area. It had been erected about the time of the First World War as an eventual retirement home for the MacKenzies who, by 1927, were quite elderly. It was not disused as reported in the press, but it had been little used. Indeed, when Mr MacKenzie retired, he and his wife had moved into the little house for only a short time before returning to their old home where they were residing again at the time of the tragedy. The unused house was probably rather damp so Mrs MacKenzie lit a fire for her unexpected guests. The two men told her of their plans and she expressed some concern. This concern was repeated by her husband when one of the men went to their house later to ask for some salt.

The weather was unsettled, cold and rather stormy, with the constant threat of snow; the area in which Baird and Barrie proposed to stay was remote with little, if any, contact with the outside world so that they would find themselves in serious trouble if anything untoward happened. If the young men were unaware how quickly the weather could change and produce conditions of arctic intensity, the MacKenzies knew only too well. However, the effort necessary to reach the hills was great and the opportunities were few, so there was a strong temptation to venture ahead when prudence might have dictated caution. Moreover, if the young men were to visit the larger mountain ranges of the world eventually, they would have to face conditions as bad as, if not worse than, those they were likely to meet in the Cairngorms so they would do well to gain the experience of a winter stay in the Corrour bothy. Baird and Barrie listened to the MacKenzies' concern that Wednesday evening and, according to the press, tried to reassure them by saying that they carried a barometer which they would use to guide their decisions. There is no other evidence that they had a barometer but they did have a thermometer. Perhaps the MacKenzies misheard what was said. The visitors also told their hosts that they had made an excursion into the Lairig Ghru from the Braemar side the previous March intending to stay in the Corrour bothy but had failed to reach it; they had been overtaken by darkness because of the delays created by the quantity of snow on the route.

The good people of Whitewell did not see them alive again. Baird and Barrie departed into the cold of the early morning and when Mr MacKenzie rose at 7.30 a.m. he found, as arranged, some gear in a rucksack; they would return for it on the Sunday (1st January), having spent four days at the Corrour bothy from which they would climb and explore. The MacKenzies also found that the young men had left the salt cellar on the mantelpiece of the little house and before long they were to regard the request for salt as a sign of ill omen.

With their departure from Whitewell, no doubt with high hopes for the next few days, a final veil is almost drawn across the lives of the two men. Our ignorance is not quite complete, however. The MacKenzies' son, John, later that day was to see the men's footprints crossing the Cairngorm Club's bridge over the wide Am Beanaidh flowing from Gleann Einich; they were on the route to the Lairig Ghru. Almost three months later, on Saturday, 24th March, he found the men's abandoned rucksacks and Baird's contained two notebooks, one of which was used to keep a diary which reveals something of what the men did and the difficulties they had to face. This diary was brief, occupying only a page and a half, and was almost illegible, perhaps because of the conditions under which it was written. The cold in the Corrour bothy was certainly intense and this would have made writing difficult. It is also possible that the ink froze in the fountain pen that Baird carried or that the point of his pencil broke; it may be that they had difficulty with their matches and could not light candles to allow Baird to write the diary properly at night; or it could be that lack of sufficient and hot food reduced Baird's morale and made him disinclined to write much. Professor Gregory said that Baird was a most meticulous recorder of information so that, in ordinary circumstances, the diary would have extended to several pages and contained much information. The very brevity of the diary inspires questions which prove difficult to answer, a difficulty compounded by a degree of inconsistency in the published material as to the content of the diary.

After crossing the Cairngorm Club's footbridge, Baird and Barrie followed the stream known as the Allt Druidh, round the north-eastern flank of the shapely Carn Eilrig, which divides the route to the Lairig Ghru from the one to Gleann Einich, and into the narrow confines of the Lairig Ghru itself. The whole of this area was open, with only scattered remnants of the old Caledonian forest. Once in the Lairig Ghru, as revealed in Baird's diary, they encountered a good deal of snow. The pass rises gradually to its summit at 833m, a short distance beyond which lie the Pools of Dee, one of the two sources of that river. Through the pass ran one of the old drove roads which was in use by drovers with their cattle and sheep travelling from Speyside to Deeside until about 1873. Each spring, men were sent up to clear from the track boulders which had been loosened by the winter frosts and become obstructions to the movement of the animals. From just south of the Pools of Dee, the drove road had followed the east side of the infant river which rapidly broadens as it is joined by tributaries from both sides of the steep-walled pass. The Corrour bothy is built on the west side of the river Dee and in those days there was no bridge. Although the path was under snow, it is likely that Baird and Barrie followed its course and eventually were faced with crossing the river. There can be little doubt that their boots, breeches and stockings were made wet by the snow by the time they crossed the river. It would be difficult to dry boots and clothes and it may be that wet clothes were to play an important part in the events which were to ensue.

Corrour bothy, which was built as a shelter for a deer watcher on the Mar estate, sits at an elevation of about 560m immediately below Coire Odhar after which the bothy is named. Just to the south-west is Devil's Point whose east-facing nose dominates the southern entrance of the Lairig Ghru. In the early 1920s, Corrour was a most desirable mountain residence. Its floor,

Corrour bothy.   *A. C. Gray*

walls and ceiling were made of Mar fir, and bog fir for the fire was stored in
the roof space above the ceiling. The narrow entrance passage contained a
peat barrow and a tusk for cutting peats – relics of the last watcher who
occupied it in 1914. The living room was entered through a second door and
a wide stone fireplace was set into the wall on the opposite side of the room.
It was well-furnished with shelves, cupboards, forms and a table, and it had
the added refinement of a huge, home-made armchair, stuffed with straw
and covered with hessian, in which one could recline in front of a roaring fire
of bogwood. Another refinement was the box bed in the walled-off corner
and this was supplied with a straw mattress. It was without equal. However,
by the end of 1927, when the two Glasgow students arrived, those halcyon
days had gone and the bothy was in decline, suffering from the attentions of
vandals who, among other things, had begun stripping the floors, walls and
ceiling of wood for the fire. How much easier to do this than to collect bog fir

which was in plentiful supply in the neighbourhood! Baird and Barrie found it a cold and cheerless place. Nevertheless, had the two friends known a little more about the bothy, they could have made their stay a little more tolerable. The ceiling had not been wholly stripped and, as Affleck Gray says:

It would not occur to them to look above the ceiling where I would have left an ample supply of bogwood before winter set in. They might even have been able to dig up some bits sticking through the snow in the bogs, but perhaps they did not know that if one starts off bogwood with small spales [splinters] the bigger pieces will quickly ignite on account of the high resin content.

However wet they may have been, the first night seems to have been spent in relative comfort and the following day, Friday, they climbed Devil's Point whose summit, a kilometre away, was easily within reach. The diary gave no indication that they did anything else with their day and this is surprising. It is fairly certain that they would have ascended Devil's Point by way of Coire Odhar and, at most, this route would have measured a total of 5km to and from the bothy with an ascent of 444m and even if they had come upon hard snow and ice, the whole outing would have lasted no more than four hours. The two men had made a considerable effort to come to the Cairngorms; it was, therefore, surely their intention to do as much climbing as they could. Having reached the top of Devil's Point, an obvious continuation was to Cairn Toul, whose summit, at a height of 1291m, lay a mere 3km to the north-west across the gradually rising plateau. There is no suggestion that they attempted this or any other route. It may be that they were tired after their journey to the bothy or did not get under way until late in the morning or that they spent time searching in the snow for rock specimens. It is also possible that they had to contend with worsening weather, the prelude to a violent storm which swept the area during that evening and night.

It was through that storm that three men battled their way up Gleann Einich to the lower bothy which they intended to use as a climbing base and in which they would welcome the New Year. They had arrived in Aviemore on the 4.00 p.m. train from Boat of Garten with provisions, gear and a sledge and they set off into the gathering gloom of the late afternoon. They reached the home of John MacKenzie, the stalker, at Achnagoichan and spent a little time there. They left MacKenzie with the impression that they proposed to shelter in the stable attached to the bothy. However, one of their number, Affleck Gray, knew how to enter the bothy from the stable and open the door from the inside and it was this that they had in mind. Affleck Gray, then a student of forestry at Aberdeen University, was in the company of his brother, Robert, and a friend, Cecil Philip, and he wrote a vivid description of the storm in an article published in the *Glasgow Evening News* on Monday, 9th January, 1928. It is quoted here at some length partly because it illustrates a mountaineering era which has now receded into the mists of time and partly because it gives a clear impression of the power and effects of such a storm and an indication of the terrible difficulties that must have faced Baird and Barrie in the much greater storm of the following Sunday.

It was with high hopes of clear days on Braeriach and Carn Toul that we set out on our Arctic-like expedition from Aviemore on the Friday preceding the tragedy in Glen Eunach. For many days beforehand our plans and preparations had been made and revised from time to time. Profiting by the experience of former years, we employed a hand sledge to carry our sleeping bags, provisions, and a judicious supply of sticks and coal. Until we reached the croft of Achnocoichan [Achnagoichan] the going was fairly easy, but beyond that, in the depths of the forest, conditions became more trying, and it was found necessary to yoke all three of the party into the traces. After that, the snow was deep and soft, and each step became an effort. Our sledge with its heavy load on too shallow runners, sank deeply, and it was only with concentrated endeavour that we made any progress.

After hours spent thus, we gradually moved forward to the outer margin of the forest of Rothiemurchus. As we approached Windy Corner and freed ourselves of the forest's gloom, a noise as of many thundering torrents roared in our ears, and as though the furies were loosed, the blizzard, sweeping round the sudden bend from the open glen beyond, caught us in its icy fury, choking the breath in our throats and hurtling us against each other in utter helplessness. Here we were stranded for the moment, for the glen was drifted bare of snow. Behind a bank we sought shelter from the swirling spindrift to discuss our position. After a short discussion we were obliged to move, for the cold was intense. Leaving our sledge, we staggered ahead for half a mile, examining our route, but conditions were hopeless. We had no alternative but to abandon our sledge and push on with part of our baggage on our backs. Almost half an hour must have been wasted loosening knots with numbed fingers, but when at last all was ready with sleeping bags and a minimum of food, and we again faced the raging blizzard in the open glen, it was to be hurtled backwards with awful venom.

The blizzard was almost Arctic-like in its severity. . . . One part of the road, where there had been a jamb in the Beannaidh stream, was a mass of block ice, and prudence had to be exercised in crossing this treacherous surface. At 5 a.m. we crossed the wooden bridge across the Beannaidh Bheag and reached our goal, coated from head to foot with ice. The bothy was locked, but we gained admission through a hole in the broken end.

If the weather was as severe as this in Gleann Einich at an average height of about 450m, it must have been at least as bad in the Corrour bothy standing in the parallel glen of the Lairig Ghru at a height of 560m. That it was, is borne out by Baird's diary which stated that that night, 30th-31st December, was intensely cold, the thermometer they carried showing a temperature of −14.5°C in the bothy. So cold was it that it took Baird half an hour of sitting on his boots in the morning to thaw the frozen leather to allow him to put them on. Primus stoves can be difficult to start in the cold and theirs may have functioned badly; it was their only source of heat for cooking and warming the hut. The fact that Baird had to use body heat rather than heat from the primus stove to thaw out his boots confirms that the stove could not have been properly operational. The diary seems to have made no reference to using candles to thaw the boots so it may be that the men had a problem with matches, perhaps having got them or the striking paper wet. The cold and the lack of hot meals may well have had an effect on their morale. The blizzard and its evil confederate, the howling wind sweeping up the Lairig Ghru from the south, swirling round the isolated bothy and finding draughty chinks in its weakened defences, must have made the two students feel very lonely and not a little fearful.

The 31st (Saturday) also presents a problem to the investigator. An article on the accident in the Cairngorm Club Journal (Volume XII, January 1929) said: 'The entry for the Saturday is not very explicit but suggests that they may have climbed Cairn Toul.'

Edwin Davidson, an Elgin clothier and founder member and sometime president of the Moray Mountaineering Club, joined Affleck Gray's party for an outing on 1st January and on 2nd January he was in the area of the Lairig Ghru. He was, therefore, involved in the events of those days and in January 1952 he had published a short account of the tragedy under the title of *Mountain Shadows*. In referring to Baird's diary, he said: 'It was a day behind as though the previous night [31st] had been too cold for it to be written.' Clearly this conflicts with the entry in the Cairngorm Club Journal and it may be that Davidson's memory is at fault. Certainly elsewhere in *Mountain Shadows* there are one or two factual mistakes.

Rev. R. B. Thomson wrote an article for the *Badenoch Record* under his pseudonym of 'Monadh Ruadh' in which he considered the tragedy. Referring to the men's intentions once they had arrived at the bothy, Rev. Thomson said:

As to their actual plan of campaign, the conversations they had with the keeper Mackenzie afford the next best clues . . . Ben MacDhui would be attempted; as to Carn Toul, with Angel's Peak and the Devil's Point on either side of it, the return journey toward Braeriach and Glen Eanaich would include all they would consider worth while, or find themselves fit for, the going being such as it was, under arctic conditions.

That Ben MacDui as well as Cairn Toul was on their programme is stated also by Professor Gregory in the short article already mentioned. Whether, on the Saturday, the men made an attempt on Cairn Toul or on Ben MacDui or did something else will probably never be known. Accepting that for some good reason they were unable to reach the summit of Cairn Toul the previous day, it would be surprising if they attempted it again on the Saturday when it is likely that they had decided that their return route to Whitewell on the Sunday would take them over the Cairn Toul-Braeriach plateau into Gleann Einich. The weather on the Saturday was tolerable: Affleck Gray said in his article in the *Glasgow Evening News* of Monday, 9th January that,

Saturday was calmer, but Braeriach and the cliffs of Sgoran Dubh were clouded in dense volumes of mist that were hurried eastwards to Ben Macdhu and Cairngorm.

It is, therefore, possible that they made some kind of an attempt on Ben MacDui, although they may have been deterred by the problem of crossing the Dee, particularly if they had met such difficulties on their arrival on the Thursday. However, if their morale was already rather low, it is possible that they felt disinclined to do much that day and spent a good deal of their time in the hut – and perhaps, in consequence, eating their way through more of what was left of their meagre provisions than they would otherwise have done.

The night of Saturday-Sunday (31st December – 1st January) was another freezing experience for Baird and Barrie. There is no reference to it in the diary because there is no entry for 1st January. However, Affleck Gray, in an article published in *The Courier and Advertiser* on 1st February, 1968 commemorating the fortieth anniversary of the tragedy, said of that Sunday morning in the lower bothy in Gleann Einich:

We arose early to find intense frost festooning the bothy window, and scintillating on the walls. Laboriously, we thawed our boots in a ring of candles, and prepared breakfast with sharpened appetites . . .

The Cairngorms were cloudless but, according to Edwin Davidson in *Mountain Shadows*, there was a red dawn and snow-laden clouds were massing. Davidson has the storm break upon the Cairngorms at 10.00 a.m. and this is too early so perhaps the menacing clouds were not to be seen at the time of the red dawn. Whether they were or not, since the Lairig Ghru is confined within steep, high mountain-sides to both east and west, it is probable that Baird and Barrie were unaware of any sign of the impending storm and may well have been grateful for a fine, clear day on which to return to Whitewell. They would make the most of it. The route over the

Cairn Toul-Braeriach plateau must have seemed quite feasible to them and, although they were evidently low on food, they could not have foreseen any especial risk in the decision to take this way. They would be encouraged in this decision by a heavy accumulation of snow with deep drifting in the Lairig Ghru: on the plateau, swept by the wind in the previous days, the snow would be much less exhausting and Gleann Einich was wider and shallower than the Lairig Ghru so that the snow should not be so deep. It had, moreover, a road and would avoid the tedium of returning by their outward route.

From the Corrour bothy to Whitewell through the Lairig Ghru is 16 km with little ascent, while the route via Gleann Einich is 18 km and involves ascending 730m. The additional distance and climbing was by no means excessive for fit, young men and would be compensated by the easier conditions underfoot. There was no habitation of any kind between Corrour and Whitewell by the Lairig Ghru route but, if need be, they might hope to gain entry to one of the bothies in Gleann Einich which was only 8km distant over the plateau. That they took this route must indicate that they felt fit enough to accomplish it since, if they had doubts, there was open to them the shorter and easier journey to the stalker's cottage at Luibeg and Derry Lodge. Of course, calculation may have played a minor role in the decision: perhaps their youthful enthusiasm, an ignorance of the real dangers of the Cairngorms in winter and a wish to achieve something worthwhile encouraged them to take the bold – and, as it turned out, fatal – course of action.

Superficially, the evidence revealing the time of arrival of the storm which was to kill the two men is conflicting. Professor Gregory said in his article in the S.M.C.J. (art. cit.):

The morning of 1st January opened with continued fair, calm weather, and the two men probably left the hut at daybreak and climbed Braeriach. . . . The fact that he [Baird] reached Glen Eunach utterly exhausted, and that he had been caught in the blizzard which broke over the mountain about 4 p.m., and began at Aviemore about 7 p.m., shows that he had been engaged in the late part of the Sunday in some strenuous effort.

In *Mountain Shadows*, Edwin Davidson said:

At daybreak the Cairngorms were cloudless but the sky gave warning of the approaching storm. As I walked up Gleann Einich I watched the storm break on the Cairngorms and at 10 a.m. the clouds were down to 3,000 feet and the furies were in mad hunt. The spindrift coming off the Sgoran Dubh was tremendous.

The timings given in both these accounts can be treated as unreliable if, as they do, they disagree with times provided elsewhere. A study of the weather maps for 1st January gives the following general information. During the day the wind blew from the south, about Force 6 at sea level, but increasing as the day progressed. At 7.00 a.m. the sky was fairly clear but by 1.00 p.m. it was overcast and by 6.00 p.m. it was snowing, these being the times of issue of the weather maps. Marjory Roy, former Superintendent of the Edinburgh Meteorological Office, says:

Pressure was high over northern Europe and low over the eastern Atlantic with southerly winds over Scotland. A depression developed to the west of Ireland and deepened, causing a strengthening in the southerly winds over Scotland. This depression moved away northwards on the 2nd and winds eased. The period of strongest winds was likely to have been between 13 hours and about 21 hours.

The meteorological information agrees fairly well with evidence from other observers at the time. The report in the Cairngorm Club Journal (art. cit.) stated:

The weather on the Sunday was fine to begin with but broke down in the afternoon, a blizzard coming on when the men were probably still upon the hill.

William Marshall was head forester at Nethybridge and was involved in the search for Hugh Barrie. In his diary he recorded:

On Sunday January 1st, 1928 wild day of drifting snow started with hard south to south-west wind about 2.00 p.m. (loud noise on hills) and died down about midnight. ['Loud noise on hills' indicates that Marshall could hear the storm in Nethybridge.]

Affleck Gray has provided information about the morning and early afternoon in Gleann Einich:

On the morning of the tragedy when I looked out at daybreak to study the sky, the spindrift was rising in a plume from the summit of Braeriach in a stiff S.W. wind. It was fairly calm in the glen but I decided to abandon setting out for Braeriach immediately after breakfast and wait for a bit to see what the weather was going to do. We decided to walk as far as the top bothy and see what thickness of ice lay on Loch Eanaich. It started to snow quite heavily as we reached the bothy somewhere about midday. We sheltered there for a bit to see if it would clear but the snow continued to fall heavily and the wind rose to near gale force. It was now about 2 p.m. and blowing a blizzard. It took us two hours to reach Dunc's bothy, two miles down the glen.

It is clear from the evidence that the storm had struck the area by 2.00 p.m. and that there was a strong wind blowing across the plateau from a southerly direction from daybreak. Affleck Gray says that heavy snowfall had

begun in upper Gleann Einich 'somewhere about midday' and this leads to
the conclusion that the blizzard must have started on the Cairn Toul-
Braeriach plateau itself at that time.

How strong was the wind over the Cairngorms? A comparison can be
made with the wind in the area five years later, on 2nd January, 1933 for
which there is slightly more information. On that day the wind, which was
also southerly, was between Force Seven and Force Eight on the coast and
Force Nine at Dalwhinnie where, by then, there was a weather station.
Dalwhinnie lies about 35km distant from, and some 760m lower than the
Cairngorm plateau. If it was Force Six and more on the coast on 1st January,
1928, by analogy with the 1933 figures it must have been Force Eight at
Dalwhinnie. Marjory Roy says that the direction of the wind may be
particularly significant. There is good evidence to show that, when winds
blow from a southerly direction, they can be unusually strong over the
Cairngorm plateau, much stronger than would be expected from the general
wind speeds in the area. The explanation may have something to do with the
topography of the area, but it also seems that, when the wind flows from a
southerly direction, warm air higher in the atmosphere may act as a lid
containing colder air below. Air flowing over the mountains is then trapped
beneath the lid and the wind speed can increase dramatically as the air is
squeezed between it and the plateau. Thus, if the wind speed on 1st January,
1928 was Gale Force Eight at Dalwhinnie, it may well have risen to Storm
Force Ten and even Violent Storm Force Eleven on the plateau in the
afternoon and evening. Indeed, the wind on Tiree had increased to Strong
Gale Force Nine by 6.00 p.m. and this suggests that it could have attained
speeds of Hurricane Force Twelve on the Cairngorm plateau.

At 1.00 p.m. the sea level temperature in the west of Scotland was about
4.5°C but on the eastern side it was still as low as 0°C. These figures indicate
that the air temperature on the Cairngorm plateau would have been no
higher than −4°C. Taking into account the wind-chill factor for winds of
Force Ten, the cooling effect on the bodies of the two men as they crossed
the plateau would have been equivalent to their being in a still air
environment in which the temperature was −30°C. This is close to the
temperature at which exposed flesh will freeze. Added to this dreadful
situation, even before the arrival of the snow about midday, the increasing
wind would have created storms of stinging, swirling spindrift. With the
onset of the blizzard, the situation became desperate.

Baird and Barrie probably left the bothy soon after daybreak as daylight
would be short and they had far to travel. They would have climbed Coire

Odhar and reached the plateau, 400m above the bothy, between 9.30 a.m. and 10 a.m. In the corrie, they would have been protected to some extent from the wind and may have realised its true force only when they neared the plateau, by which time a change of plan would have been difficult. From there, presumably they made their way towards the summit of Cairn Toul, with the rising wind at their backs. The following wind would have been no advantage; indeed, in some respects they would have been better served by a headwind because the tailwind would have forced them into a constant and debilitating battle to prevent themselves being blown forward quite out of control. At times, especially during the more violent gusts which may well have lasted several minutes, they probably had to prostrate themselves and drive their ice-axes into the snow or hold on to any available rock to prevent themselves from flying headlong before the wind. When the blizzard started, there was a grave risk that the wind might separate them and, if that happened, they would be fortunate to find each other again: they would have little chance of seeing one another and the noise of the wind would make it very difficult for them to hear shouting. It was perhaps because of this danger that they brought their short length of rope into operation: when the packs were found the following March, the rope had a loop tied at each end.

Once they had passed by the top of Cairn Toul, they would have to turn westwards to be subjected to the wind blowing hard from their left and doing its utmost to drive them towards the precipitous northern faces of the mountain. This must have been a terrifying experience, exacerbated by the blizzard. The plateau was devoid of all shelter. How desperately distant the croft of Whitewell must have seemed; how warm and friendly the sheltering walls of the little corrugated iron house. There was no alternative to continuing towards Whitewell: their food supply was very low and, even if this had been sufficient, the wind and the snow driving into their faces would have made it well-nigh impossible to return to Corrour bothy. After fighting their way in this westerly direction for 2km, they would have been able to turn in a northerly direction again to have the wind at their backs and cross Einich Cairn. Whether they knew where they were or were able to take any bearings in such atrocious conditions is debatable; indeed, their eventual route of escape from the plateau may well be best explained by their being quite lost and simply desperate to get down at any cost. It is doubtful if they knew they were descending Coire Bogha-cloiche which would bring them down close to the upper Gleann Einich bothy; even if they did, they would have had great difficulty in finding the bothy in the storm.

It is difficult to estimate when they made the northerly turn towards

Braeriach and Gleann Einich.   *Donald Bennet*

Einich Cairn, but the state of exhaustion which was to cause them to
abandon their rucksacks in Coire Bogha-cloiche must have been beginning
to manifest itself. Apart from their increasing physical debility, the wind
itself would have been making progress very slow as they struggled to
maintain some little control of their movement. Affleck Gray's party at the
lower and more protected level of Gleann Einich was contending with the
same wind and it took them two hours to cover the 3km from the upper
bothy to the lower bothy. Baird and Barrie could not have exceeded this rate
of progress, and were probably significantly slower. Therefore, it could well
have been after 1.30 p.m. when they turned north; and it was from 1.00 p.m.
until about 9.00 p.m. that the wind was at its strongest. The wind would have
tended to drive them down the northern side of Braeriach but they did not

want to take this route. Their safest line of descent from the plateau into Gleann Einich was down the north-west shoulder of Braeriach which is not steep and would have taken them close to the lower bothy. It was because of the likelihood of this descent route that this section was chosen as one of the main search areas. That they turned west at or beyond the level summit of Einich Cairn and in so doing had to contend again with the wind and the blizzard blowing hard on their left side suggests that they had become lost and quite possibly disoriented or that they were absolutely desperate to escape from the plateau and reach lower ground. There is the possibility that they had some idea of their position and decided to make for the upper Gleann Einich bothy, perhaps being aware that the stable was open, but they knew that the bothy itself was locked and might be difficult to enter and they must have known that it would be difficult to locate in the blizzard and almost impossible in the dark.

Whatever their reason, they made their descent from the swirling cauldron of the plateau by way of the narrow corrie known as Coire Bogha-cloiche which descends 600m or so to the northern end of Loch Einich and close to the upper bothy. They may not have descended directly from the steep headwall of the corrie but rather left the plateau close to the top of Einich Cairn and been blown by the wind diagonally downwards towards Coire Bogha-cloiche. There is no doubt that they descended this corrie because their rucksacks were found almost half way down by John MacKenzie, the stalker, almost twelve weeks later. By the time the mountaineers started their descent, it must have been at least 2.30 p.m.

After its steep headwall of about 150m, Coire Bogha-cloiche fans out and the angle of descent becomes fairly gradual until its final steep section of about 140m down the centre of which there is a fine triple waterfall. At the bottom of the corrie, the ground slopes easily down to the floor of Gleann Einich which, being quite wide and flat, has large areas of peat and moss hags.

The men's rucksacks were jettisoned in the more gently sloping middle section of the corrie. One, containing apparently only a few light articles, was dropped at a height of 915m and the other, which contained the rest of their gear and was heavily laden, was 90m lower down and left carefully beside a boulder with a stone placed on top, as though to mark its position. It is almost certain that the light pack was being carried by Barrie and the heavy one by Baird. The abandoning of the packs shows how exhausted both men had become. Whether they maintained contact with each other on the way down the corrie or became separated because of the blizzard, or by a fall, a glissade, a snow slide or soft snow avalanche or even by the onset of darkness is not known. The rope was found in the light rucksack and this shows that they were not roped together for much, if any, of the descent of the corrie. The fact that only one ice-axe was found by the searchers and Baird was found the next day with Barrie's walking stick could indicate a fall or some kind of avalanche.

There is another factor to consider. Dr Balfour was the medical practitioner in Aviemore and he examined Barrie's body after it was found towards the end of March. He had a bruise on his temple and he had a sprained ankle. The sprained ankle could be significant. It would seriously delay the men's progress, not least because the violent wind would make it so very difficult for Barrie to protect the ankle as he walked and he may have required regular and frequent assistance from Baird. It may well be that it was the damage done to Barrie's ankle that forced Baird to carry most of the gear. Certainly, the descent of the corrie would have been extremely difficult if the mishap had already happened. It may be that Baird was bearing the heavy pack because Barrie had become very tired. It is inconceivable, however, that Baird would have left Corrour that morning with such a heavy burden: if Barrie was already so weakened that he could manage only a light pack, the men would surely have made for the Braemar side of the Cairngorm massif.

By this time Affleck Gray's party had regained the lower bothy after their two hour battle with the elements. Affleck Gray, in his article in *The Courier and Advertiser* on 1st February, 1968, described their experience in the bothy during the later part of that awful day:

All afternoon and evening the storm raged. The bothy trembled and creaked, and we feared it might be flattened. We did not venture outside for water and, for cooking, melted snow that drifted in under the door. While we had been stumbling down the glen, two tragic figures must have been groping their way across the plateau in a raging blizzard of wind, snow, and spindrift . . . Later, secure, well-fed, and warmed by a blazing fire, we never dreamed that near the bothy where we had sheltered earlier in the day a young man of our own age approached his last sleep in a peat hag, and another was stumbling to within calling distance of us, only to tumble over a snow wreath in utter weariness, and die almost on our door-step.

Affleck Gray has added detail to this grim picture and takes events on to the following morning when they left the bothy to return to Boat of Garten:

Just about half a mile south of Dunc's bothy there was an enormous wreath across the road stretching from the high bank above to the Beannaidh. It was over this wreath that the exhausted Baird tumbled never to rise again. By daylight next morning a warm air blew from the west and a very rapid thaw set in. . . . My brother thought before we left for home that he would walk up to the wreath and see how much it had sunk, but fearing a 'rocket' from me for leaving us to pack the sledge he remained with us. What a pity! But for my intransigence he would have found Baird, and as we had some fuel and food left over we might well have revived him.

That storm of 1st January, 1928 is still remembered by the older local residents of the area. Jock MacKenzie, another member of the MacKenzie family, was sitting with his family in their house at Tullochgrue, only a short distance from Whitewell, when the south-east facing window of the room was blown in by the force of the wind. Jessie MacDonald, who lived at Whitewell until her death at the end of 1990, resided at Loch an Eilein in those days and that Sunday she and her family had a visit from friends who walked out from Inverdruie. The blizzard came on during the afternoon and the snow piled up to the level of the windowsills. So great was the snowfall that their visitors were obliged to spend the night with them. The fact that they made the journey is a clear indication that the severity of the storm was quite unexpected.

At 6.30 a.m. on Monday, 2nd January two young men from Perth left that city by train bound for Aviemore. They were Alastair Cram who was seventeen and Edward Maconachie, a nineteen-year-old bank clerk. During the previous summer, they had enjoyed a camping and walking holiday near Aviemore and they were looking forward to seeing Loch Einich, which was one of their favourite haunts, under wintry conditions. They were to take the road up Gleann Einich and in the course of time they met Affleck Gray's party returning with their sledge to Aviemore. The thaw was exposing much of the road which caused problems with the sledge. *The Strathspey Herald* of Friday, 6th January, 1928 contained a full description of the adventure that befell Cram and Maconachie after they left Aviemore for Loch Einich.

They set off across the moors, making direct for the loch. They had covered about seven miles by mid-day, and were on a moorland track, when they came across the body of a young man. In an interview Edward Maconachie said: 'Alistair [sic] and I saw a man lying by the side of the track. When we examined him we found he was unconscious. We tried by rubbing his hands and forcing something between his teeth to bring him back to consciousness, but, although he moved slightly as if trying to get up, he did not come round. His hands and legs were badly bruised. We wondered what to do with him, and seeing a bothy on the hillside about 400 yards away we decided to carry him there. He was heavy, and it was a stiff job getting him over the hillside. When we reached the hut the door was shut, and we had to smash it in with a stone. Inside we tried again to do something to revive him, but there was no response to our efforts, and at length we decided that one of us should remain with the man

while the other sought assistance. Alistair set out for the nearest 'phone, which was at
Coylum Bridge, some five miles away. I was left to look after the man, and it was a
lonely vigil. . . .'

Alistair Cram then took up the story: 'I knew when I left the hut,' he said, 'that it
was a case of life or death, and it was the very possibility of saving the unfortunate
man's life that spurred me on over the worst and hardest of roads. It took me about an
hour and a half to cover the six miles to Coylum Bridge, from which place I
telephoned to Dr Balfour at Aviemore. . . .'

Dr Balfour, who was, incidentally, a cousin of Robert Louis Stevenson,
was also interviewed by the newspaper and his account added further detail,
including some interesting insights into a Highland medical practice in those
years:

The doctor, in an interview, said he received the call shortly after two
o'clock. . . . Unfortunately all of the available cars in the village were on hire . . .
Eventually the doctor obtained a car and set out on his journey. At Coylum Bridge he
was met by Cram, his young informant, who had walked to meet him. The doctor was
disinclined to take Cram in the car, but yielded to his entreaties to be allowed to go
and rejoin his companion whom he had left in the bothy with the unconscious man.
As they went along Cram, who was in his 'teens, said that he and a companion named
Maconachie, both of whom belonged to Perth, were walking through Glen Eanich,
and had passed the first bothy by about 400 yards when they saw a man in breeches
lying near the roadside partially in a pool of water. At first they thought he was drunk,
and they passed on. But something in the posture of the man caused them to retrace
their steps. . . . Cram had scarcely finished his story to the doctor when the motor car
stuck in a snowdrift, 100 yards long, in the Forest of Rothiemurchus. All attempts at
progress proved unavailing, and the car had to be turned back to the village of
Inverdruie, where, after a search causing more delays, the doctor obtained a horse
and sleigh, and the journey was recommenced. . . . When the doctor entered the
bothy the scene told its own story. The unconscious man had died. Maconachie gave
the simple information that two minutes after his companion had left him the man
had expired, and he had been left alone for four and a half hours in the hills with the
corpse. The body of Baird, as it later turned out to be, was placed on the sleigh, and
the tragic party commenced the journey through the forest once more, back to
Aviemore, where the grim burden was placed in the mortuary. By the side of the
sleigh walked the doctor and his two companions. At 10.30 p.m. Aviemore was
reached. . . . Both lads were convinced that Baird had left to secure assistance for his
companion, who must have met with difficulties. The knees of Baird's breeches were
badly torn. He had no kit beside him apart from the waterproof jacket which he wore.
His clothes were completely soaked, and the absence of kit convinced the boys that
Baird had discarded all heavy material wherever his companion lay in order to help
him in his rescue efforts.

Alastair Cram has the following to say of the events of that day. As he now remembers, Baird had little visible injury.

I still can recall most of the journey I made in January 1928. A point in the newspaper description I should like to alter is that one of us told the reporter that, having found Baird, we went on and then came back to him. It is of course correct to say we went on but only a pace or two before returning and attending to him. Baird was lying on his back, fully clad, without gloves, ice axe or rucksack. Apart from a few scratches he had no visible injuries. As we lifted him from the ground, a prolonged rattle sounded in his throat. . . . On the way back [from the lower bothy to Aviemore to summon assistance for Baird], I employed a combination of loping run and walking pace which brought me on fast without need to halt. . . . At Coylum Bridge, the postmistress plainly held an opinion that I was drawing a long bow and required prepayment for my 2d [one penny] telephone call. Instead of setting in train an equipped rescue party, I had to lope into Aviemore to find and persuade the police and the doctor that I was not wrong in the head or was seeking publicity. The old doctor, however, proved a trump. He told me how to order a horse and a sleigh, along with blankets and a horseman. He himself was recovering from near pneumonia yet setting out on a journey which might prove fatal for him. The horseman and I walked, the doctor wrapped in blankets rode on the sleigh. . . . Once back at the hut, I found Ted had made a fire and the hut was warm. The doctor continued to make a thorough examination of the body, presumably with an inquest in mind. With time on my hands, I went outside uneasily conscious that a companion could be a victim of the storm. I walked up the line of the road to where I knew a long, shallow scoop descended the lower part of this 4000 foot corner buttress of Braeriach which an exhausted man might choose to follow down. Opposite to the scoop was a wilderness of peat trenches. Into this I went a little way before calling loudly to no response. This was the area where, after some time, the body of Barrie was discovered, lying in a trench in the hag.

Thomas Baird's identity was provided by the letter found in his pocket and the authorities soon ascertained that he had been in the company of his follow student, Hugh Barrie. It was clear that Barrie must still be somewhere in the hills; the problem facing the searchers was his location. It was known that they had left Whitewell with the intention of staying in the Corrour bothy and, although it could not be known for certain that they had used it, there was general agreement that they had been there since the Thursday, especially after the upper Gleann Einich bothy was reached and found to be locked, with no evidence of having been used. John MacKenzie had seen footprints, evidently theirs, in the snow on the Cairngorm footbridge on the way to the Lairig Ghru and, in any case, there was nowhere else they could, within the realms of reasoning, have stayed. There was the possibility that Barrie had been injured or taken ill during the stay in the Corrour bothy and that he had been left there while Baird made his way for help; it was, however, only a faint possibility since assistance would have been more easily and quickly summoned from the Braemar side. Nonetheless, a party would set out from that side to try to find the missing man. If he was not at Corrour, he must surely be somewhere between there and the lower Gleann Einich bothy, somewhere along the route taken by his friend.

That Baird was found near the lower bothy made it certain that he had made his way over the plateau; uncertain, however, was the route by which he had travelled. Bearing in mind the violence of the storm which had raged for so much of the previous day and the fact that they may well have been lost, they could have descended from the plateau almost anywhere along its western and northern flanks. This was an extensive area which would be difficult to search properly even in good conditions with a large body of searchers; in bad conditions and with limited manpower, there was little chance of success. By struggling down the glen in his valiant effort to survive, Baird had widened the search area: if he had succumbed near the upper bothy, the area would have been considerably more restricted.

With the manpower available, it was decided initially to concentrate the search in Gleann Einich and, on both the Tuesday and the Wednesday, a party of ghillies and police searched the glen as far as the upper bothy. On the Wednesday, close to the place where Baird was found, they discovered a thick woollen sock, a silk handkerchief lying on a snowdrift and a stick in the shape of a crook in a nearby pool of water. Barrie's sister, Nancy, travelled from Glasgow to Aviemore on the Wednesday and she was shown the items. She recognised the stick as her brother's and the silk handkerchief as being like one that he possessed. This led to speculation that Barrie had died before Baird had left him and Baird had taken these personal items to give to Nancy, the sole surviving member of the Barrie family.

The weather was very wild and by the Wednesday it was certain that Barrie, if he was lying in the open, would be covered by the snow and that he must be dead. On the Thursday the weather was so stormy, with heavy snowstorms from the south-west, that no search was made from the Aviemore side, but it had improved somewhat on the Friday so another party of ghillies, accompanied by Police Constable MacLean of Aviemore, proceeded up Gleann Einich. Three of the eight members went no further than the lower bothy, but the others reached the upper bothy and were able to go a short distance towards Coire Dhondail before being driven back by the weather. P.C. MacLean discovered a box of matches and a piece of string in the snow and apparently some faint footprints, but there was no way of telling if any of these had to do with the two Glasgow students.

If the weather was too bad to permit a further sortie from Aviemore on Thursday, 5th January, it was little better in Braemar. However, there was the chance that Barrie was in the Corrour bothy so an attempt was made to reach the bothy from that side. The plan was for a party consisting of police, stalkers and ghillies to assemble at Derry Lodge and to make their way through the Lairig Ghru to the Corrour bothy and, if Barrie was not there, to search the hillsides above the bothy towards Cairn Toul and Devil's Point. If they drew a blank, their intention was to return to the area the following day. *The Sunday Post* of Sunday, 8th January told the story of the attempts on both these days:

Inspector Cooper, of the Aberdeen County Police, led the party of six men which left Braemar on the Thursday morning, and struggled through a snowstorm to Derry Lodge, a distance of eight miles. There they found the conditions so unfavourable that they were compelled to shelter the whole day at the lodge. Next morning they set off in spite of most unpromising weather to cover the last lap of five miles. During four terrible hours the party battled on in the face of a howling blizzard. They plunged through drifts of snow which took them up to the armpits, and in which one member or another frequently became embedded, and had to be pulled clear by his comrades. At last human endurance could brave the storm no longer, and with a bare four hundred yards separating them from the Corrour Bothy the men came to a standstill. Chagrined in the extreme at being foiled when so near their goal, the men dispiritedly turned their backs to the gale, and ploughed back through the snow to Derry Lodge, at which they arrived in an exhausted condition, and barely able to lift one foot after another. One of the party, Mr John Harkness, whom a *Sunday Post* representative interviewed to-night said: 'The snow was lying very deep among the hills, and we never knew what we were walking on. In several instances we found ourselves waist-deep in water, owing to the fact that several of the mountain burns were covered with a thin layer of ice and snow, and were invisible to the naked eye.'

In *The People's Journal* of Saturday, 14th January, Alexander Grant was quoted as saying:

This is the first time that I have had any connection with a tragedy in the mountains and I was very sorry to turn the party back when within a quarter of a mile from Corrour Bothy, but it was humanly impossible to have gone any further. We could not see the River Dee, which must have been near to us, and another step farther would have been extremely dangerous. . . . It is very evident that disaster overtook the two men somewhere between Corrour Bothy and Aviemore. If they had met with disaster near Corrour Bothy one of the men would have come down here [to Luibeg] for help.

Alexander Grant's son, Iain, was one of the party and he remembered the expedition:

The party of police spent the previous night with us at Luibeg. The 6th January was an awful day. I never faced a worse blizzard. My father was in the lead and his moustache was frozen and part of his face coated with ice. We were well round into the Larig but never caught a glimpse of the bothy. We would have made it with a struggle. The police, however, would take no risks. Two or three of the younger fellows offered to make a dash for it but the Inspector would not allow.

If the men from Deeside were to place themselves rather unwittingly in such peril on the Friday, it was to be the turn of others on Sunday, 8th January. During the week following the finding of Baird, Professor Gregory had organised a search party to travel from Glasgow to join the local volunteers for a major effort on the Sunday (8th January). Sixty men, far more than hitherto, took part in the most atrocious of conditions; so bad, in fact, that the searchers placed themselves at considerable risk. As *The Glasgow Herald* of Monday, 9th January said:

The weather yesterday at once made the operations a fiasco and extremely hazardous and trying for those taking part. The men were half-blinded by driving snow, which froze to ice on their clothing. High on the mountain the gale was estimated to be travelling at 80 miles per hour.

Shortly after 8.00 a.m. the party left Aviemore for Gleann Einich and the lower bothy which was to be the base for operations. Many made their way to the bothy by car since the Gleann Einich road was by then fairly clear of snow. Four car loads came from Boat of Garten and five from Aviemore. The searchers ranged in age from some in their teens to Mr Carr, head stalker on the Rothiemurchus estate, who was seventy. The press representatives had seen to it that a supply of coal was taken. John MacKenzie, the second stalker on the Rothiemurchus estate, was in charge of the sixty men and he organised the plan of campaign which was set in motion at 10.00 a.m. The press reports were rather confused and conflicting in their descriptions of this plan, one reason for this probably being that the newsmen were unfamiliar with the area and another being that they preferred to stay in or close to the lower bothy, with its coal fire and hot drinks, rather than venture far into the storm. The report in *The People's Journal* purported to come from the pen of a member of the search party and it made good enough sense; it also inspired rather more confidence than the others in that it gave the correct spelling of the places mentioned in contrast to some rather eccentric anglicised spellings favoured by the other reports, the most amusing of which is Corbuncle for Coire Dhondail.

It seems that MacKenzie divided his forces into three main groups, with a

John MacKenzie at Dunc's bothy.   *A. C. Gray*

fourth under P. C. MacLean searching the flat ground along the floor of the glen between the lower and the upper bothies. The smallest of the main groups, under James Reid, the Coylumbridge ghillie, worked its way up the Beanaidh Bheag stream to examine Coire Beanaidh, one of the sources of the stream which flows down the northern flank of Braeriach to join Am Beanaidh itself beside the site of the lower bothy. MacKenzie himself led a party up Gleann Einich to ascend Coire Dhondail, the north facing corrie to the east of Loch Einich which MacKenzie was sure was the line taken by the two men as they fought their way down. The third and largest party, under the direction of Rev. R. B. Thomson, undertook a search of the western flank of the mountain approximately between the lower and upper bothies, ultimately working towards Loch Coire an Lochain lying in the most westerly of the three great northern corries. It was hoped that all three parties would be able to make their way over the plateau to the Wells of Dee where they would rendezvous and return across the plateau and down the western flank of Braeriach in open order to conduct a final thorough search. In this way, the whole area over which Baird and Barrie could have been expected to travel would be covered. It was not to be: the ferocious wind and the blizzards that it swept along denied them any access to the plateau and negated the efforts that they made at the lower levels.

The writer of the report in *The People's Journal* to which reference has been made was a member of the group led by Rev. Thomson. In the course of the article he said:

The wind was now increasing in violence [as they ascended the western flank]. It was impossible to toil upwards while the gusts lasted. We could only crouch camel-like with our backs to the blizzard, which formed an armour of frozen snow on our clothing . . . Our greatest handicap was the powdered spindrift, which blotted out everything more than a couple of yards away, froze on our faces, and compressed in an icy vice the exposed parts of the neck and head. An eerie 'whee-rr' above us gave us warning of these sudden squalls, which either threw us down to the ground or sent us hurtling forward a dozen yards or so until we had regained our balance, and we soon learned from the sound to crouch for shelter behind the nearest boulder. . . . Still we toiled onward and upward until at a height of about 3,000 feet we encountered the worst blizzard of the day. For about 15 minutes it lasted, while we crouched behind a rock, unable even to open our eyes because of the drift. At this point we were within a very short distance of Loch Coire-an-Lochan, the highest loch in Scotland. 'Fancy a gale ten times worse than this!' Mr Smith [Donald Smith, a farmer and former stalker], who was crouching beside me, shouted in my ear. 'I reckon that the gale last Sunday was ten times worse than this. Nobody could have lived through it at this height.'

Although undoubtedly an exaggeration, this comment by Donald Smith does make the point that the conditions and dangers facing Baird and Barrie the previous Sunday would have been worse, perhaps much worse, than they were to be a week later.

'The minister's party for Coire an Lochain'. 'The Courier', Dundee

Others suffered from the conditions. *The Glasgow Herald* of Monday, 9th January, which had Rev. Thomson being 'blown over in a somersault by one fierce gust', reported that Professor Gregory 'was completely toppled over by a blast of wind, and saved himself from rolling down by the adroit use of his alpenstock' – which *The People's Journal* referred to as an ice-axe. The same *Glasgow Herald* report mentioned that another search leader 'slipped and tumbled furiously down the slope, turning catherine wheels for 150 yards towards a heap of boulders' but, fortunately, he was saved by a patch of soft snow; one party, nearing the plateau, was caught by the fury of the wind and swept up about 45 metres on to the edge of the plateau and found themselves being blown upwards even when they lay flat on the snow; and a youth collapsed from exhaustion at 762m and was revived with hot drinks from vacuum flasks and an onion, the eating of which was regarded as a panacea by shepherds and stalkers.

Affleck Gray, who was a member of John MacKenzie's Coire Dhondail search party, described his experience that day in *The Strathspey Herald* of Friday, 13th January:

Mr Gray states that after searching the floor of Coire Dhondail, an attempt was made to gain the plateau by the steep wall of ice and snow. 'Towards the foot the snow was fairly soft, and good footing was obtained, but as one ascended the surface gradually became harder, till each step was a menace. Every step I had to cut with the aid of the pike, and by kicking through the concrete-like surface with the toe of my boot. The only arm which could be used gradually weakened in such a cramped position. Ever and anon a fierce sweep of the blizzard flattened us to the field; a false move would have meant destruction, or at the least great injury. And while I toiled and perspired freely my companions, a youth of my own age, and John MacBain, an old stalker, following in my steps were numbed to the bone. . . .'

At another point in the search, after discussion with MacKenzie, Gray with his brother, Robert, and two others broke away from the main party and managed to reach the plateau by way of the ground between Coire Dhondail and Coire Bogha-cloiche. The blizzard at that altitude was so fierce that it would have been folly to have done other than retreat to lower ground, but not before Robert Gray was blown away from the other three and disappeared in the spindrift. It was with relief that they glimpsed him momentarily and grabbed hold of him.

All these endeavours were for nothing. It was clear that any further search was futile until the weather improved and the snows subsided and no further searches of any size took place from the Aviemore side until after John MacKenzie had discovered the men's rucksacks towards the end of March. However, one further effort was made to reach Corrour bothy from Deeside to check the bothy for the presence of the missing Barrie and, if he was not found there, to search the ground above the bothy.

On Saturday, 14th January, taking advantage of a break in the severe weather which had prevailed in the Braemar area for the previous fortnight, Alexander Grant, the stalker from Luibeg, and his son, Iain, set off for the bothy. Iain Grant wrote:

. . . I think Baird and Barrie had been short of food on their last journey. When my father and I went into the bothy we found no food there which was unused. There was an empty milk tin and a small bean tin in the fireplace. This had been presumably their breakfast, but by later inquiries we learned that those tins had been left full by two Dundee chaps who were there a short time previous. We found Baird and Barrie's tracks frozen in the ice leading away from the bothy towards Cairntoul by the Coire Odhar.

Whether or not these were the tracks of the unfortunate men cannot be known for sure. The Grants were little more than an hour ahead of two young men from Glasgow, George Robertson and James Wilson, who had travelled overnight to spend the weekend at the bothy. During their stay they ascended Coire Odhar to the plateau but found no evidence of Baird and Barrie. Yet another party reached the bothy that Saturday: a team, organised by the Aberdeenshire police, which included a group of five Dundee members of the Grampian Mountaineering Club led by Robert Ower. They left Braemar in the dark at 7.00 a.m. and motored as far as Derry Lodge, after which progress was made on foot. It snowed continuously. Shortly after 10.00 a.m. they reached a point opposite Corrour bothy where they were faced with the problem of crossing the river Dee. Fortunately the bed of the river was piled high with an accumulation of ice on which the snow was lying and on this they worked their way over on their hands and knees. They knew from the smoke curling up from the bothy chimney that they were not the first to arrive and within minutes they were sitting round the fire with the young men from Glasgow. Before returning to Braemar, the police team made a search of the slopes leading upwards behind the bothy but without result.

The weeks passed. Stalkers and walkers out in the area were alert to any signs which might betray the whereabouts of Barrie's body but still nothing was discovered. Then on Saturday, 24th March, John MacKenzie found the two rucksacks in Coire Bogha-cloiche. MacKenzie marked the positions of the rucksacks but left them where they were for inspection by P.C. MacLean the following day when their contents were examined. The only food in Barrie's rucksack was some porridge in the billycan and attached to this pack was the small rope with the loops at both ends. Among the contents of Baird's rucksack were two university sweaters and, in one of these, a thermometer was carefully wrapped. There was a wallet containing a fountain pen, a map measurer, a pencil and two notebooks, one of which was Baird's diary. There was no food and attached to the rucksack were two raincoats and two blankets. That the men had been carrying clothing which could have been worn is an indicator that their thinking had been affected by hypothermia; however, it could be that it had been simply too windy on the plateau to struggle into this clothing.

As a result of the discovery of the rucksacks, John MacKenzie considered that there was a likelihood that Barrie's body would be found somewhere lower down the mountain-side. Two parties resumed the search the following day. The first consisted of six men from Nethybridge and was led by William

Marshall, the forester and naturalist, a man well acquainted with the Cairngorms who wrote about them under the pen name of 'Mam Suim'. The other party, under the leadership of P.C. MacLean, left from Aviemore and included two Dundee members of the Grampian Mountaineering Club, Robert Ower and a Mr A. Soutter, who met John MacKenzie adventitiously at Aviemore station when they arrived there in the later part of Saturday.

The Aviemore party set out first and searched the low ground from the point where Baird was found to the upper bothy but discovered nothing. Then they made their way up to the rucksacks in Coire Bogha-cloiche, MacLean and Soutter first making a brief diversion to examine the ground at the bottom of the Allt Coire Dhondail, the stream which drains the corrie of that name. The first pack was Baird's and while they were examining its contents the Nethybridge party arrived. Then they went together up to Barrie's smaller pack. William Marshall wrote of their experience in *The Northern Scot and Moray and Nairn Express* of Saturday, 31 March:

At daylight the mist was low down on the mountains, and we had little hope of getting much done on the tops. . . . From the burn near where Baird was found dying we made a line on the slope of Braeriach. The top man was at the edge of the mist, and the lowest on the broken ground near the road. Slowly we moved westward [sic – it should be southward], searching systematically every burn and hag. The day was mild and calm, but through a rift in the mist fresh snow showed on Sgoran-dhu. In front, dark Loch Eanaich lay brooding, with just a catspaw of wind rippling its far corner. A pair of ptarmigan, still in white winter plumage, rose from a patch of scree, and occasionally a white hare hastened uphill from the intruders. There was a huge wreath of snow, perhaps forty feet deep, in the burn above the top bothy, and we paid particular attention to every broken edge of that. From there, the lowest man kept the pony path and the rest of us searched the scree above, on towards Cor-dhondail. In Cornaclach [Coire nan Clach which lies just to the north of Coire Dhondail and must be a misreading for Coire Bogha-cloiche] we joined up with the Aviemore party. We then combed the floor of the corrie ere moving lower down. There is a great quantity of snow in all the high corries of the range, in fact I have never seen so much. The finding of the two packs indicated that both men had got below that point, so we decided to lunch at the top bothy and search the floor of the glen carefully in the afternoon. On the way down we extended a line from the path to the lochside and moved slowly eastward [this must be an error for westward]. In a moss hag, Mr Slessor – second from the left – noticed his Labrador get the wind of something, and went over to see what attracted its attention. There, in a shallow rut, lay the remains of the ill-fated Barrie. We all closed in, each with a feeling of satisfaction that the search was over, but with a strange stirring at our hearts as we looked on the body which had lain hidden for exactly twelve long weeks. He lay naturally on his back, untouched by vermin, head to the west, gloveless hands on his breast. His wrist watch had stopped at 7.45, but whether a.m. or p.m. it is difficult to say. From the bothy, which was 400 yards away, we procured an old ladder and improvised a stretcher. Reverently, and with some difficulty owing to the broken moss, we carried the body up to the hut. It was now about 2 p.m., so after lunch we moved, in subdued spirits, down the glen to the car and arrived at Nethybridge soon after five o'clock.

In a letter to Edwin Davidson, William Marshall gave the following additional information about Barrie's body:

There was a spot of fungus on one of the hands, otherwise the body was in wonderful condition after 12 weeks. Barrie's breeches were down. Probably he had been so exhausted that he was unable to pull them up again. There was a bruise, nothing serious on his temple. [Victims of hypothermia are known to remove their clothing.]

Barrie's body, which was found between the old sluice at the northern end of Loch Einich and the upper Gleann Einich bothy was left in the upper bothy overnight and the following day, Monday, it was brought to Whitewell and, with somewhat tragic irony, placed in the little house where he and Baird had spent the night before their departure for the isolated bothy in the Lairig Ghru.

On Friday, 6th January, long before Barrie's body was found, the burial of Thomas Baird took place in the churchyard of Baldernock Church, near Milngavie. Barrie's funeral took place on Tuesday, 27th March, two days after his body was found. The grave lay about 300 metres from Whitewell in ground given for the purpose by the laird of Rothiemurchus, Major J. P. Grant.

For approaching eighteen months, Barrie's grave was marked off only by a wooden fence while the preparations were made for the building of a cairn over the grave. Two large boulders of reddish Cairngorm granite were hauled from Am Beanaidh at Windy Corner in Gleann Einich and dragged by horse up the slope to the track above; one was to be set on the top of Barrie's cairn and the other was to be put on a rectangular granite block to mark the final earthly resting place of Thomas Baird. The boulders were taken down Gleann Einich on a slipe – a triangular-framed sledge pulled by a horse – and Baird's was transported to Glasgow by train. Masons came from Glasgow to construct the cairn. The large granite memorial stone was cemented on to a concrete pillar about one and a half metres high, and around this, effectively concealing the pillar, the drystone cairn was carefully built to withstand the rigours of the weather. On Saturday, 7th September, 1929 the memorial cairn was unveiled. On the front of the stone facing the Cairngorms are the words:

Erected in proud and affectionate memory of Hugh Alexander Barrie M.A. interred here and Thomas Baird M.A. interred at Baldernock who lost their lives on 2nd January 1928 while climbing these hills

Find me a wind-swept boulder for a bier

Bier - handbarrow or portable frame on which corpse is placed or borne to grave

Attached to the memorial stone is the crest of the Glasgow University Officers' Training Corps. The grave is situated on open moorland with an impressive panorama southwards towards the Cairngorm massif. Especially prominent, beyond the little corrugated iron house with its few sheltering trees, is the great bulk of Braeriach with the Lairig Ghru to its east and Gleann Einich to its west.

The granite memorial stone marking the grave of Thomas Baird in Baldernock Parish churchyard is tapered on the right and in the top right angle, there are the words:

A wind-swept boulder from the Cairngorms

The rest of the stone reads:

In proud and affectionate memory of Tom Baird M.A. aged 22 – interred here – and of his friend Hugh A. Barrie M.A. interred at Tullochgrue, Aviemore who lost their lives in the great blizzard which swept the Cairngorms 2nd Jan. 1928.

Baird's memorial stone, like Barrie's, has the crest of the Glasgow University O.T.C. attached. The granite base on which Baird's stone rests has inscriptions in memory of both his father and his mother.

Some time after the men were found and laid to rest, John MacKenzie was offered a gold pocket watch and chain. He asked that it be given to his father, Alexander, who, with his wife, had given shelter to the two friends before they set out on their last visit to the hills. The watch, which is now in the possession of Brock Nethersole-Thompson, has the interlinking letters 'A' and 'M' on the front of the case which opens to reveal a face with black Roman numerals and black hands. Inside the rear cover is an inscription in English and Gaelic. The MacKenzies did not speak Gaelic, although they understood it. In English, the inscription reads:

Hugh A. Barrie   *Thomas Baird*
To
Alexander MacKenzie
As A Remembrance
For Your Valued Service
January To March
1928

The quotations on both memorial stones came from the verse Barrie had published in the summer 1927 edition of the *Glasgow University Magazine*, no more than six months before his death. Barrie was not granted his wish not to be buried in the dark earth but, in a society which prefers burial or cremation, the disposal given to his body was as close to the wish he expressed as was possible.

Lines

When I am dead
And this strange spark of life that in me lies
Is fled to join the great white core of life
That surely flames beyond eternities,
And all I ever thought of as myself
Is mouldering to dust and cold death ash,
This pride of nerve and muscle – merest dross,
This joy of brain and eye and touch but trash,
Bury me not, I pray thee,
In the dark earth where comes not any ray
Of light or warmth or aught that made life dear;
But take my whitened bones far, far away
Out of the hum and turmoil of the town,
Find me a wind-swept boulder for a bier
And on it lay me down
Where far beneath drops sheer the rocky ridge
Down to the gloomy valley, and the streams
Fall foaming white against black beetling rocks:
Where the sun's kindly radiance seldom gleams:
Where some tall peak, defiant, steadfast mocks
The passing gods: and all the ways of men
Forgotten.

So may I know
Even in that death that comes to everything
The swiftly silent swish of hurrying snow;
The lash of rain; the savage bellowing
Of stags; the bitter keen-knife-edge embrace of the rushing
wind: and the still tremulous dawn
Will touch the eyeless sockets of my face;
And I shall see the sunset and anon
Shall know the velvet kindness of the night
And see the stars.

                              BAH (Hugh A Barrie)

Baird also had turned his mind to poetry and had had the following poem published in the *University Verses, 1910-1927.*

> *Via*
> This road that wanders through the pines
> Has strangely aided in the growth of me;
> Its landmarks are the outward signs
> Of thought educed in walking reverie.
> These lines of beeches on the hill
> That glow with leaf cascades in Spring
> Had once the witching power to fill
> My mind with wondering at the burgeoning.
> But now the wood nymphs all have died
> And I, emotionless, can pace the road between
> With thoughts refined and clarified
> To calm approval of their vivid green.
> And on this stretch betwixt the burns
> I well remember how I plotted out
> The problem of a God, by turns
> Inspired by hope, and taught us to think by doubt.

This, then, is the story of two determined spirits who left Whitewell against advice and in weather that was far from ideal for the hills they loved. It remains to attempt to provide an explanation of what happened to the men after they left Corrour bothy on Sunday, 1st January, 1928. This is no easy task since the amount of reliable evidence is limited and such evidence as exists is capable of differing interpretations. However, with care and some qualification, a description of the likely course of events can be given.

Baird and Barrie had set off for Corrour bothy on Thursday, 29th December with insufficient food for their stay, a deficiency which was almost certainly aggravated by the failure of their primus stove to function properly. Lack of food would weaken them both physically and psychologically and this would have been compounded by the weather which was generally cold and, at times, very cold. They had little or no heat in the bothy and it is quite possible that their clothes and boots were damp for much of the time. It is perhaps rather surprising that they did not decide to change their plans and return to Whitewell on the Saturday. In the early days of the search for Barrie, Professor Gregory did consider the possibility that they might have left for Whitewell on that day and become benighted, but neither he, subsequently, nor anyone else took this seriously and it is almost certain that they did not do so. Bearing in mind their shortage of food and their probable general condition, it seems also rather surprising that they went by way of the

Cairn Toul-Braeriach plateau and Gleann Einich rather than by way of the Lairig Ghru which was slightly shorter and involved little climbing. The inference to be made from their decision to remain at the bothy until the Sunday and to make for Whitewell rather than for Luibeg, which was much closer and more easily reached, is that they were not unduly concerned about their situation. Unfortunately, after they had gained the plateau and could not well turn back, they were struck by two pieces of almost demonic ill fortune which were to alter so radically the factors in the equation of survival. These were the violent storm and the sprained ankle.

It is probable that they left Corrour bothy at daybreak or soon after when the weather seemed set fair, another factor which may have encouraged them to take the high route. It is unlikely that the damage to Barrie's ankle happened during the ascent of Coire Odhar or on the earliest part of the crossing of the plateau as, if it had, almost certainly they would have returned to the bothy and then made for Luibeg and Braemar. Once they had made some progress over the plateau, that option would diminish almost with each step and the mishap to the ankle could have occurred anywhere thereafter. As indicated earlier, it is almost inconceivable that the two men left the bothy with rucksacks loaded as they were found. After they were well under way, something must have happened to cause them to minimize Barrie's load. This could have been the onset of fatigue on Barrie's part or an injury to his ankle. It may also have been caused by Barrie becoming hypothermic. Both men were cold during their stay in the bothy and Barrie's central core temperature may already have been below normal when the two men left in the morning. Lack of food, damp clothes and the ferocity of the wind would soon further reduce this temperature with pernicious results. The re-allocation of loads must have been done while Baird still felt fit enough to carry the added burden and, since he abandoned his pack about half way down Coire Bogha-cloiche, it is improbable that this took place in the corrie itself or on the last stage of the journey across the plateau. It seems, therefore, that it occurred when they had still some considerable distance to travel across the plateau and their speed, already slow owing to the storm, was further reduced, in consequence of which they were overtaken rather early by darkness.

It is not possible to tell where they were when dusk came to that blizzard ravaged inferno, but it seems likely that they managed to escape from the plateau while they had at least some light, although it may be that failing light made them choose their descent line down Coire Bogha-cloiche. They may have bivouacked at the place where Baird left his pack, Barrie, who had already dumped his pack, being unable to go any further. If so, by morning their condition, particularly Barrie's, would have been still very serious, and Baird may have abandoned his load in order to expedite the struggle to reach safety. However, Barrie's rucksack was simply dropped in the snow and this indicates that he was probably hypothermic by then; if they bivouacked at that point half way down the corrie, the likelihood is that Barrie would have died there. It is probable, therefore, that they continued their progress downwards after discarding the rucksacks in a desperate endeavour to go as far as possible before stopping for the night. If they knew their approximate position, they would be aware that to reach Gleann Einich would offer some hope of finding one of the bothies in which to shelter. Eventually, they came to a halt at the start of the wide area of fairly flat ground, cut by numerous peat and moss hags, at the bottom of Coire Bogha-cloiche. It was perhaps one of these hags, quite possibly the one in which Barrie's body was found, which was to offer the men shelter for the night – if they were still together.

Only one ice-axe was discovered during the operations to find Barrie. It is not known whose axe was missing but Baird was using Barrie's stick when he was found about midday on the Monday close to the lower bothy. He had injuries to his hands and knee and it could be that these happened in a fall when he lost his ice-axe. On the other hand, Barrie may have fallen and lost his axe and, in the morning, Baird took the stick to make his way along Gleann Einich since it would be of greater use in deep snow and drifts than an ice-axe. There is no doubt that one or more falls may have happened, particularly on the steep upper and lower sections of Coire Bogha-cloiche.

There is one other point to make. It was presumed by everyone at the time that Baird fought his way down Gleann Einich through the blizzard during the evening of the Sunday only to collapse about 366 metres from the lower bothy which was occupied by the brothers Gray and Cecil Philip. He lay there exhausted, hypothermic and exposed to the elements, initially in the blizzard and then in the thawing snow and was found at about midday on the Monday lying, clear of the snow, partly on a snow drift and partly in a pool of water – and he was still alive. This is really quite unlikely. Much more convincing is that he found somewhere fairly sheltered and there spent the night to resume his efforts to reach Whitewell at first light the following morning. In all probability, he was not already lying where he was found when the three men departed from the lower bothy on the Monday morning; it is much more likely that he had collapsed there within an hour or so of the arrival of the young men from Perth.

Perhaps the best guess is that the light began to fail as they descended

Coire Bogha-cloiche and this increased the need for as rapid a descent as possible. Both men, but especially Barrie, were close to exhaustion and Barrie was in pain from his injured ankle. Barrie was becoming seriously hypothermic and he jettisoned his rucksack; Baird, whose condition was rather better, decided to abandon his own a little further down, perhaps to facilitate assisting Barrie or to accelerate his own progress, although in his case too it may have been the result of exhaustion. At some point in the corrie Baird – and possibly Barrie also – suffered a fall in which he injured his hands and knee, lost his ice-axe and possibly also his gloves, but the two friends maintained contact and resumed their descent. By the time they reached the bottom it was dark and the blizzard continued relentlessly so that they had no chance of finding the upper bothy, even if they knew where they were. Barrie was quite unable to continue any further so the men spent the night sheltering in a peat or a moss hag, probably the one in which Barrie was found. Although they were fairly well clothed, they were rather ill-supplied with waterproofs and their clothes must have been quite wet; during the evening and night almost certainly they grew colder.

The night was long and miserable but eventually the new day dawned. Barrie was dead and Baird did what he could to lay him out, folding his arms across his chest. It may be that Baird took Barrie's silk handkerchief as a personal memento for Nancy but it may have been taken as offering some protection to Baird's injured hands. Cold and wet, hungry and exhausted, having eaten little for twenty-four hours, Baird left his friend in the moss hag and struggled down Gleann Einich. But it was all too much for him and, sometime between 10.00 a.m. and 11.00 a.m., when so close to the lower bothy, which by then was empty and locked, he staggered over the wreath of thawing snow and fell, never to rise again.

All this, however, is speculation. What is not is the unadorned and brutal fact that Barrie died within 400 metres of the upper bothy and Baird died within the same distance of the lower bothy.

MacKenzie and Ferrier on Cairn Gorm. New Year, 1933

Five years after Thomas Baird and Hugh Barrie perished in the Cairngorms, an old two-seater Morris Oxford convertible could have been seen leaving Grantown-on-Spey on its way south towards the same mountains. On board were Alistair Russell MacKenzie and Duncan Alexander Ferrier. Alistair MacKenzie was thirty-five years of age and was one of the seven children of John MacKenzie. In 1881, at the age of twenty-six, John MacKenzie had moved from Kirriemuir to Forres where he started an ironmongery business. The business prospered and in 1930 a branch was opened in Grantown, the management of which was placed in the hands of Alistair who was a partner in the family enterprise. John MacKenzie was a keen businessman and contributed to the civic life of the community through his involvement with the Forres Horticultural Association and with the local Scout association. All five of his sons had joined the movement in their boyhood and Alistair had retained his interest. At the age of eighteen, Alistair MacKenzie had enlisted in the Royal Field Artillery, had seen service as a gunner in France during the First World War and was to be gazetted as a lieutenant, an indication of his soldierly abilities. He accepted his father's precepts of industry and service to both customers and the community and was widely respected. He enjoyed the outdoors and would sometimes take himself with a companion or two into the hills. One of his great interests was the Scout movement to which he gave much of his free time and he continued his responsibilities as scoutmaster of the First Forres Troop after he moved to Grantown.

His assistant scoutmaster was Duncan Ferrier. Ferrier was almost eighteen and captain and senior prefect of Forres Academy. He had a young sister, Betty, whose sixth birthday on 3rd January, 1933 fell on the day after her only brother should have returned from his New Year expedition to the hills. He was captain of his school's badminton and cricket teams and was competent on the bagpipes; academically he was strong in mathematics, science and French, and he was due to start training as a chartered accountant with a firm in Elgin on 9th January of that year.

Alistair MacKenzie and Duncan Ferrier:
Cairn Gorm, 1st - 2nd January, 1933.

Route taken by MacKenzie and Ferrier on 1st January _ _ _ _ _ _ _ _ _ _
Return route from Shelter Stone on 2nd January _ . _ . _ . _ . _ .

High St. Forres,
1914.   Alex Fraser

The expedition began about 9.30 a.m. on Sunday, 1st January, 1933 from Tyree House, the home of Mrs MacIntyre and her daughter with whom Alistair MacKenzie had lodgings in Grantown. MacKenzie shared these lodgings with another young man from Forres, Jim Hyslop, whom MacKenzie had befriended when the boy's father had died. When Hyslop had left school, MacKenzie had offered him a position in the ironmongery business. Hyslop eventually was to marry MacKenzie's sister, Sheenac. Also sharing the lodgings in Tyree House was Captain R. H. Glass from whom MacKenzie had borrowed a walking stick, carved with the initials 'R.H.G.'. It had been intended that Hyslop take part in the expedition but he had withdrawn at the last moment as he was not fully recovered from an infection. There was to have been a fourth member, David Banks, who was then a student in London, but he was unable to return north in time to participate. He knew the Cairngorms better than MacKenzie and it is possible that his presence would have prevented the forthcoming tragedy.

MacKenzie and Ferrier left Grantown with a plentiful supply of provisions, sufficient for three to four days according to Mrs MacIntyre, contained in three packs. It seems that one of these was a commodious rucksack of fairly heavy construction and the others were of lighter make, at least one of these being more of a haversack and slung over one shoulder. In addition to the food, they carried blankets, cooking utensils, a stove and its fuel, a small camera, two torches and even reading material. When their packs were found and examined, it was discovered that they contained much of the food that they had taken with them. In view of subsequent events it is unlikely that these supplies were carried as a precaution against an enforced extension to their stay at the Shelter Stone and one is left to conclude that their failure to strike a satisfactory balance between sufficiency of supplies and lightness of load was the result of lack of experience of mountain expeditions. There can be no doubt that the weight being carried was excessive and this may have played a role of some significance in tiring the men as they fought their way back the following day.

Their aim was to drive to Glen More, ascend Cairn Gorm, continue onwards across the plateau to Loch Avon and spend the night at the Shelter Stone. There they hoped to be the first to make an entry for the year 1933 in the Shelter Stone visitors' book. In this they were to succeed but the message they left was to be their last contact with humanity. The following day, Monday, 2nd January, their intention was to return across the plateau and reach Grantown in time for MacKenzie to attend a dance in the company of Jim Hyslop. Ferrier would return by train from Grantown to Forres where his young sister planned to meet him.

When they set forth on New Year's Day, the two men had little reason to suspect the elemental storm that awaited them. For several days in the last week of 1932, the weather had been sunny and mild; spring was in the air as the old Morris made its way out of the town. Indeed, the Cairngorms themselves had a rather thin and patchy covering of snow and it may have been the rather unseasonable weather which decided the two men to dispense with heavy, warm clothing and ice-axes. MacKenzie wore breeches, an army tunic and a light raincoat with a pair of unnailed shoes; Ferrier wore only a Scout uniform with its short trousers, a light pullover, a light trench coat and ordinary shoes with a few protectors in the soles. They had gloves, but neither man had any protection for the head. In addition, MacKenzie carried the stick lent by his friend, Captain Glass. In making comment upon their clothing and footwear, it is well to remember that in those days there was little specialised mountaineering equipment generally

John MacDonald's home, where MacKenzie left his car.   *Author*

available and most of those who took to the hills, whether as gamekeeper, walker or rescuer, did so in their workaday clothes. Nevertheless, Ferrier's clothing is little short of astonishing. The Cairngorms are clearly visible from Grantown and the residents of the town, of whom MacKenzie was one, would know how quickly mild weather could be replaced by cold, with snowfall on the mountains. That they went on a two-day expedition thus clothed, without ice-axes and wearing shoes which would be quite inadequate for dealing with hard snow and ice, makes it clear that they were sadly unaware of the conditions they might meet.

They left their car in the yard of John MacDonald, the head stalker on the Glen More estate, at Glenmore Lodge not long after 10.30 a.m. Before leaving, they spoke to MacDonald and told him of their plans, mentioning that they would return to their car the following day. Apparently they left the car parked with the hood down – a clear indication that they expected a continuation of the fine weather of the previous few days. It is most unlikely that they had heard or seen any weather forecast before they left Grantown. Alistair MacKenzie knew Cairn Gorm to some extent; in fact, he had climbed it in the company of his father, John, the previous August when the old man was already seventy eight.

Cairn Gorm and An t-Aonach ridge, from Meall a'Bhuachaille.   *Donald Bennet*

MacKenzie and Ferrier would have taken the stalkers' path along the right bank of the Allt Mor, the wide stream which drains the waters from three of the northern corries of Cairn Gorm – those of Coire Cas, Coire an t-Sneachda and Coire an Lochain. This would have taken them through the wooded area of the Glenmore Forest and on to the open, rising slopes beyond, following the approximate line of the modern ski road. It is almost certain that they would then have worked their way up to An t-Aonach ridge, the eastern flank of Coire Cas, passing on the way the remarkable giant erratic block known as the Clach Bharraig. This is a lonely and isolated relict, incongruously marooned by the receding ice of the last ice age, overlooking Loch Morlich and Glen More. Once they attained the ridge, they would have been faced with nothing more than an easy walk along its gentle gradient to the summit of Cairn Gorm, although they would have had to contend with a strong southerly headwind that was increasing in strength and was harbinger of the great storm to come. The distance from Glenmore Lodge to the top of Cairn Gorm is about 8 km with an ascent of approximately 905m and they probably reached the summit of the mountain about 2.00 p.m., three and a half hours after saying farewell to John

MacDonald. In view of the wind and the rather scanty clothing that the men were wearing, it is unlikely that they spent much time by the summit cairn, preferring to continue on their way towards their billet for the night, the Shelter Stone beside Loch Avon, one of the highest and loneliest of the many lochs in Scotland. Their destination lay just over 3km from the top of Cairn Gorm.

It is evident from MacKenzie's entry in the Shelter Stone visitors' book that the wind impeded their progress across the plateau and that they also met with difficulties on account of ice. In view of the lateness of the hour and the deteriorating weather, they probably headed in a southerly direction to make their descent from the plateau by way of Coire Raibeirt, a narrow and fairly steep corrie on the north side of Loch Avon. They would have come upon icy patches on the plateau itself but probably it would have been on the steep sections of the corrie that they would have had to contend with any difficulties presented by ice. MacKenzie was not given to overstatement and the brief reference made to ice may conceal to some extent the problems they had, poorly shod as they were and lacking an ice-axe. Once at the loch, a short walk would have taken them to the Shelter Stone near the south-west end of the loch. This they reached at 3.30 p.m. as dusk was approaching.

The Shelter Stone, or Clach Dhion in Gaelic, is possibly the best known of all the mountain shelters in Scotland. It is the largest of the many boulders which lie, scattered over a wide area, at the base of the Shelter Stone Crag from which they tumbled in one or more gigantic rock falls. The enormous Shelter Stone boulder itself came to rest on four smaller boulders, thus forming a roomy chamber underneath, offering sufficient space for seven or so in reasonable comfort, while in an emergency up to thirty could huddle together safe within its confines. The entrance, which faces north-north-east is narrow and low but this makes for less draught and the shelter has been made fairly wind-tight by packing stones, sods and heather into the chinks in its defences. Positioned as it is close to the cliff and protected by the neighbouring slopes which descend steeply from the plateau, the Shelter Stone is fairly well protected from wind, although there is no escape from the incessant noise of the water of the Garbh Uisge pouring down from the plateau over the rocks and into Loch Avon. The roof of the howff slopes upwards towards the back so that one can stand almost erect in that part of the shelter, a pleasure not permitted nearer to the doorway. A liberal bedding of heather makes for considerable comfort during the long hours of darkness within. The famous Cairngorm mountaineer and writer, A. I. McConnochie, measured the Stone to be 13.4 metres long, 6.4 metres

The Shelter Stone.   *Donald Bennet*

wide and 6.7 metres high and he estimated the weight as 1.700 tonnes; later, in 1926, Dr W. Bulloch measured it, giving slightly smaller dimensions, and a sample of the Stone later analysed in London provided a total weight of 1361 tonnes, based on Bulloch's figures.

By 1933, the Shelter Stone already had a long history as a mountain shelter; in fact, in the Statistical Account of 1794 it was described as a sanctuary for freebooters which could hold eighteen armed men. Ramsay MacDonald, the first Labour prime minister, on several occasions spent a night there, and in the summer of 1931 he took the whole of his family to it, walking in from Tomintoul. The Shelter Stone has a special place in the history of Scottish mountaineering as it was there on the morning after the golden jubilee of Queen Victoria in June 1887 that the Cairngorm Club, the earliest surviving mountaineering club in Scotland, was founded, preceding the Scottish Mountaineering Club by two years. In 1924 a tin box containing a visitors' book was placed within the refuge, a practice that continues to the present day. Completed volumes are kept in the library of the Cairngorm Club in Aberdeen. The year 1933, for which MacKenzie and Ferrier made the first entry, had a particularly fine summer which encouraged as many as

523 people to visit the Stone and sign the visitors' book in the month of July, with as many as 129 on one day alone; for the whole year there were 1018 signatures and no doubt some paid visits without signing the book.

If the two men who squeezed through the narrow entrance of Clach Dhion that New Year's Day knew about its history, they certainly had little inkling of events to come. No doubt they were grateful to be able to unburden themselves of their loads and to cook a meal. It must also have pleased them to find the shelter unoccupied and no entry for 1933 in the visitors' book. Their entry, written in pencil, gives some idea of the conditions they had met on the journey there and during their stay in the refuge:

January 1st, 1933. Happy New Year, To all who come here. A. R. MacKenzie, Grantown, D. A. Ferrier, Forres. Arrived here 3-30 p.m. after a stiff climb over ice & against a fierce head wind. Found Shelterstone rather draughty so fixed blanket across entrance feeling it of more service there than on the bed. Before settling down we heated a stone which served the purpose of a foot warmer so spent a comfortable night. 2nd dawned wilder than 1st. Mist driving before a fierce gale. Setting out for Glenmore. 11 a.m.

With the difficulties of the crossing and the deterioration of the weather, it must be wondered if any concern about a safe return was forming in the mind of either man; if so, there is no evidence of it in the entry. Clearly, the entry was made just before their departure from the Shelter Stone for Glen More and there is only limited information about the hours they spent there. With the wind coming from the south, it is rather surprising that they had trouble with a draught entering through the doorway. However, it is quite possible that the wind was subject to local deflection in the area of the Shelter Stone. In all likelihood they would have settled down to sleep quite early and, with their scouting experience, it is probable that they slept soundly, little disturbed by the sounds of the wind and the rushing water of the Garbh Uisge. Whatever their concerns about the weather, their entry in the visitors' book shows that they were aware of the strength of the wind in the morning. By all accounts, that day – 2nd January, 1933 – was witness to the wildest storm experienced in the Cairngorms for a long time. William Marshall, the head forester from Nethybridge who had played a leading part in the search for Hugh Barrie in 1928 and who was to occupy a similar role in the search for MacKenzie and Ferrier, said that the wind which blew all that day was certainly worse than the one that had claimed the lives of Baird and Barrie. In the *Forres, Elgin and Nairn Gazette* of Wednesday, 11th January, 1933, Marshall was quoted as saying: 'And such a gale I have not

At the Scout Jamboree, Birkenhead, 1929. Middle row: centre – Alistair MacKenzie, right –
Jim Hyslop. Back row: right – Duncan Ferrier.   *Jim Hyslop colln.*

felt in 21 years. The blizzard was worse when Barrie and Baird died, but the
gale was not so devastating.'

Mae Marshall, William's niece, reports that Dr Ross of Dulnain Bridge, a
noted ornithologist, entered in her diary on 2nd January: 'Great gale sprang
up suddenly after a fine day. MacDonald, Glenmore (stalker), told me he
could not stand at his front door without holding on.'

So great was the wind that trees were blown down in Glen More itself.
Robert Campbell, who was booking clerk at Aviemore station and who
helped in the search for MacKenzie and Ferrier, well remembers, 'having to
give assistance to a rather stout elderly Grantown lady who got stuck on the
overhead footbridge at the station because of the exceptionally strong wind'.

The storm did not confine itself to the Cairngorms and the surrounding
area: much of Scotland suffered from its devastating power. Tom Weir,
whose experience of the Scottish mountains extends to over half a century,
has a clear recollection of his ascent of Beinn Dorain above Bridge of Orchy.
He and his companion, Matt Forrester, had to crawl the final 122m both to
and from the summit and were lifted off their feet lower down after
venturing to stand upright. It was one of the worst two winds he has ever
experienced. Nineteen km to the east of Beinn Dorain, Iain Ogilvie, another

mountaineer with extensive experience whose adventure on An Teallach in 1966 is treated later in this book, ascended Meall Ghaordie above Glen Lochay as part of the New Year meet of the Junior Mountaineering Club of Scotland. The S.M.C.J. (Volume XX, April 1933) contained a description of the day's activity:

In contrast to the previous day's weather we were greeted with a morning of driving rain and sleet. . . . one and all arrived on Meall Ghaordie, which soon began to resemble Princes Street on a busy morning. All went well until the summit plateau was reached and then the Meet found that it could not reach the cairn only a few yards away. The parties had climbed on the lee-side of the hill, and as soon as the top was reached it was found impossible to stand up. Hence the undignified spectacle of members on hands and knees crawling over the final 20 yards to the cairn. Some fifteen reached the cairn in this manner and immediately crawled back again to the shelter of some rocks; others with more sense subdued their pride and retraced their steps. With the wind at their backs very fast progress was made downhill, one party doing the first 1,000 feet in just under seven minutes. Every one was back by 1 o'clock, which must constitute a record, even be it an unenviable one.

The summit of Beinn Dorain stands at an elevation of 1074m and that of Meall Ghaordie at 1040m. The Cairngorm plateau which MacKenzie and Ferrier were to cross rises to a height of about 1130m while the summit of Cairn Gorm is at 1245m. There can be little doubt that the effects of the wind on MacKenzie and Ferrier were at least as great as, and probably significantly greater than they were on Tom Weir and Iain Ogilvie.

In 1933, there was a weather station at Dalwhinnie, about 40km from Cairn Gorm. For much of 2nd January, 1933 there was a Strong Gale Force Nine wind blowing consistently from the south. Reference has been made to the fact that winds from a southerly direction can be unusually strong over the Cairngorm plateau. Thus, a wind blowing at Force Nine in Dalwhinnie, whose altitude is about 760m below that of the Cairngorm plateau, may well have been Hurricane Force Twelve on the plateau.

If they had some appreciation of the dangers of their situation, MacKenzie must have felt a keen and lonely responsibility for making the decisions of that day. Their relatively late departure from the Shelter Stone may indicate considerable uncertainty as to the correct course of action. Undoubtedly, the concluding two sentences of the entry in the visitors' book make it clear that they were aware that there was a 'fierce gale' blowing on the plateau, but it is equally evident that they had no conception of how violently they would be handled by it at that exposed height: otherwise they would not have ventured anywhere near the plateau. This error of judgement may have been caused partly by conditions at the Shelter Stone itself. They would see the mist and cloud scudding presto furioso northwards in the direction they would be going, but it is likely that the wind in the protected area around the Shelter Stone was in no way exceptional and this may have deceived them into giving insufficient thought to possible conditions on the plateau. For certain, they had no personal experience to warn them and guide them; indeed, it is probably fair to say that in those days few people did. Dr Ross of Dulnain Bridge, in a diary entry of 9th January, 1933, made a relevant, if somewhat hostile, comment on the men's failure to realise the true nature of the wind on the plateau:

Did they [MacKenzie and Ferrier] not hear the wind roaring above them in the corries above the Shelter Stone and, if so, kept down Loch Avon with the wind behind them over the Saddle and down Strath Nethy in comparative shelter? Amazing how stupid people can be on the hills.

When a loud noise was heard from the Cairngorms, Strathspey residents knew that there was a fierce wind blowing on the hills. It is almost certain that the wind sweeping across the plateau was sounding loudly at the Shelter Stone and MacKenzie, himself a Strathspey resident, and Ferrier may have delayed in the hope that the wind would moderate, but by 11.00 a.m. were forced to accept that it had no intention of doing so and by then felt that the amount of remaining daylight necessitated a return to Glen More by the shortest route. They had ample supplies to allow them to remain at the Shelter Stone for one or even two days. However, they could have had no idea how long the storm would last and it must have been of concern to them that, if they delayed their departure until the Tuesday or the Wednesday and the weather continued stormy with blizzards blowing up, they might be quite unable to escape. They were ill-supplied with clothing to withstand such weather and their footwear and lack of ice-axes would have made difficult a return in snow of any depth. As it transpired, the following day the storm relented somewhat and, had they waited, they might well have emerged from their adventure alive.

There would also have been consideration of their family and friends – and, for MacKenzie, business commitments. They were expected to have returned to Grantown by the Monday evening and a failure to do so would cause mounting alarm. They might also cause a rescue operation to be mounted, putting others at possible risk, when in fact they were safe in their refuge. If they braved the elements, they might avoid both eventualities – and perhaps as they made their way towards Glen More the storm would abate.

'Early morning mist above Loch Avon taken from Shelterstone, 1932'.   Alistair MacKenzie

These are objective considerations which may have weighed with them as they decided what to do. There could well have been other factors too, factors psychological, powerful in their effect, driving them out into the storm. It is no pleasant thing to be trapped in such a lonely, high place with the hostile elements as one's constant companions and with no idea when they will depart. Why not make a dash for it and escape the anxiety and the uncertainty of waiting? It is so easy to succumb to such emotions and it takes a strong mind to resist them – or an experienced one. Today, with so much more known about the correct procedures to adopt in an emergency in the hills and with the existence of an efficient search and rescue service, often involving helicopters, it is not so difficult to sit tight and, if necessary, await help. In 1933, if one got oneself into difficulties, one had to get oneself out of them. And that, from what is known of their character, would have been the attitude of these two men.

It may be that the two friends thought and responded in these ways, but one would expect some hint of their anxieties and deliberations in their entry in the visitors' book. This entry, although undoubtedly not sanguine, shows no especial concern about the weather and their safe return to Glen More and this leads to a more probable explanation of their fairly late departure and the route they took. They were experienced in sleeping out of doors and, in the comfort and darkness of the Shelter Stone, they may not have awoken until 9.00 a.m. or even after. They would not be concerned about this since they were merely retracing their route of the previous day. Then, they had left Glenmore Lodge at about 10.30 a.m. and had reached the Shelter Stone at 3.30 p.m. despite 'a fierce head wind'. The return journey would have more descent than ascent and it would be aided – so it might seem to them – by an even fiercer tail wind so that, in leaving at 11.00 a.m., they should surely be able to return to their car by 4.00 p.m. They quite failed to realise the awful power of such a wind, the way in which it would hurl them about, the chilling effect it would have on their bodies, especially once their clothes had become wet, and the sheer exhaustion it would soon induce in them.

Dr Ross indicated in her diary entry that, had they been more experienced or knowledgeable, they would have returned to Glenmore Lodge by way of the Saddle, at a height of about 807m, and Strath Nethy which would have kept them at a lower altitude and have offered some protection from the wind. Nevertheless, there is no certainty that the Strath Nethy route would have saved their lives. It may have been sheltered from the worst of the savage wind which screamed across the plateau 300m above the Saddle. However, it is by no means sure that the wind would have been much less severe. The glen runs northwards from the Saddle and the southerly wind may have been funnelled down the glen, thus increasing its intensity; and the rough terrain in the glen would not have made easy going. Bearing in mind that trees were blown down at the lower levels in Glen More, the wind in Strath Nethy would have been severe, even without any funnelling effect.

Further, the Strath Nethy route was about 5km longer than the direct route over the Cairngorm plateau and the men were carrying fairly heavy loads. This, together with the rough terrain which may have had some areas of deep, soft snow, could well have fatigued them long before they had regained Glenmore Lodge and quite possibly before they could reach either Badfeannaig bothy, a lunch hut with adjoining stable situated at the point where the road from Nethybridge and the Ryvoan bothy met the Lairig an Laoigh footpath some 10km from the Shelter Stone, or the Ryvoan bothy itself 2km further on, both of which they could have used in an emergency. After all, the two friends were to collapse after no more than 5km of the route that they were to take. There is also a danger in taking the Saddle route in a storm: in poor visibility, there can be a tendency to miss the point where the Saddle is crossed and therefore, unless great care was taken in navigating, they might have missed it and, in consequence, been driven into the Caiplich where the chances of survival would have been slim.

The initial efforts to find the men were handicapped by uncertainty about the return route they would have taken in the conditions; in fact, there was a chance that they had remained at the Shelter Stone, although this possibility was largely discounted when they failed to appear on Tuesday, 3rd January when the weather had improved. There was a fairly general opinion that they would not have attempted to cross the plateau, an opinion which was reflected in part of a report published in *The Courier and Advertiser* on Thursday, 5th January, three days before the bodies were found. It should be noted that the report erroneously indicated that the wind was more westerly than southerly. It read:

When MacKenzie and Ferrier left the Shelter Stone they might have chosen any of the following routes –

(1) Along the north bank of Loch Avon, with the wind at their backs, following the River Avon at a height of about 2000 feet towards Faindouran Lodge. [This was a disused lodge on the river Avon about 11km east of the Shelter Stone. It would have been fairly easy to locate even in poor weather, but it was unlikely that the men would have gone in that direction.]

(2) Up the Feith Buidhe, a steep burn falling between Cairn Gorm and Ben Macdhui, and then down into the Lairig Ghru by the March Burn. This would probably be too much for them against the gale [It would also have made for a long journey of 16km or so to safety, whether to reach that safety the men headed towards Glen More with a tail wind or towards Derry Lodge and the keeper's cottage at Luibeg into a head wind. However, this distance was no greater than that to Glen More by way of Strath Nethy and, at least if they made for Derry Lodge, they would reach Corrour bothy after about 8km.]

(3) Up the Garbh Uisge, a similar burn leaving Macdhui, or into Corrie Etchachan, and so into Glen Derry. [Any attempt to reach the south side of the Cairngorm massif would have forced the men to fight their way into the violent wind and progress at times would have been impossible.]

(4) Down Loch Avon, round the shoulder of Cairn Gorm into shelter from the wind and along to the Garbh Allt, which leads to Strath Nethy and eventually to Nethy Bridge. [This is the route over the Saddle already mentioned.]

The long ridge from Macdhui to Cairn Gorm would have been quite impossible in the gale, and it is most unlikely that they would have returned over Lurcher's Crag, which is a common way home under ordinary circumstances.

In reality, only the fourth of these possibilities could have been seriously considered by the men, the more especially if they were to return to their car and minimise concern for their safety.

By which route did the mountaineers make their return from the Shelter Stone? It is fairly definite that they reascended Coire Raibeirt with the wind at their backs. It is probable that they began to be affected by the real violence of the wind when they were little more than half way up the corrie by which time it would be moving towards noon and rather too late to make changes of plan, unless they were going to return to the Shelter Stone. In any case a further 2km would have brought them across the plateau and into upper Coire Cas – and, as they might hope, out of the worst of the wind. Even if they went over the summit of Cairn Gorm, the distance was just over 2km; and from the top of Coire Raibeirt, where they would come on to the gently upward-sloping plateau itself, it was even less. Nonetheless, it was in that short distance that so much of the damage was done.

MacKenzie had an oil-filled compass and seems to have been a good navigator. The bodies were found in Coire Cas, in the bed of the stream called Allt a' Choire Chais and, as it happened, in an almost straight line from the top of Coire Raibeirt to Glenmore Lodge. It might seem, therefore, that MacKenzie set a course for Coire Cas from the top of Coire Raibeirt. However, even if, in those awful conditions, he managed to set a course, the only route they could have taken would have been the one dictated by the wind and that was in the direction of the top of Cairn Gorm itself. It is not known whether they were blown up the summit slopes and from there were able to work their way down into Coire Cas or whether they succeeded in exerting sufficient control over their fate to skirt round the summit slopes to the west and then down into the corrie. The search party which reached the Shelter Stone by way of the summit of Cairn Gorm on Wednesday, 4th January reported finding footprints travelling in both directions; the footsteps were regular and apparently indicated that those who had made them had been progressing well. It is possible that the footprints heading south in the direction of Loch Avon were those of MacKenzie and Ferrier on their outward journey, but those travelling north most assuredly could not have been theirs on their return, playthings as they were of the hurricane. Whatever the route along which they were actually driven, they must have been desperate to escape from the exposure of the plateau and have battled with every remaining joule of their diminishing energy to reach the apparent sanctuary of the corrie. However, that devastating wind would have swept onwards and downwards into the corrie with no great diminution of strength and they would find themselves still driven and battered as they descended. The natural topography of the corrie would lead them to the snow-covered stream where their bodies were found together, frozen into the snow and ice.

The first signs of the tragedy which had happened came when Duncan Ferrier did not alight at Forres station and Alistair MacKenzie failed to appear at the dance in Grantown. Hyslop became anxious and tried to telephone Glen More but the telephone line was out of order owing to the storm. It was 1 p.m. on Tuesday before he had a message from the head stalker at Glen More, John MacDonald, who had been the last to speak to the two men before they set off, saying that nothing had been seen of them. Knowing that MacKenzie had some experience of the Cairngorms, MacDonald had not been unduly concerned when the two men did not return as intended on the Monday as he thought that they may have remained at the Shelter Stone. But when there was no sign of their showing up in the better weather of the Tuesday, he became concerned for their safety. The relatives in Forres were informed and on the Tuesday evening two brothers of Alistair MacKenzie, George and Ian, went to Grantown in an effort to organise a search party for the next day. Ian, a minister from Methilhill in Fife, had arrived in Forres the previous day to visit his ailing father and he now became active in the search for his brother and young Ferrier. In happier times he had himself visited the Shelter Stone and this was the name he had given to his manse two years before.

On Wednesday, 4th January four parties set out to search the most likely of the routes by which the men may have made their return; two of these parties started from Glen More, one from Nethybridge and one from Braemar, but only one of the Glen More parties found anything of substance. The weather conditions during the day conspired to make the search difficult: drifting snow, blown in clouds by the wind, combined with banks of mist to limit visibility and it was so cold on the higher slopes that the searchers' clothing froze. The Nethybridge party was led by William Marshall, the head forester, and they searched the Strath Nethy route and visited the Ryvoan and Badfeannaig bothies but without any sign of the missing men.

The first of the search parties which set off from Glen More was led by Edwin Davidson from Elgin, president of the Moray Mountaineering Club. They made their way over Cairn Gorm following the route taken by the two missing men. They traced regular footsteps going in both directions but there was no telling by whom they had been made. They reached the Shelter Stone at midday in the half hope that they would find the men there. It was not to be. Rev. Ian MacKenzie entered alone and found the entry in the visitors' book; now there could be no doubt that his brother and Duncan Ferrier had perished on their attempt to return to Glen More. The searchers made their own entry in the visitors' book. It read:

T.M. Crowley W. Forsyth R.K. Forsyth Rev Ian MacKenzie John MacDonald Edwin Davidson. Party arrived S Stone Noon in search of above not heard since 1/Jany.

It appears that they took a copy of the missing men's entry, which was immediately above their own one, since the press gave fairly accurate transcriptions of it the following day. The five men did not return to Glen More without mishap. R. K. Forsyth, a well-known Forres businessman and sportsman, who was to make a major contribution to the search over the next few days, sprained his ankle and Tom Crowley, an exciseman, fell down a rock about 100 metres from the Shelter Stone and gashed his leg badly. He was unable to reascend to the plateau so he made his way back to Glen More by way of the Saddle and Strath Nethy which at least offered the advantage of providing another search of that area. The wound to his leg required several stitches when he returned to Forres.

When it became clear that both the Nethybridge and the Glen More search parties had failed to locate the men, another party set out from Glen More to go to Faindouran Lodge to discover if MacKenzie and Ferrier had, in fact, gone there. They left in the twilight and it was late at night before they returned to report no trace of the men.

The Braemar effort was inspired by Miss Betty Rushby who was organiser of mountain activities at the Fife Arms Hotel in Braemar. When news reached the hotel during the Wednesday morning that the two men were missing, she immediately suggested that a search be mounted from the Braemar side. This diversion may have come as something of a relief to her since the weather conditions were presenting her with some problems. On the Monday, she had tried to take a party up nearby Morrone which rises to a relatively modest 859m, but they were forced to retreat. Three guests from the hotel – one from Paris, one from Switzerland and one from Edinburgh – offered to assist in the search and Police Constable Bell, the village policeman, agreed to lead the party, which motored as far as Derry Lodge. To begin with the weather was quite fair, the going was not difficult and they followed the course of the Luibeg Burn and its tributary, the Allt Carn a' Mhaim, to gain the higher ground to the north. At a height of 600m they spread out to begin a search up the ridge known as Sron Riach, but had ascended only a further 75m when mist came sweeping down. The decision was taken to return to Derry Lodge: after all, it would hardly be right for the hotel to lose one or more of its paying guests. On their way back, they met two young men from Aberdeen who had been staying at Corrour bothy since the previous Saturday and climbing in the vicinity. They said that the wind had been extremely violent during their stay and that, on the Sunday and the Monday, there were times when they feared that the roof of the bothy would be blown off. The only people they had seen were two men from Dundee and two members of the Cairngorm Club; there had been no sign of MacKenzie and Ferrier.

The following day, Thursday, 5th January, the search was resumed. Although the message left at the Shelter Stone indicated that the missing pair had set off for Glen More, it seems that some people considered there was a chance that the men's plan had been subsequently changed and that they had directed their course southwards towards Derry Lodge and Braemar, unlikely though this was in view of the ferocious headwind through which they would have had to fight their way. Four parties left Derry Lodge to search the most probable routes; they spent nine hours on the hills, greatly hampered by swirling snowstorms, before abandoning the search when darkness fell. No further search was made from the Braemar side because it had become clear during the day that the men had, indeed, made for Glen More.

From Glen More, the search concentrated on the north side of Cairn Gorm and its summit area, this now considered to be the men's most likely way of return. The searchers, who included William Ferrier, Duncan's father, were divided into two groups, the smaller, under the leadership of John MacDonald, taking An t-Aonach ridge towards the summit. The larger group, under William Marshall, undertook a search of three of the northern corries of Cairn Gorm, beginning with the easterly one known as Coire Laogh Mor. During the earlier part of the day's activity a driving snowstorm sprang up and the snowflakes swirled in huge eddies round the heads of the searchers, minimising visibility. After about an hour, however, the storm abated to some extent and this presented the searchers with better prospect of success. *The Courier and Advertiser* of Friday, 6th January contained a description of the efforts of Marshall's team:

The larger party slowly combed the precipitous slopes from Choire Laoigh Mor, where they could hardly keep their feet on the long reaches of hard ice. They drew a blank and then proceeded to make a complete circuit of the corrie on the east side of the summit and ridge of Cairn Gorm [Coire na Ciste]. Knowing that darkness would be upon them within a couple of hours they began to retrace their steps towards Glenmore Lodge, spreading out into fanlike formation so that every acre of the ground would be covered. [By this time they had worked their way into Coire Cas, although this is not made clear in the report.]

A piercing snow-laden wind was blowing, chilling the searchers to the marrow, but they carried on indomitably. As the party were slowly moving down one of the numerous little burns which run into Loch Morlich, two of them caught sight of a large dark object lying in the snow. On reaching it they discovered that it was a bulky webbing haversack of army type. It was so firmly embedded in the snow that considerable force had to be exerted in order to move it. The haversack was similar to one of the three with which MacKenzie and Ferrier left Grantown on Sunday, and there is no room for doubt that it belonged to MacKenzie. It contained several large objects, with blankets rolled in a waterproof sheet on top. [It contained also food sufficient to have lasted the men at least two days.] Whether accompanied by Ferrier or not, MacKenzie had managed to make his way a good deal further than had been expected. In the teeth of the wind and snow he had struggled half way between the Shelter Stone and Glenmore Lodge. The haversack had not been dropped inadvertently. It had been thrown away on purpose, because it would considerably impede the progress of the person who was wearing it.

Two sets of footprints were faintly discernible leading to within ten feet of the abandoned haversack. There were no tracks leading away from it. They may have been obliterated by the recent falls of snow, but the accepted theory is that MacKenzie and Ferrier both reached the point where the haversack was thrown away, and soon afterwards fell dead or dying in the snow. [It is also possible that the footprints were obliterated by the wind or that the wind had blown the pack the 3 metres from where it had been abandoned.] The search party formed into open order and moved along the burn, expecting to find a body or bodies, but they could not penetrate the deep snow drifts without adequate equipment, which they will take with them to-day.

The pack was found just over 6km from Glenmore Lodge and about 5km from the Shelter Stone. It was evidently simply abandoned with no attempt made to leave it in a position from which it could be easily recovered, as Baird had apparently done five years before. A little later in the same report reference was made to a search of the area carried out by two R.A.F. aeroplanes from Leuchars.

In fact, there were three aircraft involved in the search that Thursday: the two from Leuchars and the other hired by *The Scottish Daily Express* and piloted by Walter B. Caldwell. That newspaper, on Friday, 6th January, contained a detailed description of the flight, given by Caldwell himself and it is worth quoting as it is an early example of the use of aircraft in mountain search and rescue.

I have searched – at times just a hundred feet above ground level – miles of the ground between Cairngorm and Braemar, round the south-west shoulder of Cairngorm and Ben Macdhui. Once I caught a momentary glimpse of a party of searchers – small specks on the unbroken covering of snow. There was no other sign of life, not even an animal. . . . I was flying for long stretches under the 'roof' – dense black clouds 3,000 feet high – between the sheer white walls of the mountains, battling against violent hail and snowstorms. Hailstones the size of peas blinded me. Fierce currents and numerous air pockets rocked my Moth airplane incessantly. I never saw the top of a mountain. Clouds and mists obscured everything more than 3,000 feet high. Once, just above Braemar, I tried to climb above the cloud. At 4,000 feet it was even thicker, impenetrable. . . . I cannot tell how many degrees of frost my thermometer recorded, but I felt the gripping coldness of the winds cutting through my coats, leather jerkins, and sweaters. . . . I turned west at Braemar along the valley of the Dee – a thin, black crack wriggling over the marble floor of the earth. Each cut I saw in white walls to the north I crawled up, turning only when the mountains forced me. My passenger and I searched every possible foot of the snow. No trace . . . I was doing about eighty-five miles an hour then. I saw two Royal Air Force machines then, doing as I was doing, carefully following each gully in turn. The three of us, in single file, banked, swerved, and crawled along the mountain sides. We tried to get round to Cairngorm by Glen Feshie, but the cloud beat us back, and I could not see a yard. A rift in the pall led me to Loch Einich. I could see the lower slopes of the Cairngorm, and searched the ground with my binoculars. White, blinding white snow for miles . . . .

The next day, Friday, conditions were worse with high winds and fierce blizzards sweeping the hills; 10 to 15cm of fresh snow fell and new drifts a metre or so in depth had formed in many places. In spite of the difficulties, almost every available able-bodied man – and some women – in the locality, generally reckoned to total sixty, went out, with the search concentrating on the area around and below the point where the rucksack had been found. Probes and shovels, some of the steel-headed probes having been made in Aviemore the previous evening, were used. *The Courier and Advertiser* of Saturday, 7th January contained a full report with some interesting information about the search and some of the searchers. It said:

. . . The weather yesterday was so severe that one experienced climber had to turn back, utterly exhausted. Others were forced to lie down with their faces to the snow in order to breathe freely. Icicles hung from the searchers' moustaches, and all their clothing was covered with frozen snow. While the blizzard raged in the morning the conditions were fearsome. Yet in the afternoon, when a pale sunset cast its long rays across the mountains, bathing the virgin snow in a weird iridescent light, there was a wondrous beauty on Cairn Gorm. One hated it for its cruelty, but could not but admit its fascination.

The search party set out about ten o'clock, with Mr John Macdonald, Glenmore Lodge, as guide, and spent six hours on the hills. Ferrier's father did not accompany them, nor did either of MacKenzie's brothers. They have now given up hoping. The search party had with them a Highland garron, which was stabled in a hut halfway up the mountain-side, but there was no occasion to use the animal. Ernest and Ian Russell, two youths in their teens, walked seven miles through the snow from Aviemore, where their father is schoolmaster, to join the party at Glenmore Lodge. Another volunteer, a gentleman belonging to Carr Bridge, who knows Cairn Gorm in all its moods, walked in his kilt and plaid from his hotel at Aviemore, joined the search party, and covered the same distance back on foot, after being out on the hill all day. On his return from the 26 miles tramp he gave the *Courier and Advertiser* a description of the search. 'We were all covered with snow from head to foot,' he said. 'It was bitterly cold on the top, and you could not risk standing for long. Everybody had a long stick or pike, and they prodded in every direction. By pure chance they might have come across the tip of a boot protruding from the snow or perhaps touched a body with a probe. But there is no real hope of finding the remains of MacKenzie or Ferrier until the thaw comes. The snow alongside the stream is from 15 to 20 feet deep in many places. Most of it is fresh snow, which has piled high since MacKenzie and Ferrier were there. The snow on top is soft, but a few feet down it is frozen as hard as rock.'

In the *Forres, Elgin and Nairn Gazette* of Wednesday, 11th January, R. K. Forsyth gave a detailed account of the search that day:

Setting out from Glenmore shortly before 10 o'clock, we made the spot in Coire Cas where MacKenzie's pack was found our objective. There were between 40 and 50 of us, and after getting clear of the wood we walked two miles to the point where the footprints were seen on the previous day. We advanced roughly within 15 yards apart, the line of searchers covering some 600 yards, and then swung over the higher ground of the summit. Arriving at the point which we had set out to attain, we gathered together and made a concentrated search right down the corrie which, in the opinion of Mr Macdonald, our guide, was the most likely way to have been chosen by the missing men.

The footprints seen earlier in the week could not be traced. Most of us were armed with long iron spikes, and although moving in close formation, so that we were actually touching each other, and probing every yard, we hit upon nothing. Having repeated this mode of search down both glens, the party again spread out on either side of the burn, and continued the search after the manner we had begun, right down to the woods above Glenmore. It was snowing so heavily, however, that the heather and rough were entirely covered up, and to add to our difficulties the snow was coming down in whirling clouds so thickly that we could scarcely see more than a couple of yards ahead. The conditions on the mountains to-day were certainly the worst that we have experienced in any of the searches, and it would have been fatal to attempt more than we did on such a day.

In spite of the dreadful weather, another aeroplane ventured to assist in the search. It belonged to the Scottish Motor Traction Company and left Turnhouse, near Edinburgh, piloted by Squadron Leader Malet. However, the weather denied it any chance of success.

On the Friday it was decided that the search for the missing men should be abandoned until a thaw came to clear much of the existing snow and this, it was confidently expected, would not happen for a considerable time. In this they were deceived with the change arriving the next day when a rapid thaw set in. As it became evident during the Saturday that it would be possible to resume the search on the Sunday, efforts were made during the later part of Saturday to recruit a sufficient number of volunteers to search the area where the men were almost certainly lying. Notices were posted by the police in Grantown with the appeal shown below.

This appeal alone seems to have produced about 200 volunteers and similar appeals in other villages provided perhaps a further hundred. These figures may be somewhat inflated, but there were certainly about 250 – the largest search party that had ever gone into the Cairngorms. Indeed, had it been required, a saturation search of the area could have been mounted.

NOTICE.

·····················

It is proposed to organise a Search Party to proceed to Glenmore Lodge on SUNDAY, 8th JANUARY, to leave Grantown at 8 a.m.

Physically-fit men are requested to hand in their names to Mr STUART, Bookseller, on or before 8.30 p.m. to-night.

All persons willing to provide motor transport are asked to co-operate by granting use of motors.

It is specially requested that only fit men take part. One day's rations to be carried.

7th January, 1933.

Courtesy of Robert Campbell

One of those who responded to the call was Stubbert, the chauffeur of Dr Ross of Dulnain Bridge, one of whose duties was assistant bird-watcher. Stubbert's presence is known from his employer's diary where mention is made of the birds he saw while he was in Coire Cas and on the top of Cairn Gorm on Sunday, 8th January. *The Northern Scot and Moray & Nairn Express* of Saturday, 14th January described the departure of the Grantown contingent:

> The Square at Grantown resembled that of a large city on Sunday morning. . . . Thirty motor cars and a number of lorries conveyed the party from Grantown to Glenmore, where 300 men had gathered to take part in the great comb out of the hills.

The volunteers from over the wide area made their way to Glen More not just by car and lorry, but also by charabanc, by bicycle and on foot. Miss Mairi McSween, whose father was among the searchers, can recall how willingly these people gave of their time and money, some paying sixpence each to hire a lorry from Willie Hay, who had the garage in Aviemore, to take them to Glen More, while railway workers did extra unpaid hours to allow their colleagues to go out on the hill. *The Strathspey Herald* of Friday, 13th January gave the following description, provided by one of the searchers, of part of the day's action:

> It was an excellent day for climbing, and it was an impressive sight to see the large party winding through the forest led by Mr John Macdonald, head stalker at Glenmore, and Mr Marshall, chief forester at Nethybridge. They and Constable Sutherland had been indefatigable in helping to trace the lost climbers. The party included several Rover Scouts from MacKenzie's troop, all the local stalkers, ghillies and shepherds. When the party reached the edge of the timber line a council was held. The searchers were detailed to move in an extended line to Coire Cas. Slowly the line advanced. Every dip and hollow was examined. Our beat lay about 200 yards up on the hillside above the Coire Cas burn [Allt a' Choire Chais]. Just before 11 o'clock a shrill whistle rang out on our right. The whole line stopped. Somebody had discovered something. Then a handkerchief waved from our side of the burn and we concentrated at that point. The search was over.

From the *Aberdeen Press and Journal* of Monday, 9th January came this account of the finding of the bodies:

> . . . As on Friday, the search was thoroughly systematic. The task was rendered much more easy by reason of the fast melting snow. It fell to Hamish Reid, a Rothiemurchus ghillie, to make the tragic discovery. He it was who on Friday came upon the haversack belonging to MacKenzie. To-day he was one of a party of seven who set off ahead of the main body of searchers. Making straight for the spot where

the haversack was found, the small group concentrated round this part of the Coire Cas, prodding every yard of the way. Suddenly came the cry from Reid. 'They're here.' He had seen a knee protruding from the snow. Beneath was found lying, face upwards, on the edge of the burn, the body of Alistair MacKenzie. Two yards away, with his face looking towards Glenmore, and with only one finger visible above the snow, lay the body of Duncan Ferrier. The latter carried a light haversack. The large-hearted MacKenzie had apparently relieved Ferrier of the heavier pack, throwing away his own before the two made a last desperate effort to reach shelter. The ice had to be broken in the burn, and it was only after considerable difficulty that the two bodies were retrieved. From their state it was apparent that the two men had received a terrific buffeting. In the burn near them was found a walking-stick that MacKenzie had carried, which belonged to Captain Glass, Grantown. On it were carved the initials, 'R.A.G.' [sic – it seems that it should have been 'R.H.G.']

There are some inconsistencies in the details about the finding of the bodies. Some reports said that the bodies were found in the Allt a' Choire Chais, while others said that they were lying in the snow on the bank of the stream. Some said they were found about 800 metres from the abandoned rucksack, while others gave only 18 metres. Some stated that the knee which Hamish Reid saw belonged to MacKenzie, while others stated that it was Ferrier's. The number of fingers visible varied from one to three. However, there was general agreement that Ferrier's body was about 2 metres nearer to Glen More.

Robert Campbell, who was one of the party of seven who came upon the bodies, recollects events in some particulars rather differently from many of the accounts in the press. He says:

> It was Ferrier's bare knee that protruded above the snow (MacKenzie wore breeches). The three finger tips above the snow were also Ferrier's because he [Ferrier] was lying face upwards. MacKenzie was on his side facing Glenmore, completely snow covered, just a shade downstream. There was little or no difficulty recovering the bodies – the stream was well below the snow they lay in. . . . I clearly recollect the finding and recovery of the bodies.

It should be said, however, that although MacKenzie did wear breeches (and Ferrier wore shorts), one leg of his breeches was apparently badly torn so that the knee could have been his. Some of the press reports stated that the party which found the bodies were advancing along the line of the stream probing as they went. Certainly they had probed on the Friday, but Robert Campbell says:

> My recollection is that while we were making for higher up the corrie, Hamish Reid, who was in front, just accidentally made the discovery. I don't think any probing was being done – the quick thaw made probing less necessary. There was,

however, evidence of probing having been done in the area previously – the probe holes, having been enlarged by the considerable thaw, were visible.

Both men had haversacks which were lighter than the one that had been discarded; these two haversacks contained together, among other things, a primus stove and paraffin, two electric torches, a small camera, cigarettes and the latest book by George Bernard Shaw. To leave food in the abandoned rucksack and to carry the unnecessary weight of the stove and other items is a measure of how exhausted and confused the men had become. According to the press reports, the men were held fast in ice and hard snow which had to be broken to release them and it was only after much effort that the bodies were recovered. It was believed that if they had been able to cover a further 100 metres they would have been clear of the snow then lying and would have come on to lower ground, more sheltered from the wind. It was also thought that, if the bodies had not been found when they were, they might have been carried well down the mountain-side by the spate waters of spring. It should be said that the evidence provided by the rucksacks suggests that the two men were hypothermic as they descended Coire Cas and, even if they had managed to reach the lower ground which was apparently clear of snow, probably they would not have survived. The report in the *Aberdeen Press and Journal* on Monday, 9th January, went on to describe the physical state of the men whose bodies showed every sign of the dreadful hammering they had taken from the ferocious wind:

Ferrier's legs and knees were bruised, cut and flayed of all skin. His spectacles were missing. His gloves were worn to tatters, and his hands and fingers skinned and bruised, the finger tips being chafed flat with crawling desperately over snow and rocks. The left side of his face was cruelly injured, evidently by being blown against a boulder. MacKenzie's leg and hands were severely cut and he had a huge gash on his left hip. His nose appeared to have been bleeding. . . . When word of the discovery speedily spread around, the great body of searchers scouring the shoulder of the mountain gathered round the tragic spot, where a short, simple service was held by the Rev. R. B. Thomson, the bareheaded company joining in the Lord's Prayer. Before returning to Glenmore the company built a memorial cairn, each man placing a stone on the pile to mark the spot. Rough stretchers were then formed with crooks and walking sticks. . . .

Whereas on the Friday, a horse had been taken to a hut about half way to the area of the search in anticipation of finding the men, this was apparently not done on the Sunday and two of the searchers had to go down to Glen More to fetch one for the conveyance of the bodies. The horse could not be taken further than the end of the stalkers' path since the ground beyond was too rough for a horse bearing a load. While the horse was being brought, others went up the hill to recall those searchers who, in ignorance of the finding of the bodies, had gone far ahead towards the top of Cairn Gorm. Perhaps one of these was Stubbert, the chauffeur.

It is not easy to trace events during the final hours of MacKenzie and Ferrier. Leaving the Shelter Stone at 11.00 a.m., they would be afforded some protection from the full strength of the wind as they walked along the north side of Loch Avon. Once they began their ascent of Coire Raibeirt, the wind's strength would have increased quickly and by the time they were half way up – and this would have been at about midday – they must have been contending with a wind of great fury; when they reached the open plateau, they would have been exposed to a wind of unbridled savagery. It becomes very difficult to estimate times once the men found themselves subject to the full ferocity of the wind because it is impossible to know how much time they spent simply clinging on to objects, and perhaps to each other, to try to prevent themselves from being blown away. It is highly probable that much of the men's progress across the 2km or so of the open plateau was accomplished by crawling: it is inconceivable that they could have walked erect for anything other than the shortest of stretches and the condition of their hands and legs suggests that they spent much of the time on all fours. Not that this prevented them from being hurled and tossed by the hurricane to be smashed against rock and ground. MacKenzie was reported in the press as having sustained a large gash in his left hip. Brock Nethersole-Thompson, who lives today in Whitewell (the house occupied in 1927/28 by Mr and Mrs MacKenzie who had given shelter to Baird and Barrie before they departed for the Corrour bothy), was told by one of the men who saw the bodies that one of them (presumably MacKenzie) had the whole side sheared off one of his buttocks. The headwall of Coire Cas is fairly steep and it is possible that some of the men's injuries were sustained in a fall or slip there.

Once the men attained the plateau, there was simply no shelter from the infernal wind until they reached Coire Cas; and even then it would still be violent. Bearing in mind the wind and the fact that the snow and ice conditions in Coire Raibeirt may have been difficult, it is quite possible that it was 1.00 p.m. before the men reached the top of Coire Raibeirt and it could well have taken them a further two hours to reach their point of descent into Coire Cas. They were able to travel a further 2km down Coire Cas. Considering the soft snow in the corrie, the physical condition and mental state to which they had been reduced and the continuing fierceness of the wind, this last stage may have taken an hour and a half and more. Thus, it could have been 4.30 p.m. when the two friends reached the point where they died. Darkness would have been falling across the land as surely and relentlessly as it was falling upon their lives.

Not long after arriving on the plateau, if not before, MacKenzie and Ferrier would have been assailed by a mixture of driving sleet and snow which must have soaked their clothing in no time. The wind-chill factor was very high. The actual air temperature on the plateau was about 1.5°C, but the effect of the wind would have been to reduce this temperature to $-20°C$ in terms of its influence on the body's rate of heat loss. With their wet clothes, the two men must have experienced rapid chilling. Poor Ferrier in his Scout uniform must have been suffering intensely from the cold and this, combined with increasing exhaustion and an inevitably diminishing morale, would lead quite rapidly to incipient hypothermia. In view of the conditions, it is remarkable that the men managed to struggle as far as they did. Moreover, unlike Baird and Barrie, MacKenzie and Ferrier did not have a rope, in the absence of which it is equally surprising that they were able to keep together in the hurricane and the blizzard.

What happened to the men at the end? As reported in *The Strathspey Herald* of Friday, 13th January, William Marshall, the head forester from Nethybridge, believed that,

they came down into the gully where the snow was lying thick, and stumbling among the boulders, sometimes on their hands and knees, they were overwhelmed, and were blown over the slope into the bed of the burn in which they were found.

Rev. R. B. Thomson had a somewhat different view which was expressed in the same issue of *The Strathspey Herald*:

He [Rev. Thomson] visualises the two men following the bed of the burn which runs through Coire Cas. Up to a point they had firm footing, and another 100 yards would have brought them to safety, out of the snow line. Then they came to where the banks are nearly eight feet apart, and they found themselves falling through the snow, into a kind of trench. Breathless and benumbed after hours of exposure, their scanty clothing having been drenched soon after they left the Shelter Stone, they failed to regain the firm ground.

It is of some significance that they were found together. The cause of death of both men, as certified by the Aviemore physician, Dr Balfour, was 'cold and exposure'. In view of his age and quite inadequate clothing, it is probable that Ferrier was the first to become hypothermic. It may be that, if the young man had reached the point where he could go no further through a combination of exhaustion and hypothermia, his older companion decided to remain with him rather than struggle on in an effort to obtain assistance which he would probably know could not come in time. If MacKenzie had become sure that Ferrier had died and felt able to continue himself, it seems likely that he would have made some attempt to do so and the two men would not have been found together. These same considerations would apply in the more improbable event that MacKenzie was the first to succumb. The fact that they died in the same place makes it likely that they died within a short time of one another.

Their being found together is best ascribed to one of two terminal events. The first explanation is that the two men, assisting each other as best they could in the terrible journey from the Shelter Stone, reached exhaustion at about the same time and, perhaps with the onset of darkness, lost the will to continue. If this was the course of events, MacKenzie and Ferrier would have simply lain down in the snow and succumbed peacefully and painlessly to hypothermia. If they were close to the surface of the snow when they died, they may well have tended to sink lower into it and closer to the bed of the stream over the next few days, particularly after the thaw of the Saturday set in; they were, of course, covered with the new snow which fell. The other explanation is that, as they struggled downhill, they fell into the stream through the snow which had formed something of a bridge over it. Their hypothermia would have been worsening and their morale diminishing. In their state of fatigue, especially with no ice-axe to drive into the bank as an aid, they would be able to obtain no purchase for their feet or hands and struggled in vain to escape until first one and then the other slipped, completely exhausted, into unconsciousness and death.

As already mentioned, the press reports were confused about the location of the abandoned rucksack in relation to the position of the men's bodies: some newspapers stated that the pack was found about 800 metres from the bodies, while the others placed it only 18 metres away. The abandonment of this large and heavy rucksack indicates that they were seriously fatigued, although apparently not to the extent of feeling the need to jettison all three packs. If the rucksack was 800 metres distant, no particular significance can be made of it, except that the men were able to make this further distance before meeting their end. However, if the pack was only 18 metres away and it had not been blown there from a point considerably further up the corrie, it may indicate that the men met with some sudden catastrophe almost immediately after abandoning it since it is unlikely that they would have delayed discarding the load until they were so close to almost complete exhaustion. This could lend support to the suggestion that they fell into the stream and were unable to climb out of it.

The funeral took place in Forres on the Wednesday following the discovery of the bodies. The date was 11th January. It was made the more poignant because Alistair MacKenzie's father, John, was laid to rest in the same ceremony. He had been seriously ill for a week before finally passing away only a few hours before his son and Duncan Ferrier were found on the Sunday. He died without knowing that his son was missing, his wife and family having taken great care to withhold from him all intelligence of the matter. The funeral was the largest that had ever been seen in the north with people attending from a wide area; shops were closed and blinds were drawn. It was estimated that about a thousand people packed the Church of St Laurence, with many more standing outside, the doors of the church being left open so that they could take part in the service. The funeral cortege made its way to the spruce-clad slopes of Cluny Hill whose cemetery had been laid out some seventy years before. *The Northern Scot and Moray and Nairn Express* of Saturday, 14th January concluded its account of the interment of the three men in the following way:

> The Boy Scouts and Rovers formed a guard of honour as the wreath-covered coffins were slowly carried from the waiting hearses. The body of John MacKenzie was the first laid to rest, and then side by side, as they had battled through the blizzard on the mountains, the bodies of Alistair and Duncan were lowered into the grave.... [The mortal remains of Alistair MacKenzie and Duncan Ferrier were placed together in a single grave, adjacent to that of John MacKenzie.]

Not long after, in a terrible thunderstorm as chance would have it, a granite slab was taken from Coire Cas and laid as a simple memorial on the grave of the two men. The cairn which marked the spot in Coire Cas where the two friends were found was about 1.2 metres high. Almost twenty years later, on Sunday, 3rd August, 1952, Alistair MacKenzie's brother, George, and twelve others fixed to the cairn a metal plaque with the words:

> *Alistair MacKenzie*
> *Duncan Ferrier*
> *January 1933*

The plaque was attached to two iron angle supports which projected from the top of the cairn. By 1963, the cairn had fallen apart and the plaque had become detached from its metal supports which had become a hazard to skiers and were removed. Mr T. J. Paul, the general manager of the Cairngorm Chairlift Company, salvaged the plaque and some years later fixed it to a granite block which rests on a small pile of rocks within a metre or so of the original cairn. Today this is close to the second station of the White Lady chairlift but is rather inconspicuous.

The engine of the old Morris Oxford which had taken Alistair MacKenzie and Duncan Ferrier on their fateful journey to Glen More could still be seen in 1989 in MacKenzie and Cruickshank's ironmongery shop in Forres. Little did Alistair MacKenzie think when he stopped the engine in John MacDonald's yard in the morning of 1st January, 1933 that he would never start it again.

Kirkus and Linnell on The Castle.
March, 1934

In March 1941, there was published a most readable little book on climbing, part instructional and part autobiographical, by a writer whose conversational prose has an effective simplicity and directness. The book opens with a description of a moonlit ascent of Snowdon.

It was cold and bleak when I reached the summit of Snowdon at 5.30 on Easter Sunday morning. I had been climbing all Saturday, and had returned in the evening to the little climbers' hut in the Ogwen Valley, where I was staying. Most of the others were drifting off to their bunks, but it was such a lovely night – starlit and frosty – that it was more than I could resist. So I collected a little food, pulled on my sodden boots, found my ice-axe, balaclava helmet and gloves, and set off, a little after midnight, with a strange feeling of high adventure. It was wonderful to be walking across the crackly frozen bog, all alone at night. I experienced a satisfying sense of freedom and all sleepiness was driven away by the keen air; I felt I could keep going for ever.

Soon I reached a slope of hard snow and had to cut some steps. I cut with a steady rhythm, and got very hot and sticky with the hard exercise. It was almost as light as day, with the moonlight on the snow, and I had no difficulty at all in seeing where I was going, until I got into the shadow. Then a kind of chill seemed to descend on me and all the snow looked even and featureless. I had a short rest when I reached the crest of the rounded eastern ridge of the Glyders and then set off on the 1,500-foot descent to Pen-y-Pass. It was very rough and stony, and the moonlight played queer tricks. I would step on to a firm-looking rock and find it was a deep hole, or else I would prepare to jump down a drop of four feet, only to be brought up with a jolt after a few inches. After a little practice you learn to take up these shocks in your knees, so that you can run quite safely, even in the dark, down a rough slope, without any danger of a sprained ankle. The fact that you are wearing heavy climbing-boots instead of shoes makes a great difference, of course.

I passed by Llyn Cwm-y-ffynnon, a beautiful little tarn, now half frozen over, and reached Pen-y-Pass (the top of the Pass of Llanberis) at about 3 a.m. It was quite an eerie business, climbing over the rickety stone wall with all the caution of a cat-burglar, so as not to arouse the sleeping occupants of the hotel. My nailed boots made a loud ringing sound as I crossed the main road and set foot on the Snowdon massif, which was my objective. The rest of the expedition was pure joy. I made my way, first along the crazy path and up grass slopes, and then up slopes of snow where sometimes I had to cut a few steps. Then came the rocks, a mere scramble in summer-time and not difficult even now, though they were glazed with ice in places. And finally a narrow snowy ridge brought me to the summit of Crib Goch.

Crib Goch is in many ways the most lovely peak of Snowdon. It is just over 3,000 feet in height, and from Pen-y-Pass appears as a sharp cone. But on the other side is a narrow ridge, which is justly famous among mountain-lovers. I shall never forget crossing the ridge this Easter morning. The hard snow was piled up to a knife-edge on the crest, while on the right it dropped in an almost vertical wall of white. The slope on the left was easier, but still quite steep. The snowless valleys were almost invisible, so that there was nothing to be seen in front but this narrow gleaming moonlit edge, dropping down into nothingness. I felt as though I was poised in the air, on the very top of the world. All around were snowy summits, dropping weirdly into the inky blackness beneath; they looked almost like clouds. Yet there was no atom of danger to take my mind off all this magnificence; I knew the place well and felt perfectly at home.

I was feeling warm and exhilarated as I made my way through this enchanted scene, over the spiky pinnacles and up the rocky ridge of Crib-y-ddisgyl, and on to y Wyddfa, the summit of Snowdon. It was 5.30 now and beginning to get light. The moon seemed to have lost its brilliance, and the snow was a dead unearthly white, cold and spectral. A chilly wind had sprung up and I shivered as I forced my way into the old wooden hut on the summit. The door was jammed with frozen snow and it was a tight squeeze to get in.

There was no furniture inside nor glass in the windows, and the floor was covered with a thick sheet of ice. I ate a little food, but my fingers got frozen as soon as I took off my gloves, so I just stamped my feet and shivered and waited for the sunrise. The east window was almost covered by a framework of feathery icicles, and I kept watch through a ragged hole that was left in the middle. All the valleys were filled with mist, with the peaks standing up clear above, like islands. It got slowly lighter, but no warmer. Then presently a scarlet glow appeared above a level purple bank of cloud lying on the horizon, and soon the red sun, looking queerly oval, came into view. As soon as it rose above the cloud it changed to gold and made the icicles in the window gleam like diamonds. I could feel its warmth immediately and grew cheerful and comfortable again in an instant. Half an hour later I was descending to Glaslyn in a sweltering heat, the great snowy bowl of the cwm acting as a kind of giant reflector.

I have begun with this description to try and let you feel something of the spirit of the mountains. . . .

This passage shows so clearly the writer's fine sensitivity towards the mountains in which he took such delight, whether British, Alpine or Himalayan. It reveals his self-reliance and there is also, perhaps, a hint of physical toughness and mental courage. He has throughout the book a profound desire to share his experience with others in an endeavour to enourage them to take to the hills. The book is *Let's Go Climbing!* and the author was Colin Fletcher Kirkus.

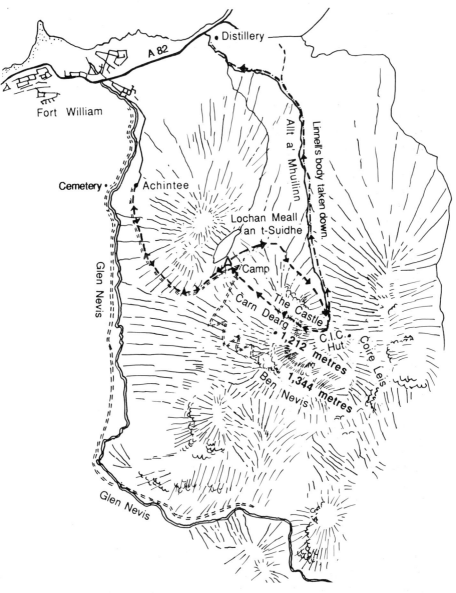

Colin Kirkus and Maurice Linnell
Carn Dearg Easter Saturday/Sunday 1934.

Distillery

A 82

Fort William

Cemetery • Achintee

Allt a' Mhuilinn

Linnell's body taken down.

Lochan Meall
an t-Suidhe

Glen Nevis

A Camp

Carn Dearg
The Castle
• 1,212
metres

C.I.C.
Hut

Coire Leis

Ben
Nevis
1,344
metres

Glen Nevis

Kirkus and Linnell's route from Achintee to the Castle   – – – ▶ – –
Kirkus's descent from the top of the Castle to Achintee   – ◀ – – –
Route taken with Linnell's body.   –·––·––·–

The mountains, however, are not always so well-disposed or rewarding to those who tread their slopes or climb their crags. Another Easter, another place, and the beauty became brutality and the richness of life became the coldness of death. Soon after midnight on Good Friday (30th March) 1934, Kirkus and his friend, Maurice Linnell, left Linnell's family home just outside Kendal for Fort William where several English climbing clubs were holding their Easter meets. Among these were the Liverpool-based Wayfarers' Club of which Kirkus was a member and the Manchester-based Rucksack Club of which Linnell was a member. Kirkus was also a member of the Climbers' Club. Both men were leading rock-climbers of their generation and had done much climbing together. Kirkus, a native of Liverpool, was 23 years old and worked in that city with the Liverpool and London Globe Insurance Company. He did not derive much satisfaction from his job and found his mind often wandering to the hills. As he said in Chapter Eight of *Let's Go Climbing!*:

> When I first started climbing I could think of nothing else. Cooped up all week in an office, I would just long for the next week-end. On a photograph of some cliff I would have all the known routes marked with dotted lines. The blank spaces in between fascinated me. Here was unexplored country; I longed to be the first to set foot upon it. I used to sit, pretending to work, with the drawer slightly open, so that I could see the photo inside. Then I would plan a route. Here was a chimney to start, but could I reach that little grass ledge 100 feet higher up? It might be possible; it all depended on the steepness of the rock. If I could find a way of connecting the next three ledges, then victory would be mine.

Along with Menlove Edwards, he was one of the giants of rock-climbing in the 1930s which were themselves an evolutionary period in the sport. He was a gifted climber, completely fearless, with a remarkable ability as a route-finder and an equally remarkable self-discipline. At Helyg, the Climbers' Club hut in north Wales, in September 1928 he met A. B. Hargreaves who, at twenty-four, was six years his senior and who did much to influence his development as a rock-climber. They became firm friends and climbed together a great deal. It fell to Hargreaves to write the obituary for Kirkus in the Climbers' Club Journal of 1943 after he had been lost on a bombing mission to the German city of Bremen.

Kirkus's experience went beyond the shores of his own country. He visited the Alps where he climbed some long and difficult routes and he was a member of Marco Pallis's Gangotri Glacier Expedition in 1933. The Gangotri glacier was virtually unexplored and its neighbouring peaks were unclimbed. Kirkus proved himself to be equally competent on rock at these much higher altitudes, the highlight being the six-day ascent of the arduous Central Satopanth Peak whose summit stands at an altitude of 6726m. Maurice Linnell was two years and a day older than Kirkus and was the son of a retired solicitor. He was an assistant chemist with Ellis Jones and Company, Manufacturing Chemists, in Stockport. Linnell had been a chemistry student at the University of Manchester where he had begun rock-climbing seriously and had quickly shown quite exceptional ability and technical skill. Wilson Hey, the founder of the Manchester University Mountaineering Club, wrote a memorial article for Linnell in the Rucksack Club Journal of 1934. In this he said:

Maurice Linnell   *Bonnie Phipps*

It is obvious that he would be present at the birth of the Manchester University Mountaineering Club, and in its earlier years all the activities of that Club were centred in him. He was its pillar of strength, first as its treasurer, and then as its secretary. He made men come to its meetings and later made them climb. In his short span he made many mountaineers. This year he became a Vice-President. . . . Although heart and soul in the Club, his individualistic personality prevented him from being a real 'club-man'. . . . In the early cautious days of the M.U.M.C. the edict went forth that members, as members of the Club, should not climb 'very difficults'. Linnell immediately retorted by ascending his first 'severe'. After this his record is one long list of week-ends in the mountains, with scarcely an interval – a striking record of conquest after conquest. . . . In achievement he must have been one of the half-dozen best of our younger climbers, and potentially he was perhaps only excelled by his last climbing companion. . . .

In 1931, Kirkus and Linnell formed a close climbing partnership which constantly tested itself to the limit and pushed ever forward the frontiers of the sport. There can be no doubt that risks were taken as they must if progress is to be made, but there were those who feared that the two men, with such a positive drive to climb increasingly demanding and dangerous routes, would meet with some terrible accident. It seems that Linnell was aware of this: in an article, entitled *Falling from Rock*, in the Manchester University Mountaineering Club Journal of 1933 Linnell said:

> The first consideration is the choice of party, and the route to be followed. The only danger likely to beset those who climb together regularly is that ambition may run away with discretion. . . . a fall means bad judgment, defeat with dishonour.

Work finished for the Easter weekend on Thursday, 29th March, 1934 and shortly after midnight the two friends left for Fort William. Not for them the luxury of four-wheeled transport; they sped north over Shap and the Scottish border on Linnell's motor-cycle, laden down with climbing and camping equipment – and with skis. Not for them either the warmth and comfort of the Highland, Palace or Waverley Hotels in Fort William where others among the muster were to stay; their billet was a small tent which had seen service with Kirkus on the Pallis Gangotri expedition and which was to be pitched beside the frozen Lochan Meall an t-Suidhe on the col half way up Ben Nevis. They wished to be as close to the mountain as possible and to do as much as they could in the holiday weekend. When they arrived, the prospects for the weekend must have seemed good: it was cold and there was a lot of snow on the Ben. Alan Hargreaves watched them set off from Kendal and as he did so he experienced a feeling that some awful event would overtake the two; his foreboding was not misplaced.

On Good Friday the two men went ski-ing in the course of which Linnell broke his skis. On the Saturday morning they left their tent beside the halfway lochan apparently at about 8.00 a.m. They were heading for the Castle Buttress on Carn Dearg. The day was fine but overcast and the weather data indicates that it was not particularly cold, even at 7.00 a.m. at which time the temperatures close to sea level north of the Scottish central belt were in the region of 4.5°C. The weather station closest to Ben Nevis was Dalwhinnie, 50km to the east and at a height of 359m. There, at 7.00 a.m. the temperature was 0°C but this figure reflects a measure of temperature inversion caused by the calm overnight conditions; by 1.00 p.m. it had risen to 5.5°C. The overall pressure pattern suggests that the wind may have been a moderate south-easterly at the summit of Carn Dearg and this would have made the snow on Castle Buttress a little firmer as it blew along the line of the cliffs. In the morning, temperature inversion would also have affected the glen of the Allt a'Mhuilinn above which stands the buttress. It is probable that the temperature at the top of The Castle was slightly below freezing all day, there being little diurnal variation at the tops of mountains unless winds are very light.

Taking into consideration that they were quite close to the climbs and that, with the weather set fair, darkness would not descend until 7.00 p.m., this was an early start and may indicate that they planned to make an ascent of another route before the day was out. The lochan lies at a height of about 565m and the men would have contoured round the north-west shoulder of Carn Dearg and into the glen of the Allt a'Mhuilinn for a distance of 3km and to a height of 650m; this would bring them below The Castle, so named after its crenellated upper section, which they intended to scale. In terms of vertical height, The Castle is a 240m downward-pointing wedge-shaped buttress which, from a distance, seems to be suspended from the shoulder of Carn Dearg. It is set in a small corrie enclosed by the walls of the main mass of Carn Dearg and Castle Ridge; viewed from below, it is bounded by South Castle Gully to its left and North Castle Gully to its right. Its actual climbing length is at least 320 metres and its average angle is about 49 degrees to the horizontal, although there are some sections considerable steeper than this. By today's standards, the ascent of The Castle is not especially difficult but, in 1934, it was regarded as one of the more testing winter routes.

In winter, the start of the climb is often made rather hard by a section of steep ice, although this pitch can be obliterated by an accumulation of snow or avalanche debris. After the initial difficulties, the route moves on to a relatively easy snow slope which leads to a rather more demanding vague groove about half way up the climb with a slightly steeper snow slope beyond. The route ascends this slope, moving somewhat leftwards to avoid a direct assault on the 30m rock band which is a prominent feature of the upper part of The Castle, and towards a conspicuous block under which there is a good stance. From here, the climbing becomes considerably more difficult. A rightwards traverse from the block reaches a steep 30m groove, icy in its lower section and, after flattening a little and then steepening again, snowy in its upper section. Above the top of this groove, there are two steep chimneys leading directly to the top of The Castle. The route ignores these chimneys, instead traversing rightwards below them along snow covered ledges to a stance some 15 metres beyond the top of the groove. This is the final belay of the climb: the route continues traversing upwards to the right to a snowy bowl or recess which gives access to the cornice at the top about 18 metres above the final belay. On Easter Saturday 1934 there was a lot of hard snow and ice and a cornice at the top, but there was also, in places, some softer and unstable snow lying on the hard surface underneath.

When Kirkus and Linnell started their climb it is probable that there were few, if any, other climbers to be seen. Certainly, they had the route to themselves and there is no evidence that they were witnessed as they made their ascent. They would be able to move fast, and not just because of their ability. Generally – and this was certainly the case with Kirkus and Linnell – winter climbing was done Alpine-style with belays found quickly and with rather less concern for belay security than there would be today. Moreover, there would have been a complete absence of running belays to reduce the risk of a long fall. It is interesting to note that in his book, *Let's Go Climbing!*, Kirkus makes no reference at all to running belays which have become so important in climbing security. Although in use on the continent, these and other aids were spurned by the British climbing fraternity. Generally, the anchorage to the mountain was no more than the long wooden-shafted ice-axe thrust as far as it would go into the snow. The rope from the waist was passed round the ice-axe shaft, once only, and then a shoulder belay used by the climber. At other times the climbers had to devise the best belays that were available to them. The chances of holding a long fall were, therefore, quite restricted.

There are various accounts of the accident that befell the two men and of the subsequent events. It might be thought that these would be broadly consistent but this is far from the case; indeed, at times they come close to being contradictory. Among climbers at the time there was quite widespread annoyance with the sensational manner in which the accident was reported. Carl K. Brunning, the editor of the *Mountaineering Journal*, who was present in Fort William as organiser of the Wayfarers' Club meet and who was unhappy with the press coverage, indicated in a critical article in his journal in the summer of 1934 (Volume 2 Number 3, June-August, 1934) that some of the press descriptions of the accident and the efforts to reach Linnell 'were apparently given to them by two freelance journalists who happened to be on the Ben at the time'. It is not just the problems of sensationalism and of several newspapers using – and sometimes adapting – material from a single source that can provide difficulties for the investigator of later years. The reports were almost certainly filed from Fort William by telephone and this could have resulted in transcriptional errors occurring quite innocently

South Castle Gully (left), The Castle and North Castle Gully.   *Noel Williams*

through a poor quality telephone line.

There are two main accounts of what happened and these, while not being directly contradictory, are remarkably divergent at central points in their description of events. One is provided by Alastair Borthwick in an article published in the *Glasgow Weekly Herald* of Saturday, 7th April, 1934, one week after the accident. As he stated in this article, Borthwick was one of the first to come upon the injured Kirkus and was present throughout the sustained, but abortive, effort to reach Linnell on the Saturday, making a contribution of some note himself. Indeed, he was one of the party which escorted the injured Kirkus on a stretcher down the Ben late in the day. Although his account was written within a day of the accident, it is unreliable at certain points and it contains some evidence of journalistic licence. However, apparently Borthwick's account was not one of those which so annoyed Brunning because he has no recollection of having seen the article by Borthwick until many years later.

The most obvious error made in this article was that Borthwick had Kirkus and Linnell climbing 'Castle Gully' when it should have been clear to him that they had been climbing Castle Buttress. He was at the beginning of his mountaineering career and that day was the first time he had been on Ben Nevis; he was unfamiliar with the names of most of the features of the Ben and he heard the gully in question called 'Castle Gully'. However, it is almost certain that he was talking about South Castle Gully. There are three reasons for this. Firstly, in his description of the place he said, 'For 500 feet the gully was bounded by the sheer walls of The Castle itself'; this can only be South Castle Gully. Secondly, he described a large cornice at the top of the gully and it is unusual for North Castle Gully to have a cornice of any size – and to judge from photographs taken on the day it appears to have been largely cornice-free. Thirdly, an attempt was made by four members of the Rucksack Club in the late afternoon and evening of Easter Saturday to reach Linnell. It is known that they made their effort by descending North Castle Gully and Borthwick, who described their endeavour in his article, said:

> They [the four men] descended a gully on the other side of the Castle rock. They had to. The gully up which Kirkus had fought his way single-handed was deemed by this strong party to be unjustifiably dangerous. The easiest approach lay down the other gully.

Borthwick's conviction that Kirkus and Linnell had been climbing South Castle Gully appears to have been caused partly by Kirkus himself who, according to Borthwick, said that Linnell was lying in 'Castle Gully' and partly by the existence of steps, mentioned by Borthwick but not by others, cut into the snow and ice and apparently marked with traces of blood, which ascended the gully from the most distant point in the gully visible from the top. These footsteps surmounted the cornice and continued to the spot where Borthwick and the others had come upon the injured Kirkus. Kirkus and Linnell were climbing the Castle Buttress and not South Castle Gully: this is irrefutable. However, the steps seen by Borthwick are important as they cast considerable confusion on the route by which Kirkus reascended after the fall. The general view at the time was that he had reclimbed The Castle itself, forcing his way through the cornice at the top to reach the plateau beyond − a herculean achievement, considering his physical condition and the fact that his ice-axe shaft had broken. That he had reached the top by this route was the opinion expressed or implied generally in the press and the journals of the time and it was reinforced by Kirkus himself. After he regained consciousness, his memory of events seems to have been fairly clear and, in a statement to the press at the time of his release from hospital nearly three weeks later, he said:

I cut the rope [linking him with Linnell], as the knot was too tight to undo, and continued up to the top of the cliff, shouting for help at intervals and cutting steps with my ice-axe, which I had found sticking in the snow.

There is no indication here of an exit into South Castle Gully. It would be convenient to dismiss Borthwick's bloodstained steps in South Castle Gully as dramatic fiction which would make good newspaper copy. However, they cannot be treated so summarily. Even today he can recall many of the details and has the following observations to make upon the description he gave in 1934:

As my account states, I back-tracked Kirkus' route from the place on Carn Dearg where we found him, by way of tracks and bloodstains, to a gap in the cornice and 30 feet down the gully, from which point I saw bloodstained steps continuing downwards until they disappeared round a corner. These are facts and I am in no doubt about them. [Borthwick descended the 9 metres down the gully on a rope before abandoning the attempt to go any further. He estimated the corner round which the footsteps disappeared to be 152 metres from the top of the gully.]

In the article in the *Glasgow Weekly Herald*, he said of the cornice at the head of (South) Castle Gully:

. . . a slope which steepened at the top to 70 degrees, and which was surmounted by a cornice of solid ice which overhung by three feet and was four feet thick. I saw what was left of that cornice. Three feet below it were two steps chipped in the ice. They were about three inches deep by four inches wide. On these two tiny ledges, Kirkus must have stood for close on an hour while he hacked his way through the cornice. And he did it all with only half an ice-axe. Bleeding from a dozen cuts, he had carved his way through, inch by inch.

Today on the subject of the cornice he says, referring to the suggestion that the bloodstains may have been left by 'some other climber':

Consider the state of the cornice. Blood had fallen in sufficient quantity to soak into the snow and spread. These were stains more than a foot across. It is inconceivable that they could have been made by anyone capable of leaving the mountain unsuspected and undetected. And remember, I followed an uninterrupted trail from Kirkus to the cornice and saw an uninterrupted trail from the cornice down the gully. My narrative is accurate. There was no 'some other climber'. Kirkus climbed the gully.

Borthwick implied that the bloodstains were visible down the gully for the entire 152 metres to the corner round which they vanished. However, when, in consequence of the information provided by him and quoted above, he was asked specifically if he had been able to see the bloodstains coming all the way from the corner, he said he could not remember.

What can be made of all this evidence? The route by which Kirkus reascended is not a minor detail. Even if Kirkus made much of his reascent by way of South Castle Gully it was still a heroic feat. Frank Bennett, one of the four members of the Rucksack Club who made the descent of North Castle Gully later on the Saturday to try to reach Linnell and who was one of the team which recovered his body on the Sunday, is in no doubt that Kirkus made his reascent entirely up Castle Buttress. Linnell lay about 76 metres from the top of the 240m Castle Buttress. Bearing in mind that this distance, which is based on the most reliable of the estimates of those who were present, probably represents actual climbing length, Linnell was lying three quarters of the way up the buttress; even if it was a vertical height estimate, Linnell's fall had still come to a halt no more than a third of the way down. There are only two feasible exit points from the buttress into South Castle Gully and these both come low down on the buttress. In early February 1991, an experienced Fort William climber, Noel Williams, in the company of a climbing companion retraced the route taken by Kirkus and Linnell with a view to making some observations relevant to their ascent, an effort that was supplemented by an examination of the buttress from both the north and the south. On the possibility that Kirkus may have escaped from the buttress into South Castle Gully, Williams says:

We made a point of looking for places where it might be feasible to gain South Castle Gully. The only place where we thought this was a reasonable proposition was after two full pitches (i.e. after about 90 metres of climbing). There was another possible place after a further pitch but this looked rather more difficult. There was nowhere on the upper half of the climb where we thought it likely that anyone would attempt to enter the gully. If Kirkus fell a total distance of some 90 metres on the final pitch, then he would have fallen over an obvious rock band before coming to a halt, but he would still have been a long way up the climb. In my opinion, it would have been much easier for him to reclimb the last two pitches of The Castle rather than for him to try and enter South Castle Gully and climb that route.

It is interesting to note that in the 1936 S.M.C. Guide for Ben Nevis, Graham Macphee, the writer of the guide, said in his description of South Castle Gully that there were two exit points from The Castle into the gully quite low on the buttress, probably those seen by Noel Williams and his friend, but he mentioned no higher point at which an escape was possible. A further indication of the improbability that Kirkus escaped into the gully is to be found in W. H. Murray's *Undiscovered Scotland*. In this classic mountaineering book, Murray gives an account of an attempted ascent of The Castle he made with his young friend, Douglas Laidlaw, in January 1940. The snow and ice conditions on the day presented some difficulties but eventually they reached the slabs at the top of the climb. Murray however, did not like the look of the snow lying on them so he pitched a large stone on to it as a test. The snow cracked and was considered by Murray as much too unsafe to venture across. Under the constant threat that the snow, whose hold on the slabs Murray had weakened, would avalanche down upon them, the two men retreated all the way to the bottom of the buttress with no thought of making an exit at any point into either South Castle Gully or North Castle Gully when these would have offered easier and much safer lines of descent.

Alastair Borthwick still has the impression of a steep-sided gully and, when asked if he thinks that Kirkus made an exit from the buttress into the gully somewhere up the 152 metres visible to him from the top of the gully, he says:

I have a strong feeling of sheer walls. I don't think there was an escape route. I could easily be wrong. But I certainly did not see signs of one being used – no steps, no blood.

This largely confirms Borthwick's original opinion that Kirkus had ascended the gully from a point which was, in fact, well below where the fall came to a stop. It is inconceivable that Kirkus would have descended any significant distance to find an exit into the gully – and the minimum distance would have been 90 metres, 120 metres being more probable – then to climb to the top of Carn Dearg when he would have been so much nearer the bottom of the buttress and only a short distance from the C.I.C. Hut where he might have hoped to obtain assistance. Moreover, an exit presumes that he knew fairly precisely where there were escape routes and this, almost certainly, he did not. It is not known whether this was his first time on The Castle but it is highly likely that it was: coming as he did from Liverpool and being only twenty-three at the time, his visits to the Ben must have been fairly limited and he was the kind of climber who was always exploring and doing new climbs, as indeed was Linnell. In the emergency in which he found himself, rather than wander about searching for an easier way to the top, he would surely have returned over what was familiar ground, regaining and following the footsteps the two men had already made.

It follows from this discussion that Borthwick's narrative must be handled with some care, but it is a prime source and is of value, if used with discrimination. At many points it agrees with, and even expands upon, other evidence. The other main account of the happenings of that day was given by Robin (or Robert) Petrie, a student from Bearsden, near Glasgow, who, with his friend, McKinnell, also from Bearsden, seems to have been the first to reach Kirkus. The main source of Petrie's version of events is to be found in *The Scottish Daily Express* of Monday, 2nd April where he is described as the reporter of the major item on the accident on page one. Without doubt, Brunning was much irritated by a highly inaccurate item on the accident on page two of the same issue of the newspaper, but if Petrie is intended as one of the 'two freelance journalists who happed to be on the Ben at the time', Brunning is rather misguided in his criticism of him: it is fairly clear that Petrie was simply a student climber who chanced to be on the mountain that day and was able to provide a first-hand account with photographs. Incidentally, although Petrie makes no reference by name to Alastair Borthwick, Borthwick does mention Petrie; however, he calls him Colin rather than Robin.

Of the two accounts, Petrie's is probably to be preferred because his fits fairly well with that of Kirkus and with other evidence. The problem with accepting Petrie's account of events has been that it appeared chiefly in a newspaper which elsewhere in its coverage that day made entirely erroneous assertions, most especially that it had been given an interview by Carl Brunning. This interview was published on page two and was attributed to a '*Scottish Daily Express* representative' and not to Petrie. This may well have been one of Brunning's 'two freelance journalists'. The interview was, in Brunning's own words, 'quite fictitious' and the newspaper, which Brunning believed had sensationalised the event, felt obliged to publish an accurate statement the next day signed by Brunning and by Marco Pallis who was also present at the English meet. There is no doubt that Brunning had good cause for complaint about this alleged interview in which Brunning credited himself with playing a major role in the rescue efforts on both Saturday and Sunday when, in fact, he was not in any way involved. His strictures do not, however, seem to cast doubt on the general reliability of the account given by Petrie. With regard to the reliability of the sources of information, even Kirkus's own recollection of events has to be treated with at least a little caution as he was badly concussed and there is evidence that he tended to lapse in and out of consciousness for some time after the accident. All this having been said, however, a careful study of the whole evidence allows an account to be given which is probably fairly faithful to the facts.

The ascent had been undertaken with Kirkus and Linnell taking alternate leads and Kirkus was leading when the accident happened. Some reports stated that this occurred about 30 metres from the top while others said that he had reached the cornice, a variation repeated with the length of the fall which ranged from 'over 100 feet' in *The Scotsman* of Monday, 2nd April to 'about 500 feet' in other reports. Kirkus himself made a statement to the press on his discharge from Belford hospital in Fort William on Thursday, 19th April and this statement was carried in *The Strathspey Herald* of the following day and in *The Oban Times* of Saturday, 28th April. Here, Kirkus was quite specific that he had reached the cornice, having overcome the difficult parts of the climb. Thus, it is reasonable to conclude that he was standing on the snow-covered slabs immediately below the cornice at the top of the climb and directly above the 30m rock band high on The Castle, his friend belaying him about 18 metres below and to his left. The reports given in *The Strathspey Herald* and in *The Oban Times* were almost identical, except that the latter gave a longer first paragraph and it is this report that is quoted:

Maurice Linnell on Ben Nevis, 1934.
Colin Kirkus

Linnell and I were climbing the Castle,

and we had got over the difficult part, and had almost reached the top of the cliff. At this point neither of us had any suspicion of danger. Although we had reached a comparatively easy spot, we took all precautions. We took turns at leading. I was leading and had reached the cornice, when a step I had cut in the snow collapsed and slid off the very hard snow underneath.

I immediately fell down, leaning on my axe so as to try and stop myself, but I was going too fast, and I went over a cliff about 50 feet lower down. That is the last thing I remember until I regained consciousness and found myself lying some 300 feet lower down. I could not remember where I was at first, so I followed the rope, which had not broken, and found Linnell on the other end, some 80 feet higher up. The rope had caught over a ridge of snow, so that we were suspended on different sides of it. When I reached Linnell, I found the rope had slipped up and caught round his neck.

He had a spare loop round his waist, so I put the ice-axe which I found quite close to his body through this and into the snow so as to support him while I released the rope from his neck, otherwise he would have slipped down the slope. I think he was dead then, but I was not sure at the time. He was lying on a slope of about 50 degrees, and I tried to pull him up on to a ledge but had not the strength. I ran the rope out to its full length, however, so as to serve as a guide to a search party. Then I cut the rope, as the knot was too tight to undo, and continued up to the top of the cliff, shouting for help at intervals and cutting steps with my ice-axe, which I had found sticking in the snow. When I reached the ridge, I made a small cairn on the edge of the snow to indicate the spot to the searchers. . . .Where the accident took place was quite an easy spot, and we took every precaution, Linnell's axe being driven into the snow and the rope wound round it at the time of the accident.

Kirkus was quite unaware of the dangerous condition of the slabs. The snow cover on the slabs of the upper section of The Castle is now known to be generally unreliable, even when the rest of the climb is in good condition; indeed, Macphee gave a clear warning of the danger in his 1936 guide-book. Noel Williams said of his ascent of The Castle in February 1991:

On our ascent of The Castle we found that short sections of ice on the first and penultimate pitches gave the hardest climbing on the route. Apart from the final section, the remainder of the climb was on good névé and proved to be relatively straightforward. Although we found excellent conditions on most of the climb, we were rather surprised by the sudden change in the character of the snow halfway up the last pitch. It became much softer and felt much less secure. It was easy to imagine this final part of the climb on occasions being very dangerous. The snow is blown there by wind passing over the summit and lies on smooth slabs perched above a steep rock band. These slabs are approached by a rising rightwards traverse. The slabs themselves were not visible on our ascent because they were covered in deep snow, but it was from this point on that the snow became unpleasantly soft. The final section below the cornice consisted of a broad, shallow depression and could be described as a gully although it is nothing like as narrow as either South or North Castle Gullies.

Murray and Laidlaw had been equally surprised at the change in the condition of the snow at the top on the day of their attempt and Murray gives the same reason as Williams for the phenomenon.

It is difficult to be precise about the distance fallen by Kirkus and Linnell. At best, it can be said that Kirkus fell something like 100 metres and Linnell about 65 metres. Certain it is, nevertheless, that Kirkus's foothold gave way just below the top of the climb and that he was rendered unconscious after he fell over the rock band, which he called 'a cliff', immediately under the final slabs. He continued his headlong descent, taking Linnell with him, until the men's progress was suddenly halted when the rope snagged on some protrusion of ice or hard snow, probably close to the bottom of the rock band. Kirkus was unable to do anything to stop himself and he was very quickly made unconscious by a severe blow to the head. Judging from the facts that the foothold gave way, that he tried to use his ice-axe to arrest his fall and that he sustained serious injuries to his face, it seems that he descended feet first and face down, although he may have tumbled some of the way. By the time he drew level with Linnell he must have been travelling at high speed and when the rope linking the two men became suddenly taut, there was little likelihood that he would be held. If the rope did not break, the force of the impact would probably either break Linnell's belaying ice-axe or pull the axe out of the snow. As it happened, the axe was pulled out and Linnell followed Kirkus down the slope. The axe may have been caught in the rope as it was found close to Linnell.

It is not known how long Kirkus remained unconscious. However, the air temperature was about freezing level on the snow-covered east-facing buttress; on ascending to Linnell, Kirkus found that Linnell showed no detectable signs of life, but that he was still warm and this may indicate that Kirkus's period of unconsciousness was short. Kirkus also discovered that the rope had somehow become wrapped round Linnell's neck and had apparently strangled him. It is not difficult to understand how the rope would wrap around Linnell's neck. He would have been providing Kirkus with a shoulder belay and this would have allowed the rope to catch around his neck when he fell. In fact, Linnell was not killed by the rope. The Rucksack Club's Accidents Sub-Committee's report contained the following information on the cause of death:

From the medical and other evidence it would appear that Linnell fell sheer, struck the ground with the left side of the front of his head, and did not move further. The head being forced backwards by the weight of the body, the neck was broken, resulting in instantaneous death.

The Register of Corrected Entries in New Register House, Edinburgh, briefly gives as the cause of death: 'Fracture of the neck. Instantaneous.'

Kirkus also discovered why the fall had been stopped: the rope had caught on a 'ridge of snow' which was apparently somewhere near a ledge and it was towards this ledge that Kirkus tried to drag his friend. In this way Linnell's position would have been made fairly secure while Kirkus went for help, but Kirkus was obliged to leave Linnell where he was, securing him to the slope by putting Linnell's unbroken ice-axe through his waist band and driving it into the snow. Kirkus, who preferred to use a wrist loop with his ice-axe, fortunately found his own ice-axe nearby but the fall had broken its shaft, apparently near the head. Such was his concern for his friend, whom in any case he believed dead, that he denied himself the use of Linnell's unbroken axe, choosing to use it to make as sure as possible that Linnell would fall no further.

That reascent – and this would apply even if it had been made up South Castle Gully – was an astonishing achievement. In his statement to the press made on his release from Belford Hospital, Kirkus made no comment upon the difficulties he must have faced as he climbed back up to the cornice; he did not even mention that he had to use a broken ice-axe. This was quite in keeping with his unassuming nature. Having fallen to the right of their upward route, Kirkus first had to scale virgin ground to reach their earlier steps, knowing all the time that the ground might give way under his feet as it had done before – and, if it did, this time he would probably go most of the way to the Allt a'Mhuilinn, 335m below the base of the Castle Buttress itself. He was severely injured, much worse than was thought when he was taken down the mountain-side in the late evening. He had severe concussion and suffered from a fractured skull; he was badly lacerated and the wounds were reluctant to congeal; he had sprained his ankle, broken his nose and damaged his jaw; and, worst of all in the long term, he had done his right eye irreparable harm. Not only was his face generally, and the area round his eye in particular, badly swollen making vision difficult, but the eye itself had been permanently misaligned. Added to all this was a fear, amounting to a fairly certain knowledge, that his close friend and climbing companion lay dead below him.

The first others knew that something serious had happened was when Kirkus was seen and heard calling for help on the north shoulder of Carn Dearg. Kirkus's own account in both *The Oban Times* and *The Strathspey Herald* is typically brief:

It was not until I got half way down to the lochan that I managed to attract the attention of two people by the side of the lake, who came up to me, arranged for a party to look for Linnell, and took me down to my tent by the lake, after which I was carried by a stretcher party down to Fort William.

There is some dispute as to when Kirkus reached the top of The Castle. The Rucksack Club's Accidents Sub-Committee's report said, 'probably about 2.30 p.m.', while Borthwick, in his article in the *Glasgow Weekly Herald*, stated: 'At one o'clock I found Kirkus in a terrible condition, wandering on the broad shoulder of the Ben.'

Borthwick wrote his account of the day's events the day after they happened and there is no reason for him to have erred; moreover, he and his friend, Bill Thomson (W. S. Thomson who was to become well-known in the picture postcard business), were making their way towards one of the climbs on the Ben and it is unlikely that they would have been much later than this. When he and Thomson heard Kirkus's cries for assistance, they were, according to Borthwick's estimate, 305m below. Allowing for some lapse of time between Kirkus's arrival at the top of The Castle and his being heard by Borthwick and Thomson and between his cries being heard and their appearance on the scene, it seems that Kirkus would have reached the top of The Castle about noon. This may seem fairly early, but Kirkus and Linnell had started their climb by 8.45 a.m. and they would have moved up the climb quite quickly, minimal time being spent on setting up belays, so that it is not at all inconceivable that Kirkus was below the cornice by about 10.45 a.m. Certainly, when Noel Williams and his companion made their exploratory ascent of the buttress it took them just over two hours. The snow conditions were nearly perfect and, of course, they had the benefit of modern equipment, but time was spent making their observations and they would have used more time in belaying than would Kirkus and Linnell. If Kirkus's period of unconsciousness was brief, it is possible that he was able to attend to his friend and to reclimb the route by midday or soon after – although in doing so, the achievement was all the more astonishing.

The time estimated by the Rucksack Club is almost certainly too late. It is apparent that an hour must have elapsed between the arrival of Borthwick, Thomson, Petrie and his friend, McKinnell, on the scene and the appearance of the party of four from the Rucksack Club, one of whom was Frank Bennett. Time was then spent in an abortive endeavour to lower one member of this party to Linnell directly down the buttress, after which it was decided that the party should try to reach the fallen climber by descending North Castle Gully. It is fairly certain that this effort began about 3.00 p.m.

Today, as Frank Bennett recalls, his party reached the area, 'mid to late afternoon'; however, it is approaching sixty years since the event and it would not be in the least surprising if his memory on this point of detail was not wholly accurate. It is probable that the time of their arrival was about 2.00 p.m.

Kirkus made his way down the north-west shoulder of Carn Dearg towards Lochan Meall an t-Suidhe where his tent was pitched. As he went, he called out for help. Borthwick wrote in the *Glasgow Weekly Herald* of Saturday, 7th April:

> I heard a shout. It sounded very like 'Help!' Away up on the top of the shoulder, a thousand feet up, a small figure straggled along. 'Anything wrong?' I bawled at the top of my voice. No reply came, and I thought I had made a mistake. We walked on. Again came the shout, and this time there was a desperate sound about it. I shouted back, and, although there was still no reply, Bill and I decided that it needed looking into. So we set off uphill as fast as we could go.

Meanwhile, Petrie and McKinnell had also heard Kirkus's pleas for assistance. In *The Scottish Daily Express* of Monday, 2nd April, Petrie stated:

> We had got as far as the Lochan by the pony track. That is half way up the Ben. We heard faint cries for help. We stopped and listened, climbed on, and saw Kirkus. He was on his feet, but I could see by the marks in the snow that he had been crawling to look for help. When I was within thirty yards of him I saw his face was covered with blood. He said, 'I think my jaw is dislocated. I cannot see with one eye, and my ankle is hurt. Linnell is lying about two hundred feet from the summit. I am all right. Go after him.' He did not think of himself at all. 'I think,' he added, 'he is either strangled or unconscious. The rope is around his neck.'
>
> Kirkus' ice-axe was smashed in two. I soon saw why. He had performed an almost unbelievable feat of climbing in his brave efforts to get help for his friend. He told me he had put two stones to mark the spot. He had had the presence of mind for that. He described where it was, and I went up, leaving him with McKinnell. I had no difficulty in finding the spot, for I followed blood stains left by Kirkus as he crawled down. There was no sign of Linnell. The ground sloped out to a precipice with an overhang of ice and snow. I looked over. All I could see was signs of someone having climbed up the face of the precipice. It must have been an almost superhuman feat for a man in Kirkus' condition. He had made steps for about two hundred feet up an almost vertical precipice face, and then had cut a tunnel through the snow cornice overhanging the precipice to get a hand hold at the top. Then he had placed the stones.

This quotation contains two rather surprising points: Kirkus says that the rope was still around Linnell's neck when he had actually removed it and he refers specifically to a cairn of 'two stones'. However, both may be misunderstandings on the part of Petrie or later transcriptional errors: Kirkus may have said, 'The rope was around his neck' and 'a few stones'.

From below, Borthwick and Thomson could see Petrie and McKinnell. Borthwick described what happened:

> Meanwhile Colin [sic] and his friend had sensed that something was far wrong, and they too set off. They had a few hundred feet start of us, and reached the man first. It was Kirkus. Colin turned, and shouted to us in a voice that left no doubt that something pretty bad had happened. I don't blame him for sounding a little queer. Kirkus' face seemed terribly injured. Colin's pal dashed off to Fort William for a doctor, and a middle-aged gentleman who turned up stayed with Kirkus after we had put most of our clothing round him. Kirkus was past speaking, but he managed to gasp out, 'He's in Castle Gully. I think he's dead. He's hanging from the rope by the neck.' Colin, Bill, and I gave each other one look, grabbed our ice-axes, and went as hard as we could along Kirkus' tracks. There were several tracks about, but we had no difficulty in knowing which were the right ones, for there were blood-stains.

Here, too, Kirkus is quoted as saying that the rope was still around Linnell's neck, but more significant is Kirkus's reported statement that Linnell was lying in Castle Gully. Kirkus, dazed though he was, must have known that his friend was to be found on the buttress where he had anchored him with the ice-axe. There may have been no reference to a gully: it may have been an innocent gloss made subsequently by Borthwick who thought that the men had been climbing South Castle Gully.

The two accounts are not identical but can be put together to make reasonable sense. Petrie and McKinnell were probably the two men beside the lochan or 'lake' whose attention Kirkus said he was able to attract from halfway down the shoulder of Carn Dearg and when they reached him ahead of the other two he was able to talk fairly lucidly. Petrie left Kirkus in the care of McKinnell and set off for the top of the Castle Buttress before the arrival of Borthwick and Thomson (in spite of Borthwick's assertion that Petrie was still there when they arrived). By the time Borthwick and Thomson gained the spot, Kirkus had lapsed into semi-consciousness and was almost inarticulate. He was evidently badly concussed and in a state of some shock and he was also in danger of suffering from the cold so they wrapped him in all the available warm clothing and McKinnell set off for Fort William to alert the authorities and to summon assistance.

By this time others were beginning to appear on the scene, including the 'middle-aged gentleman who . . . stayed with Kirkus' mentioned by Borthwick. It is clear from other news reports that two members of the Swiss Alpine Club, some of whose members were also climbing in the area, made

an early appearance and this was probably one of them. They were Mr
Slingsby (probably Hugh Slingsby, a nephew and godson of the great Cecil
Slingsby) and Dr Alford Rogers and some newspapers, notably *The Times*
and the *Aberdeen Press and Journal*, gave credit to these two as being the first
to find Kirkus. Certainly, they seem to have escorted Kirkus down to his tent
where, after attending to him, they left him in order to round up further help
and to assist in the attempt to rescue Linnell. Borthwick and Thomson left
Kirkus in this care and proceeded upwards, like Petrie following the
bloodstained trail.

Thus far, acceptable sense can be made of the reports; it then becomes
more difficult. Borthwick's account continued as follows:

> We reached the gully. A crazy line of ice steps ran up it. It was Kirkus' route up.
> The same traces were there [i.e. bloodstains]. I shouted. There was no reply. For 500
> feet the gully was bounded by the sheer walls of the Castles itself, and it was from a
> point round the corner below the Castles that the steps came. Round that corner lay
> something, and we did not like to think what it was. From what we had gathered from
> Kirkus and from the very plain traces on the snow, it seemed that Kirkus, while
> leading up the 2000 feet ice slope, had slipped from his footholds when only a few
> hundred feet from the top. Linnell, a hundred feet below, had his ice-axe driven into
> the ice in the usual way, with the rope belayed round it. Kirkus avalanched down in a
> cloud of soft snow, and must have been travelling at a tremendous speed when the
> jerk came on the ice-axe. The ice-axe snapped [sic]. Linnell was dragged from his
> holds, and together they careered down the ice slope towards the corrie, 2000 feet
> below, dropping over several small cliffs on the way. Somehow they stopped. Kirkus
> was unconscious, and Linnell was dead.

This passage is quoted to show that, when he wrote the article, Borthwick
believed that the two men had been climbing (South) Castle Gully.
Wherever Borthwick found himself, it was decided that an attempt should be
made to descend from there to try to discover where Linnell was and
Borthwick was lowered over the edge. His account in the *Glasgow Weekly
Herald* described this effort:

> I had a 100-foot length of rope with me and this we belayed round two ice-axes
> driven up to their heads in the snow. I tied myself on the other end, and was lowered
> over the cornice to find out if anything more was to be seen from below. The surface
> was vile – soft snow on top of ice. At the slightest touch of the foot the snow slid away,
> leaving the bare ice. I didn't like it one little bit, and after thirty feet of step cutting I
> gave up and climbed back. There was nothing else to do but wait for more rope.

It must be wondered what use, if any, Borthwick made of the existing
footsteps and it is not without significance that this description of the
condition of the snow could have applied to the final section of The Castle.

Later he said:

> We could not hang about waiting for rope to arrive. It was ghastly to think that a
> man might be freezing to death while we stood about, unable to do a thing to help.
> Four more climbers clambered up to the spot with another 100 feet of rope, but still
> we had not nearly enough. I went off to raise some more.

Curiously, Petrie's account made no reference to Borthwick's descent,
nor indeed did it make any reference to Borthwick himself. It is possible that
the explanation may lie in an editorial decision, made perhaps to reduce the
length of the item or to exaggerate the role of Petrie whose story was
described as being given 'exclusively to *Scottish Daily Express* readers'.
However, this explanation does not sit easily with Petrie's assertion that,
after reaching the top of the Castle Buttress and looking down its face,

> I stayed on the spot and shouted for help but it was an hour-and-a-half before I got
> an answer from a party of climbers, some of whom were from Manchester and were
> comrades of the two men.

Presuming that there was no simple transcriptional or typographical error,
this part of Petrie's published account is bordering on the incredible: quite
apart from the evidence of various other sources, with so many parties on the
Ben that Saturday it is, a priori, unimaginable that Petrie should have had to
wait so long in the middle of the day for any help to arrive, calling out as he
did. Even if Borthwick and Thomson were at the top of South Castle Gully,
they were well within earshot. Indeed, it must be asked why he did not set off
in search of assistance instead of shouting for it from the top of Carn Dearg!
Whatever the truth, another attempt was made to reach Linnell. The party
from Manchester mentioned by Petrie may have been the four climbers who
clambered up with the additional 30 metres of rope before Borthwick left
and since Borthwick made no reference to this second effort in his own
account, it may be that it took place while he was away seeking climbers and
extra rope, although a wrongly captioned photograph, published in the same
issue of the *Glasgow Weekly Herald* and apparently taken by Borthwick,
suggests that he witnessed it. In any event, there seems to have been
available some 76 metres or so of rope which was used to lower the lightest
of those present. It is not clear from the press reports themselves where the
descent was made but the photograph in the *Glasgow Weekly Herald*,
attributed to Borthwick, and another, taken by Petrie and published in *The
Scottish Daily Express* of Monday, 2nd April, make it clear that it was done
directly down The Castle. That this effort was made down the buttress itself
shows that it was quite clear to those present that Kirkus and Linnell had

been climbing The Castle and that it was there that Linnell was lying. It follows that it must have been up The Castle that the bloodstained footsteps came. Referring to this endeavour to reach Linnell from the top of The Castle, Petrie commented:

> We were short of ropes. He [the man lowered] came up with a terrible story. He said he could see the man lying a good deal further below on his face, with arms outstretched, as if he were dead.

The Rucksack Club's Accidents Sub-Committee's report on the accident adds some detail to this part of the afternoon's activities. It read:

> Some time afterwards [i.e. after Kirkus had reached the top of The Castle], the news reached a Rucksack Club party who were standing at the top of No. 3 Gully, being passed up to them from Coire na Ciste by way of a large M.A.M. [Midland Association of Mountaineers] party led by F. G. Brettell, who were climbing this gully. The R.C. party, consisting of Bennett, Bower, Hughes (H.V.) and Taylor (H.), went off at once to the summit of The Castle. Bower climbed down for about 200 feet; but, after further reconnoitring, the party decided that in the conditions then prevailing it was impracticable to descend to the body, and that rescue work must proceed from below.

It is almost certain that Bower was the member of the Manchester party mentioned by Petrie as being 'the lightest of those present'; there is no doubt that he made his descent down The Castle itself.

Apparently, Borthwick had success in his mission. He had made for the summit of the Ben, calling out as he went.

> On the last rise to the summit, about a mile away, I saw three parties. I stopped and shouted my loudest. They stopped. They could not make out what I was saying. I ran on. Then they realised that something was wrong, and they in their turn shouted to other parties within hailing distance. Soon fourteen of us trudged back to the head of Castle Gully.

Borthwick then gave a description, confirmed in other reports, including one from Robin Petrie in *The Courier and Advertiser* of Monday, 2nd April, of another attempt to reach Linnell whose approximate location had been discovered by the previous rescue descent. It was made by four members of the Rucksack Club.

> We had then 600 feet of rope. With one 100-foot length half a dozen of us lashed ourselves to a large slab of rock, and with the remaining 500 feet lowered four experienced climbers over the edge. It was a slow business – terribly slow. Five hours we took to pay out that rope, while the rescuers cut steps downwards. They descended a gully on the other side of Castle rock. They had to. The gully up which

Kirkus had fought his way single-handed was deemed by this strong party to be unjustifiably dangerous. The easiest approach lay down the other gully.

This was North Castle Gully, but to escape from it on to the buttress proved to be much more difficult than the men had expected.

Anxiously we consulted our watches. Time was creeping on. When at last they came to the end of the rope it was eight o'clock, and, even in the snow, it was getting dark. The rescuers were still three hundred feet from Linnell. He lay below the Castles, at a point level with them. But the 300 feet was a stretch of hard ice.

The rescue team had, in fact, descended to a point considerably below Linnell before they made their attempt to reach him.

They knew that stretch meant hours of labour, but they attempted it, after taking off the rope connecting them with the top, and had actually crossed 150 feet of it before clouds obscured the moon and made their work impossible. They knew then that Linnell was dead. By the light of two torches they made their way across farther down, and followed the steps of the ill-fated party to the bottom. They reached the Scottish Mountaineering Club hut (which lies at a height of 2000 feet at the foot of the cliffs) after midnight. [This is the Charles Inglis Clark Hut which was opened in 1929.]

It may be, as Borthwick stated, that North Castle Gully was rather easier to descend than its southern sister but it also had the advantage that it debouches on to the plateau some 40m lower than South Castle Gully. The extract just quoted makes clear Borthwick's uncertainty about the buttress and its adjacent gullies, an uncertainty shown elsewhere in his article. It is not always obvious what he meant when he used the term, 'The Castles', but it seems that he intended the entire buttress, not merely its upper castellated section which is much less in height than his estimated 152m from the top of South Castle Gully to the corner round which the footsteps disappeared. He thought that Linnell lay in South Castle Gully but apparently at a level lower than the base of the buttress. Since both North and South Castle Gullies form a bifurcation at the base of the buttress, this is itself confusing but in the extract above there is a further, although related, confusion. Here, having continued to place Linnell 'below The Castles', he mentions the difficulty of the traverse towards Linnell. At first glance, this might suggest that he realised that Linnell was actually on the buttress but it is evident that he was of the opinion that the ground below the buttress was difficult and dangerous and this was not the case.

At this point it is appropriate to return to Borthwick's bloodstained footsteps in South Castle Gully to try to resolve the matter. Petrie also

followed the bloodstained tracks from where he had come upon Kirkus to
the place where they emerged from below on to the plateau – and, according
to Borthwick, but unconfirmed by Petrie, Petrie was in the company of
Thomson and Borthwick himself at the time. When he reached the point
where the tracks went over the edge, Petrie looked down and wrote as
follows about what he saw:

> The ground sloped out to a precipice with an overhang of ice and snow. I looked
> over. All I could see was signs of someone having climbed up the face of the
> precipice. It must have been an almost superhuman feat for a man in Kirkus'
> condition. He had made steps for about two hundred feet up an almost vertical
> precipice face, and then had cut a tunnel through the snow cornice overhanging the
> precipice to get a hand hold at the top.

It is fairly obvious from this description, admittedly exaggerated
in its steepness and in the distance the footsteps would have been visible
(something under 30 metres being more probable), that Petrie was looking
down Castle Buttress and not South Castle Gully: he refers to 'the face of
the precipice' and he mentions the word, 'precipice', four times; if he had
been looking down a gully with steep enclosing walls he would surely have
said so or at least have described the scene rather differently. There is
another piece of evidence that Petrie saw the steps ascending the buttress.
On the final page of *The Scottish Daily Express* of Monday, 2nd April, there
were two photographs taken by Petrie: one showed the lowering of Bower
from the top of The Castle in his attempt to reach Linnell, the other showed
the point where it was said that Petrie looked over 'the precipice' to see the
steps coming up from below. This second photograph was taken from close
to the top of the more northerly of the two chimneys which emerge on to the
plateau slightly to the south of, and at a higher level than, the actual climb on
The Castle.

It is, therefore, just possible that Kirkus used this chimney to reach the
plateau and that it was just below the top of the chimney where he fell.
Certainly, he might have been attracted to the difficult finish that the
chimneys would offer but they are very steep and would not normally hold
sufficient snow for them to be avalanche-prone. It follows that it is unlikely
that he did use one of these chimneys either on the original ascent or on his
reascent after the accident. In view of his condition after the accident,
Kirkus would have taken the easiest way to the top. It is likely, therefore, that
Petrie looked down from the chimney and could see the footsteps traversing
leftwards to the usual finish of the climb.

In his description of (South) Castle Gully, Borthwick referred to a corner about 152 metres from the top round which the footsteps came. There is no such corner visible from the top of South Castle Gully: it simply goes straight down until it disappears from view. However, the final section of the climb on The Castle, which is a broad, shallow depression that has a slight resemblance to a gully, bends to the right when viewed from the top and ascending tracks would disappear from view round this corner. It has been pointed out already that Alastair Borthwick was on the Ben for the first time that day. He says:

> . . . I had no idea what things were called. Other people talked about 'The Castles' so I did too. My description of the gully is exact, written with care within a day of the event, but since I did not know the terrain I have no notion at all of how the gully fitted into The Castles Buttress as a whole. I know only what I saw, without context. . . . Other people must have told me that the broken cornice was at South Castle Gully because I would not have identified the place by myself.

There can be no doubt that Alastair Borthwick at some point looked down South Castle Gully because the description he gave can apply only to it, even taking into account the non-existent corner, and it is quite possible that he saw tracks ascending it – a Midland Association of Mountaineers party under George Lister had climbed it the previous day. It is clear that Borthwick did see bloodstained footsteps ascending from below and that these were made by Kirkus as he struggled to reach the top. If, as is virtually certain, Kirkus reascended The Castle after the accident, Borthwick must have seen the bloodstains on The Castle and not in South Castle Gully. This is quite possible in spite of his narrative in the *Glasgow Weekly Herald*. The bloodstained trail would have led him from the injured Kirkus to the top of the climb on The Castle where he saw the evidence of the climber's ascent and from where he made his abortive attempt to locate Linnell. Later, perhaps when he went off in search of additional rope or when he took his photographs, he looked down South Castle Gully and it made a deep impression on him. When he came to write his account of events, his lack of familiarity with the topography of the area caused him to conflate the two features, having the bloodstained tracks coming up South Castle Gully rather than the shallow depression at the top of The Castle.

To return to the attempt by the four members of the Rucksack Club to reach Linnell by descending North Castle Gully, the Club's Accidents Sub-Committee's report described this endeavour with great brevity:

> They [Bennett, Bower, Hughes and Taylor] descended North Castle Gully until it was possible to break out onto the buttress, but they were overtaken by dusk before they could reach their objective.

Although it is fifty-six years since the accident, one of this party of four, Frank Bennett, can still remember many of the details of the attempt to reach Linnell on Easter Saturday and of the recovery of his body the following day. It is interesting to compare Borthwick's account with that of Frank Bennett who says:

The Rucksack Club was holding its official Easter meet that year in Fort William. Among its members were H. V. Hughes and George Bower at the hotel in Fort William and Harold Taylor and myself camping at Achintee farm, for the same reason as Linnell and Kirkus – so that we could maximise climbing time. On the day of the accident we 'imported' Bower and Hughes from the hotel by means of Taylor's car and decided to climb near Castle Buttress. I think it could be said we were a strong party with Alpine experience and proceeded via Lochan Meall an t-Suidhe into the corrie to the foot of the buttress. [Thus, somewhat later in the morning they followed in the footsteps of Kirkus and Linnell.] I cannot recall now which climb we did but only remember that at the conclusion as I was breaking through the cornice (being the leader), I was greeted by a man declaiming there had been an accident not far from where we then were. My party completed the climb by which time other men had arrived and from whence Kirkus' name was mentioned. We then knew, as we also knew they were camping together, that the man on the face must be Maurice Linnell. This was mid to late afternoon.

Here detail escapes me, but what is still vividly clear, we traversed out on to the face of the buttress at a point which turned out to be some 1/200 feet below Linnell. We proceeded upwards, myself leading, in the darkening day until within sight of Linnell and concluded that, because of the grotesque posture of the body, a temperature well below zero, and the time which had elapsed since the accident, he was dead. In any event, night was almost on us. We retreated with some difficulty off the face and stumbled into the already full C.I.C. Hut in the late and dark evening.

Meanwhile a stretcher was brought up the hillside to the tent beside the halfway lochan where Kirkus was lying. It was late on in the day before his journey down to Fort William was begun. He was placed on the stretcher and the carrying party took it in turns to bear the burden. Colin Kirkus was remarkably tolerant. The roughness of the terrain and the difficulties imposed by a torchlight descent must have jolted him mercilessly but he made no complaint. The party reached the bottom and Kirkus was put in a vehicle and taken to Belford Hospital. It was 11.00 p.m. before he passed into the safe keeping of the medical staff: twelve hours and more since the fatal foothold had given way.

Early next day, Easter Sunday, a rescue party left from the C.I.C. Hut to recover Linnell's body, an operation which took many hours. *The Scottish Daily Express* continued to give the story extensive coverage, not altogether to the satisfaction of Carl Brunning who complained in the aforementioned article that, 'It was unfortunate that it [the accident] should happen at a time when the press was suffering from a dearth of news and from their point of view it must have been a god-send.'

The Scottish Daily Express winkled out another eye-witness whose story of the Sunday rescue it published on the Tuesday. George Lister from Coventry, a member of the Alpine Club as well as the Midland Association of Mountaineers, was one of those involved. He reported:

The party which actually recovered the body was compoosed of Mr F. G. Brettell, Alpine Club, and Messrs Beck, Henn and Walker of the Midland Association of Mountaineers, and Mr G. V. Hughes (sic) and Messrs Bennett, Bower and Taylor of the Manchester Rucksack Club. This party had remained at the S.M.C. Hut at the head of Allt a' Mhuilinn and set out soon after it was light to the scene of the tragedy. At the same time Dr Sheldon of Wolverhampton, who had also stayed the night at the hut, left for Fort William. He arrived at the Highland Hotel, the headquarters of Mr Brettell's party of Midland climbers, about 9.30 when we immediately organised a strong party to go up to The Castle Rock with supplies and to support the climbers then attempting to reach the body. When we reached the foot of the rock, they had just arrived at the ledge [sic] on which the body lay. It had taken them many hours to do this and it took them many more hours to lower the body over the steep ice-coated rock into the bed of the North Castle Gully.

It was, apparently, 3.00 p.m. before the rescuers were ready to lower Linnell's body, a measure of the difficult position into which he had fallen and from which Kirkus had ascended. It was to be 6.30 p.m. before the body of Maurice Linnell was brought down to the bottom.

Frank Bennett describes in some detail the recovery of Linnell's body:

We were off again, the same four [H. V. Hughes, George Bower, Harold Taylor and himself], to resume in the morning. I am sure there were other support climbers with us but I have no recollection. In effect we repeated the Kirkus and Linnell route with myself leading until I found myself alongside Linnell's body probably around midday (sic). There was certainly a large mass of rope, all frozen very hard and extremely difficult to handle, stood in ice steps on a steep slope. There was certainly much of it round the body and there could well have been a coil round the neck but I am certain not such as to cause strangulation. Rather than bring up the others, I decided it would be easier to cope in freeing the rope and in organising the evacuation on my own. I suppose I must have been between half and a full hour in the process by which time it was possible for me to ease the body on to the ice slope and gently pay out the rope as the body slid down under its own weight to my second. He in turn passed it on to the third man whilst I returned to the second and so on until we were all gathered together as the slope eased off. The later descent was modified such that at the conclusion we were in the North Gully where a support party was awaiting. . . .

There is some evidence, most notably in *The Glasgow Herald* and *The Scotsman*, both of Monday, 2nd April, that two men were lowered from the top of Castle Buttress to try to assist in the recovery of the body but it is clear that in this they failed. However, *The Scotsman* had it that the whole operation was undertaken from above with the body being, 'ultimately hoisted to the top of the climb, after which the rope was lowered for the two rescuers who were brought to safety'. This is another instance of the surprising inaccuracies in the reporting of the incident. It is also of interest to notice that the fictitious *Scottish Daily Express* interview which so annoyed Brunning related that the rescue party, which numbered ten, reached Linnell from the top and lowered the body to the bottom. The rescuers then had to reascend and make their way, by 'a wider detour', to the base of the cliff where, 'there was a party of men ready to bring the body down the rest of the Ben'.

Linnell's body arrived in the mortuary in Belford Hospital at about 9.30 p.m.

The party which recovered Linnell's body left behind his ice-axe and the broken shaft of Kirkus's. Steve Dean, the biographer of Colin Kirkus, has had access to the personal diary of Graham Macphee, who was a friend of Kirkus, and it refers to an ascent of The Castle made by Macphee in June 1934, just over two months after the accident of Easter Saturday. To quote from the manuscript of this biography:

> At the end of June, Graham Macphee was once again up at the C.I.C. Hut working on the Ben Nevis guidebook. Typically, Graham's journey up there was highly unorthodox as he made what is thought to be the first solo (unsupported) ascent of Snowdon, Scafell Pike and Ben Nevis in under twenty-four hours! . . . The following day Macphee, in the company of George Williams, climbed The Castle.

The entry in the C.I.C. log book, dated 21st June, read simply:

> G. G. Macphee, G. C. Williams. Castle (Carn Dearg). Retrieved Linnell's ice-axe and shaft of Kirkus's. Descended by N. Castle Gully.

It is evident from the press reports of Monday, 2nd April that even on the Sunday the full extent of the injuries suffered by Kirkus were not known to the public since the newspapers stated that they were less serious than originally feared. However, the real seriousness was known by the Tuesday by which time it had emerged that, in the words of *The Courier and Advertiser* of Tuesday, 3rd April, '. . . his head injuries are so extensive that it will be at least ten days before he may be allowed any visitors.'

Indeed, initially he was not even allowed to make a statement to the police about the accident and according to *The Times* of Tuesday, 3rd April, he continued to lapse into unconsciousness on the Monday. In fact, he was allowed the occasional visitor soon after his admission to hospital: his brother, Guy, who was himself on a mountain holiday with some friends at Crianlarich about 80km from Fort William, saw him the day after the accident and Carl Brunning visited him on Easter Monday. Both men were horrified by the damage done to his face which Brunning recalls as being twice its normal size. He was eventually discharged from Belford Hospital on Thursday, 19th April, almost three weeks after the accident.

His friend, Maurice Linnell, had been laid to rest on Tuesday, 3rd April in the cemetery in Glen Nevis which had been consecrated as a burial ground only a few years before. Linnell was apparently the first mountaineer to be buried there. It stands close to the River Nevis and below the great bulk of Ben Nevis and its northern outlier, Meall an t-Suidhe, with views up the glen which is dominated at its upper end by Sgurr a' Mhaim. Linnell's father and sister arrived in Fort William early on the Monday and made arrangements for the funeral which, as requested by them, was a quiet one. Many of the climbers had left for home, but those who remained followed the cortège from Belford Hospital, where a service was held, along the narrow road through the glen to the graveyard. Later, there was erected at the grave a simple, small, grey headstone with the inscription:

> *Maurice*
> *Linnell*
> *Of Skelsmergh*
> *Kendal*
> *Died March 31, 1934*
> *On Carn Dearg*
> *Aged 25 Years*

Sadly, after that Easter Saturday, Kirkus was never again altogether the climber he had been. Alan Hargreaves referred to this in his 'In Memoriam' in the Climbers' Club Journal:

After that [the accident on Ben Nevis] he was never quite the same and the nature of his interest in climbing seemed to change. For quite a long time he did not climb at all but gradually he came back to it, preferring, however, to do ordinary courses, only occasionally going for the difficult things. He frequently took novices and oldish people up standard climbs, laying himself out to make things safe and enjoyable for them. He was care, skill and confidence embodied and there must be many who owe to him a sound introduction to climbing.

Colin Kirkus (right) with Charles Warren on the 1933 Gangotri Expedition.

It may well be that the shock he must have experienced and the loss of his close friend and climbing partner affected him psychologically to the extent that his interest in taking the risks inevitably associated with climbing at the extremes of achievement lessened; certainly the damage to his eyesight must have made climbing on small and tenuous holds much more difficult. Steve Dean, his biographer, has the following to say:

> The death of Maurice affected him very deeply, and effectively his days as a hard climber ended on that March day in 1934 when he was still only 23. One problem was that Kirkus and Linnell were almost too talented, and friends viewed their climbing together with considerable misgivings. One view put forward is that, if that accident had not happened on the Ben in 1934, it would probably have happened somewhere else. In effect their ability and boldness outstripped the equipment available at the time.

Kirkus, however, was not deterred from returning to the mountain on which he had come to so much harm. Chapter Ten of *Let's Go Climbing!* is entitled 'Accidents'. He makes no direct reference here or anywhere else in the book to the accident of 1934 which may indicate that he found the memory painful. He does, however, describe at length an accident he and three friends had on Ben Nevis on Easter Sunday 1936. There were close similarities to the earlier visit: in 1936, as in 1934, they 'had been camping by the windswept little lochan, half-way up. The snow was plentiful and very hard – almost as hard as ice.' The party, on two ropes, was ascending the Tower Gap Chimney when 'a great avalanche of stones crashed over the rocks, just above our heads'. Even so, Kirkus with a characteristic detachment could not but see humour in their situation which he expresses in his simple and direct prose:

I went head-first; it seems to be a habit of mine. I could see my camera going down in front. It was an easy winner; I never saw it again. Then I went over the 40-foot ice-wall and landed with a sickening jolt on the edge of the crevasse. Derrick must have arrived soon afterwards to complete the party. He went plonk into a hole, so that only his head and shoulders were visible. He looked rather funny. Alfred was a few feet down the slope, held by the rope. Dorothy was close to me. The stones continued for another 500 feet. I cannot understand why we didn't do likewise.

Alfred was the most cheerful of the party, although he had a broken arm and a gash that ran half-way up his face. He also had a bone broken on his ankle. He sat and smoked cigarette after cigarette. Derrick had concussion and looked grey and drawn. His hands were mangled. Dorothy had her face and one leg badly cut and various muscles strained. I had a shoulder torn so that one arm was useless. My ribs were damaged. I could not breathe sitting down and felt sick standing up. After a time the faintness disappeared and I felt quite comfortable. We had all lost our axes, so we could not help ourselves at all. It was very chilly sitting there on the snow, waiting. At intervals we shouted for help.

Our shouts were heard by Hemming and McCallum of the Scottish Mountaineering Club, who climbed up to our rescue. We owe a lot to them; they were most skilful and efficient. They retrieved our axes; mine was broken in two. The first thing was to get Derrick down. He was lowered on his back down the slope, his arms sticking out pathetically in front. I couldn't help being amused; he looked so ridiculous, although he was in a bad enough way, poor chap. The procedure was for one or other of the rescue party to carve a great platform out of the snow every hundred feet. Then the whole party would be assembled there. I managed to descend on my own, cutting steps with my uninjured arm and the broken ice-axe.

If Kirkus makes no reference to the accident of two years previously, there is at the end of this chapter a short paragraph in the writing of which Kirkus must have drawn on that experience. It reads:

A fatal accident is a very terrible thing. Don't think of yourself, but think of the effect on all your relations and friends if anything were to happen to you. Or think how you would feel if you had to meet the parents of a friend who had been killed while climbing with you.

Colin Fletcher Kirkus knew too painfully well the meaning of that.

The Rucksack Club's Accidents Sub-Committee's report of the accident of Easter Saturday, 1934, concluded with the following observations:

The most important points arising in connection with this accident concern the condition of the snow, the tactics employed by the climbers, and the conduct of the recovery party.

Many of those whose evidence is available testify to the fact that snow conditions on the Saturday afternoon were showing definite signs of deterioration, and it cannot be too strongly emphasised that snow on our British hills must be treated with as much care and circumspection as would be used in the Alps. At the same time it must be remembered that the two climbers were men of skill and experience. They were climbing in the earlier part of the day, and were not led to suspect at all the soundness of the snow they encountered; so that there seems no valid reason to impugn their judgement on this head.

The use by the party of such long run-outs on this climb is open to serious criticism. It is an extension of the tactics employed perforce on modern rock-climbs to circumstances under which they are neither necessary nor appropriate. When climbing steep snow the members of a party should never be so far separated if it can possibly be avoided; and it is especially desirable that they should be in close proximity when tackling the final section of the climb.

As far as the recovery operations are concerned, the only serious question arising is whether the party could have reached Linnell on the Saturday evening. Had they continued down the face of the Castle on their first attempt it is just possible that they might have done so. But when we consider the paucity of their information, the deterioration in the snow conditions, and the far greater difficulty of descent as compared with ascent on such ground, it becomes clear that such a course would have been not only very conjectural but also extremely hazardous. Their actual conduct of the operations showed great powers of endurance and sacrifice combined with sound mountaineering judgement.

The following are the considered findings of the sub-committee:

1.   The party should have had less rope out and Linnell should have been near Kirkus just below the final steep section. In view of the manner in which the leadership was arranged the responsibility for these mistakes must be considered a joint one.

2.   There is no reason to impute to either climber any other fault either of judgement or technique.

3.   The recovery party conducted their operations in an entirely satisfactory manner, and did all that was possible under most difficult circumstances.

Colin Kirkus was the oldest of three brothers. In September 1939 his middle brother, Nigel, was killed in the first important air attack of the war, a bombing mission on Kiel. Kirkus was deeply affected by his brother's death and he determined to enter the Royal Air Force as an aircrew member to try to avenge the death. He knew that he would fail the eyesight test but, finding himself towards the end of the queue, he had time to memorise the test card and was passed. He served as a navigator and bomb-aimer and it was his proud claim that, despite his visual impairment, he had never failed to find the target or to navigate his aircraft home. He had made about twenty-five missions to enemy territory when he was reported missing, presumed killed, after a raid on Bremen in September 1942. He was thirty-two years old.

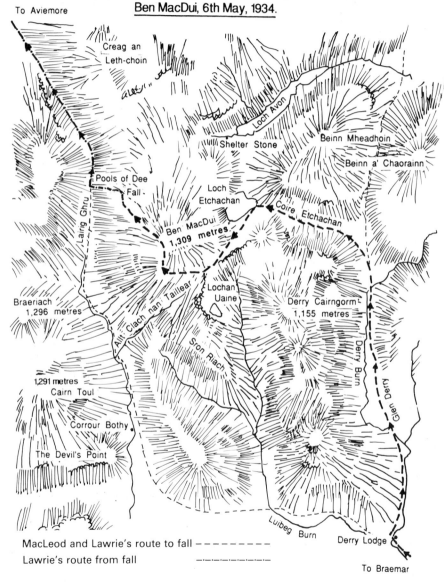

Norman MacLeod and John Lawrie:
Ben MacDui, 6th May, 1934.

To Aviemore

Creag an
Leth-choin

Loch Avon

Shelter Stone

Beinn Mheadhoin

Beinn a' Chaorainn

Pools of Dee
Fall

Lairig Ghru

Loch
Etchachan

Coire Etchachan

Ben MacDui
1,309 metres

Braeriach
1,296 metres

Allt Clach nan Taillear

Lochan
Uaine

Derry Cairngorm
1,155 metres

Sron Riach

Derry Burn

Glen Derry

1,291 metres
Cairn Toul

Corrour Bothy

The Devil's Point

Luibeg Burn

Derry Lodge

To Braemar

MacLeod and Lawrie's route to fall – – – – – – –

Lawrie's route from fall —— —— ——

Norman MacLeod on Ben MacDui. May, 1934

On the afternoon of Saturday, 5th May, 1934, two men, both aged twenty-three, boarded a bus in Aberdeen. They were setting off for a walking expedition in the Cairngorms, which had been planned for some weeks. The time was chosen because they thought that by early May the weather should be sufficiently warm and settled for their purposes. Their packs must have been heavy because, in addition to their normal hill-walking impedimenta, they carried a tent and provisions. Norman Murray MacLeod lived with his parents in Albury Street and was employed as a foreman with the joinery firm of James Blake in the city. MacLeod was a keen hill-walker who spent as much of his free time as possible walking in the Cairngorms and was anxious to introduce beginners to the pleasures of wandering and exploring in the mountains. He was a large man of strong physique who had an extensive knowledge of the history and lore of the area which made him an interesting mountain companion. He had become a member of the Cairngorm Club, itself based in Aberdeen, six months before. The friend with whom he travelled along the Deeside road was employed as a clerk in the Harbour Treasurer's Department in Aberdeen; his name was John Lawrie and he lived in Cotton Street. Lawrie was smaller than his friend but no less athletic and was soon to show that he was endowed with considerable stamina. He was less experienced than MacLeod but had made four outings into the Cairngorms in MacLeod's company.

MacLeod had a friend who lived in Aboyne to whom he wrote suggesting that he be a third member of the party. Charles Smith met them as arranged at Thistle Cottage in Meikle Inverey, the home of a well-known local lady, Maggie Gruer, who befriended so many walkers and climbers. The three friends then made their way to Derry Lodge, close to which they pitched their tent. It is not clear if Smith had brought his own tent; if not, it must have been rather crowded and this may partly account for their early departure on the Sunday morning.

They left camp at about 6.00 a.m. They headed north, beside the

139

tumbling waters of the Derry Burn and up Glen Derry, along the path which eventually takes the traveller over the Lairig an Laoigh and onwards towards Nethybridge. It was an early start but it seems that they had a full day's programme planned and it would make sense to be under way at first light. This enthusiasm may have cost Norman MacLeod his life. Their plan was to walk up Glen Derry as far as the point where the Coire Etchachan Burn comes in from the west, 6km from their camp, and then to follow the path up Coire Etchachan to the loch at its head. From there, they would make the easy ascent of 3km to the summit of Ben MacDui (1309m).

Then would come the parting of the ways: Smith would leave on his own for the Lairig Ghru and the Corrour bothy where he would spend the night before returning to Aboyne, while MacLeod and Lawrie would descend to the Shelter Stone, the famous howff beside Loch Avon. It may be that they would have spent the night there, especially if it proved to be without residents, but it appears that their more likely plan was to continue onwards towards the Ryvoan bothy which would be their refuge for the night before making their way to Aviemore or Nethybridge and a train to Aberdeen to be ready for work on Tuesday. A report in *The Scottish Daily Express* of Tuesday, 8th May, quoting Lawrie, seemed to imply that they proposed to travel all the way to Nethybridge on the Sunday, but this report is not wholly reliable in places and it is likely that the two friends would have intended to spend longer than a day in the hills over the holiday weekend.

They would have a choice of routes. They could make their way along the north side of Loch Avon and over the Saddle into Strath Nethy which would take them fairly directly to the Ryvoan bothy which, unlike many in those days, was always open – as it had been since the 'Bothans', as the occupying Grant family had been known, had abandoned the croft in the early 1900s. Alternatively, there would be the option of being a little more adventurous and ascending Bynack More (1090m) by way of the long ridge running north-east from the Saddle over A'Choinneach (1017m). They could then drop down to rejoin the Lairig an Laoigh path and thence to the bothy. There is no indication if they took their tent with them but it is possible that, as apparently they did not intend to use it again during the weekend, it was left at Derry Lodge for Smith to collect on his return from Corrour bothy.

In the published accounts of the accident, there is some doubt about the weather on that day. Lawrie was reported in the press as saying that during the ascent the weather was good; indeed, the report of the accident given in the Cairngorm Club Journal (Volume XIII, July 1934), an account which acknowledged Lawrie's assistance, referred to the weather as being 'fine and sunny', but with a high wind on the tops. However, Charles Smith, in the *Aberdeen Press and Journal* of Wednesday, 9th May, was quoted as saying: 'The weather was rather overcast, and there was a heavy wind blowing.' The same description was provided in the account of the accident in the S.M.C.J. (Volume XX, November 1934). Another piece of evidence about the weather comes from *The Courier and Advertiser* of Wednesday, 9th May:

A tragic feature of M'Leod's disappearance which came to light on the Braemar side yesterday is that on Saturday night the missing climber was urged to remain for the night because of the unsettled weather. Mr Charles M'Dougal, of Inverey, who knew M'Leod, met him making for Glen Lui Beg, and invited him to stay. He said they were to go on to the Shelter Stone, however, and be in Aviemore by Monday. [By 'Glen Lui Beg' is probably meant 'Glen Lui', at the head of which stands Derry Lodge and the gamekeeper's house, Luibeg.]

The weather maps for 6th May provide help. A deep depression moved northwards to the west of Ireland and Scotland and in the morning the barometer fell briskly. At the Dalwhinnie weather station, situated about 40km from Ben MacDui and some 760m lower than the Cairngorm plateau, the winds were generally of the order of Force Seven during the day but increasing to Gale Force Eight for some time in the middle of the day, while the temperature rose from 4°C at 7.00 a.m. to 5°C at 1.00 p.m. and to 8°C by 5.00 p.m. (All times are G.M.T.). On the weather charts, cloud cover is indicated across the United Kingdom from 7.00 a.m.; by 1.00 p.m., the time of issue of the next weather map, it was raining over the northern parts of Scotland, presumably falling as snow and sleet over the higher hills. This is confirmed by the data recorded at Dalwhinnie.

Bearing in mind the southerly direction of the wind and the magnifying effect the topography of the Cairngorm area has on winds from that direction, the wind speeds on the upper slopes of Ben MacDui and on the plateau may well have been in the region of Storm Force Ten to Violent Storm Force Eleven. With an air temperature of about 4.5°C at Dalwhinnie, the temperature on the summit of Ben MacDui would have been −1.5°C; even at the somewhat lower altitude of the plateau, it would still have been below freezing level. The wind-chill factor would have made this the equivalent of a still air temperature of about −25°C with regard to the cooling effect on the body.

Whatever the conditions, MacLeod, Lawrie and Smith made good time as they ascended the easy slopes of Glen Derry. The story of what happened next is best told in the words of John Lawrie as reported in the *Aberdeen Press and Journal* of Tuesday, 8th May:

It was about nine o'clock when we arrived at the shore of Loch Etchaichan, at the foot of the Ben, and there we deposited our haversacks in order to lighten our journey. I marked the spot with a cairn of stones. We were going to return by the same route. The weather was good as we climbed the Ben, and we found the going easy. When we reached the indicator on the summit, however, it suddenly became dark, and before we could get to shelter, a blizzard of snow and rain, and a wild raging wind practically blotted out everything. It was impossible to see more than a few yards ahead of us and, within a few minutes, we had lost all sense of direction. We had no rope, and in order to keep together we clasped hands. I thought that we were heading back towards Loch Etchaichan, but evidently we were going in the opposite direction.

Suddenly Norman began to slide, and dragged me with him. We let go hands and I lost sight of him. I am sure I slid 200 feet on my back down the snowy slope. I tried to get a grip by digging my feet into the snow, but could not make any impression on it because it was so icy. The next I saw of Norman was when he bumped on a ledge and was thrown into the air. My career stopped almost in the same place on which Norman lay, and I went to him. Although I was unhurt I found that he was unconscious and was bleeding at the hands and knees.

I lifted him into the shelter of an overhanging rock and tried to revive him by forcing whisky down his throat and rubbing his face with snow. He showed no sign of returning to consciousness. I had no idea where I was, and for over half an hour I sat beside him, during which he did not show any sign of life. For a minute the mist lifted, and below me I saw the tarns that are called the Pools of Dee. I knew that the Larig Ghru pass [sic – error for 'path'] lay near them, and I decided to try and get help by going to Braemar. I do not know how I got down the face of the cliff and made the journey in face of the blizzard, but about six o'clock in the evening I arrived at a cottage and was surprised to find that I was not heading for Braemar but for Aviemore. I borrowed a bicycle at the cottage and cycled to Aviemore where I informed the police.

Before continuing with the story of the day's activity, it is necessary to refer to the evidence upon which much of what is known depends. This evidence comes from Lawrie who resigned from his employment with the Aberdeen Harbour Treasurer's Department shortly after the Second World War to go to England and has not been traced. Lawrie's account is contained in two principal records: the newspapers of the time and the Journals of the S.M.C. and the Cairngorm Club. To be found among these records are significant differences which cannot easily be attributed to careless press reporting or journalistic licence; there are other occasions when Lawrie seems surprisingly unsure of what was happening.

The impression is formed that Lawrie may have been rather confused at the time of the events. There can be little doubt that the adventure, especially for a man of little mountain experience, was rather frightening and emotionally stressful. He would feel himself dependent on MacLeod to lead them to safety and it may be that MacLeod did not make clear to him the thinking behind his decisions, such as they were. However, there is the possibility that Lawrie was suffering from mild hypothermia, which could account for a vague and variable memory. Once under way after leaving MacLeod, Lawrie may have walked out of his hypothermic state by generating sufficient heat to raise the central core temperature; although not common, it is possible, especially if the person is fit.

The confusion can be seen in the timing of the events of the day. Lawrie does not seem to have been very reliable in his estimates of time and he appears to have been aware of this himself: when talking about the period he spent with the unconscious MacLeod after the accident, he is quoted in *The Scottish Daily Express* of Tuesday, 8th May as saying, 'I lost all sense of time'.

The first problem with the timing of events is to know with some certainty when the men reached the top of Ben MacDui. According to the reports, the three friends left their camp near to Derry Lodge at about 6.00 a.m. From there to the summit, the distance was about 13km and the height gained was 870m. Taking into consideration that they were fairly heavily laden, it is difficult to believe that they could have attained the top in much less than four hours – and this without halts of any length at all. They had the whole day ahead of them and it is more than likely that they had one or two stops on the way. In spite of this, those reports which do give a time for reaching the top offer 9.00 a.m. or 9.30 a.m. – which is in evident conflict with the time of their arrival at Loch Etchachan being about 9.00 a.m. as attributed to Lawrie in the report already quoted. Either these times for attaining the summit are too early or the men must have left their camp well before six.

The three men would have had the southerly wind at their backs as they progressed up Glen Derry but, after turning westwards out of the glen into Coire Etchachan – and until they were high on Ben MacDui – they would have been sheltered from this wind. They seem to have covered the 10km to Loch Etchachan with its ascent of 500m in good time, although probably not as rapidly as the two and a half hours generally suggested in the reports. There MacLeod and Lawrie left their rucksacks beside a small marker cairn: as they intended to return from the summit of Ben MacDui by way of Loch Etchachan on their way to the Shelter Stone, it seemed to them sensible to lighten their load for the walk to the top of Ben MacDui. They set off from the loch fairly well clad against the cold wind, although apparently without any proper protection for the head and perhaps without gloves. However, despite the amount of snow, some of it hard and icy as it turned out, they had brought no ice-axes on their expedition, a fact that casts doubt on the extent of MacLeod's experience in the colder seasons of the year. This impression of limited winter experience is strengthened by MacLeod's boots: although they were well nailed, the nails themselves were much worn and often caused him to slip on hard or frozen surfaces. Furthermore, they inadvertently left behind their compasses – possibly a fatal oversight as it transpired – and their food. They had travelled about half way to the summit before they realised that they had left their compasses but decided that it was not necessary to return for them as they did not expect any serious change in the weather. In any case, at least for the ascent, they could depend on Smith's compass if necessary.

As they ascended from Loch Etchachan, the wind would have begun to blow from their left with increasing force. They had about 365m to climb over a distance of 3km to reach the top and this must have taken over an hour to complete. Lawrie's description of the ascent as given in *The Courier and Advertiser* of Tuesday, 8th May had it that they attained the summit 'about nine o'clock', while the account given in the Cairngorm Club Journal, also produced with information from Lawrie, said 'about 9.30 a.m.' As already discussed, even 9.30 a.m. may be rather soon, 10.00 a.m. being quite conceivable.

The three men spent a short time together at the summit with its indicator stone which had been placed there by the Cairngorm Club ten years before. Smith was soon on his way down the steep western flank of the mountain towards the Lairig Ghru at the southern end of which was the Corrour bothy where he was to spend the night. He was not long gone when, to quote the *Aberdeen Press and Journal* of Tuesday, 8th May, 'a storm rose out of a clear sky . . . which only a super-man could have survived'. Certainly the blizzard which enveloped them took MacLeod, Lawrie and Smith completely by surprise. The *Aberdeen Press and Journal* of Wednesday, 9th May carried verbatim Smith's description of the arrival of the storm and the difficulties he himself encountered:

We reached the top of Ben MacDui about 9.30 in the morning. We parted there and Lawrie and MacLeod doubled back along Corrie Etchachan to retrieve their packs. It was then that the weather changed. I was going down [to] the Larig Ghru, and suddenly the visibility changed as if a blanket had been dropped before my eyes. I could not see more than a yard in front of me. I had to walk with my compass held before me, and every now and then slipped on the icy surface. 'Heaven knows what has happened to Lawrie and MacLeod,' I said to myself. I was afraid that they would be unable to get back to their packs, and I knew that they would be helpless without their compasses. To tell the truth, I became lost myself, and landed at the top of the Larig Ghru instead of the foot. However, I struggled on and eventually reached Corrour, where I spent the night. I worried a little about the other two, but consoled myself with the fact that MacLeod had a good head on his shoulders and ought to manage to reach safety.

It is questionable if the storm did materialise as suddenly as Lawrie and Smith suggested and it may be that their failure to read the signs indicates a lack of experience manifested already in the leaving of the compasses at Loch Etchachan and in their failure to equip themselves with ice-axes. Certainly squalls in the hills can creep up unannounced and strike with unexpected suddenness, but the blizzard which overtook the men was a major storm which continued into the night, almost unabated. It is hard to accept that there was no warning and it seems that MacLeod and Lawrie should have been more aware of the approaching danger, especially as they had left their rucksacks 3km away. In view of the suddenness with which the storm had apparently come and considering the time of year, it would have seemed reasonable to them to expect the blizzard to depart as quickly as it had arrived. Without a compass to guide them back to Loch Etchachan, their wisest course of action was to remain where they were in the hope of the weather clearing and revealing the route they should take. As time passed and the storm showed no sign of ending, they must have become increasingly concerned. There was no question of their staying there indefinitely as they had no food nor all the clothing they would need. They would have been growing colder by the minute. It must have been particularly troublesome for the kilted MacLeod and he must have known that it would be difficult to retain much body heat below the waist once they were on the move with his kilt flapping violently in the gale.

Eventually, MacLeod decided that they must make a move. According to press reports, they set off in what they considered the proper direction for Loch Etchachan. However, the report of the accident in the Cairngorm Club Journal had this to say:

MacLeod decided that they must make for lower ground and gave up the idea of returning to Loch Etchachan.

This is in agreement with the account in the S.M.C.J. It is difficult to know what to make of this conflicting evidence. Perhaps the truth is to be found in a combination of the two: that they made an initial attempt to find their way back to Loch Etchachan but MacLeod realised that it was too difficult a task and that, in any case, they might be unable to locate their packs in the blizzard so they abandoned the effort and set off in a direction which MacLeod thought – or hoped – would lead them quickly and in some safety to lower ground. MacLeod knew Ben MacDui and was not without experience of the hills so he could have been expected to have some idea of the best direction to take to escape from the plateau if he considered the direction of the wind. He should have realised that if they travelled on a course which kept the wind blowing from their left, as it had done as they approached the summit, they would soon descend into the Lairig Ghru following approximately the line taken by their friend, Charles Smith, and that they had a reasonable chance of locating the Corrour bothy. It would have been an arduous struggle against the wind but there is no evidence that they made any attempt to do so. It may be that they had become disoriented as they sheltered from the swirling blizzard in the lee of the cairn and when they set off into the storm were unsure which direction they were taking, or it may be that they were suffering from incipient hypothermia and this impaired their ability to make sound judgement. On the other hand, it could be that they were blown along by the wind and had little choice in their direction of travel. Certainly, so fierce did Smith find the wind that, even making constant use of his compass as he descended into the Lairig Ghru, he found himself being blown continually northwards so that he reached the pass about 2km north of his intended point. However, it is likely that Lawrie would have made some comment indicating that they were driven by the fierceness of the wind along the course they followed and he seems to have made none. Indeed, he was strangely silent about the effect of the wind on them.

Whatever the truth – and all three factors may have played a part in sending them in the northerly direction they took – they left the summit of Ben MacDui and after some time came upon the steep descent where MacLeod fell. It seems that MacLeod was not rendered immediately unconscious. *The Courier and Advertiser* of Tuesday, 8th May contained the following account of the fall, given in the words of Lawrie, and its details are confirmed elsewhere:

M'Leod was in the lead. Suddenly his feet went from beneath him on the slippery surface, and both of us slid down the mountain for a considerable distance. M'Leod suddenly disappeared down the edge of a slope. He seemed to somersault down the precipice. I did not know where I was. More by instinct than anything else I clutched a boulder. I was dazed to some extent, and when I came to myself I saw M'Leod lying amongst rocks and stones. I managed to climb down to him. Blood was flowing from M'Leod's face, hands, and legs, but he got to his feet and remarked, 'I am all right.'

Then he collapsed. While he was lying on the ground M'Leod murmured something about somersaulting, but said no more, although it was obvious he was making a strong effort to tell me something.

It is not clear how far the men fell. While the *Aberdeen Press and Journal* of Tuesday, 8th May and the report of the accident in the S.M.C.J. give 60 metres, other sources say 20 metres. In fact no one, not even Lawrie himself, can have known the distance with any degree of precision. Equally uncertain is the time when the accident happened and how long it was before Lawrie left his friend to try to obtain assistance. *The Courier and Advertiser* of Tuesday, 8th May quoted Lawrie as saying that the accident occurred at about 10.00 a.m. and that it was a further four hours before the mist lifted briefly to allow him to see his surroundings and then work his way down towards the Lairig Ghru. The account in the *Aberdeen Press and Journal* of the same day implied that he waited only half an hour with MacLeod but it gives no indication of the time of the accident. Neither the S.M.C.J. nor the Cairngorm Club Journal gave the time of the accident, but the former offered 'about one hour' as the length of time Lawrie remained with his friend while the latter provided the non-committal 'for some time'.

Nevertheless, it is possible to provide some estimate based on the postulate that the men arrived on the summit of Ben MacDui at about 9.30 a.m. Smith spent only a little time on the top before setting off on his separate way and the inference to be made from Smith's words in the *Aberdeen Press and Journal* of Wednesday, 9th May is that a short time elapsed between his departure from the others and the onset of the blizzard. If he left at 9.45 a.m., the storm must have struck by 10.00 a.m. The men would have wanted to return to collect their packs and, as has been suggested, MacLeod and Lawrie may have thought that the storm would soon blow over and that it would make good sense to remain at the cairn. The estimate of 'more than an hour' mentioned in the Cairngorm Club Journal seems reasonable. That would take the time to about 11.00 a.m. The fall occurred high above the Pools of Dee, about 2km from the summit of Ben MacDui and, unless the two men spent some time wandering about trying to find their way back to their rucksacks beside Loch Etchachan, they met with their misadventure within an hour of leaving the top. The accident, therefore, happened probably about noon, allowing some time for delays imposed by the conditions on the gradually descending plateau.

It is inconceivable that Lawrie would have remained four hours with MacLeod, who, if he was not dead, was in need of urgent help – although this was the time given in *The Courier and Advertiser*. One hour, the time indicated by the S.M.C.J., appears reasonable, although it may have been somewhat longer. In that time he did what he thought appropriate to try to resuscitate MacLeod, using whisky and snow, dragged him into the lee of a large boulder whose defences against the storm he endeavoured to strengthen by building a small wall of stones and, according to the accounts given in *The Glasgow Herald* and *The Scottish Daily Express* of Tuesday, 8th May, wrapped MacLeod's coat and scarf about him. Thus, it was probably 1.00 p.m. or a little later when Lawrie left MacLeod. Whether he waited until the brief lifting of the cloud before departing or whether this happened shortly after he had begun his descent is unclear from the published accounts. However, the reports are generally consistent in stating that Lawrie reached Aviemore about 6.00 p.m. which would give him five hours to descend into the Lairig Ghru and make his way the 16–18km to Aviemore. It would have taken the best part of an hour to work his way down to the Lairig Ghru and, in the conditions, a further four to reach Aviemore. The *Aberdeen Press and Journal* of Wednesday, 9th May gave some additional information provided by Lawrie about his journey to Aviemore:

> After a few miles he picked up footprints, which he followed. Near Coylum Bridge he overtook a party of four – two young men and two girls from Aberdeen – and told them what had happened. The two young men suggested that they might go back and look for MacLeod, but Lawrie said that the distance was too far, and ultimately they decided that it would be better to get fresh, strong, and experienced climbers, and the quickest way to get succour was for Lawrie to go on to Aviemore. Lawrie was supplied with food at the cottage at Coylum Bridge. The Aberdeen party were staying the night at the cottage, and Lawrie obtained a bicycle to ride to Aviemore.

Lawrie, then, sped on his two wheels to Aviemore to raise the alarm at the police station with the long-suffering Police Constable Murdo MacLean who, with admirable promptitude, assembled a small search party which included the equally long-suffering Dr Archibald Craig Balfour. As P. C. MacLean was the sole policeman in Aviemore, Dr Balfour was the sole medical practitioner. The team set off, presumably about 7.00 p.m., escorted by Lawrie, a remarkable testimony to his fitness and stamina and to his devotion to his friend. He must have known, as indeed would the others, that there was little likelihood of finding MacLeod without his presence, but he must have been very tired. They must have realised that, with the lateness of the hour and the fierceness of the storm into which they would have to battle, their prospects of reaching MacLeod were small and it is, therefore, all the more creditable that they made the effort. They seem to have progressed some 8km before falling darkness and the intensity of the storm forced them to give up the unequal struggle and make a disappointed return, reaching Aviemore at midnight.

The following day, Monday, 7th May, the blizzard had blown itself out. A considerable amount of snow had fallen and lay well down the hillsides with much of it having been blown into deep drifts. Sixteen men, led by Constable MacLean and John Lawrie, left Coylumbridge at 9.30 a.m. and made good speed into the Lairig Ghru. They took with them a stretcher and were accompanied by Murdo MacInnes and his pony, Katie, a surefooted Highland garron, in the hope that she would return with MacLeod on board. In clear weather the sun blazed down on the pass which trapped the heat and caused the men to discard their coats which they left at a cairn after about 8km.

Murdo MacInnes and Katie travelled as far as the summit of the pass near the Pools of Dee and waited there while the rest of the party continued onwards to the point from which they would have to climb the steep slopes, Lawrie indicating the spot where he thought he had left his friend. It is not clear if Lawrie ascended with them to the spot but when the rescuers reached the place they were astonished to find no trace of MacLeod and no sign that anyone had been there. A great deal of snow had fallen, with drifts five metres and more deep, and this had evidently concealed all trace of MacLeod and of the footprints of the day before. It does appear that they had been led to the correct place by the faithful Lawrie for MacLeod's body was found nearby three days later. It may seem from this that the search of the immediate vicinity of the rock was rather perfunctory. However, the whole area was covered with deep snow and the men did not have probes to test the ground. If MacLeod was not at the boulder where, apparently, he had been left, he might be anywhere buried in the snow.

Realising that MacLeod may have regained consciousness and tried to make his way to safety, the searchers spread out in fan formation to mount a thorough sweep search of the area but with little expectation of finding MacLeod in the deep snow. Nothing was found. In the hope that MacLeod had been able to take himself to Corrour bothy, the party reached it, a distance of over 17km from their starting point at Coylumbridge. He was not there nor was there any evidence that he had been. Nothing further could be done and the searchers retraced their steps through the Lairig Ghru to Aviemore. Lawrie became so tired that he was transported some of the way by Katie and, weary though he was, must have greatly regretted that it was he, and not MacLeod, who was being carried. The search party reached Aviemore at 7.30 p.m. and Constable MacLean telephoned Constable Bell

John Lawrie on hill pony, Katie, with owner
Murdo MacInnes.   *'The Courier', Dundee*

at Braemar to discover if he had any information on the whereabouts of the missing climber. There was none, although a search had been made on the ground to the north of Derry Lodge.

There was a sad homecoming for MacLeod's parents, Mr and Mrs David MacLeod, who had gone to Edinburgh for the holiday Monday. Efforts to locate them in Edinburgh having failed, they did not know of the misfortune that had befallen their son until their return to Aberdeen on Monday evening. It is a measure of the esteem in which MacLeod was held by his employer that the firm's owner, Finlay Crerar, on hearing the news of the accident, motored to Aviemore to offer any help he could give in the search for Mac-Leod. Meanwhile, Lawrie's superior in the Harbour Treasurer's Office told Lawrie to remain in Aviemore until his friend was found.

After a nine-hour battle with rain and heavy mist – during one hour of which they were practically lost – six stalwart hillmen returned to Derry Lodge yesterday afternoon with the packs which had been cached on Sunday morning by Norman MacLeod, the missing Aberdeen climber, and John Lawrie, his companion, when they set off to make their fateful ascent of Ben MacDhui.

Thus commenced the report in the *Aberdeen Press and Journal* of Wednesday, 9th May. Tuesday saw the search shift to the Braemar side of the mountain in weather that was considerably less kind than that which had accompanied the search from Aviemore on the previous day. The original plan was for the party to divide into two, one to make for the summit of Ben MacDui by way of Coire Etchachan and the other to proceed through the Lairig Ghru, in this way maximising the area of the search. The two parties would meet near the summit. However, the weather made such a plan unwise and the six men went together along the Coire Etchachan route. The searchers drove to Derry Lodge and set forth from there about 6.30 a.m.; they were all experienced men of the hills and were under the leadership of the local bobby, Constable Bell, and Iain Grant, the gamekeeper from Luibeg. Of the others, two were gamekeepers and two were ghillies. Rain was already falling as they left Derry Lodge and the mist was below the mountain tops. The cold intensified as they climbed higher and the rain soaked their clothing. By about 9.30 a.m. they had arrived at the east end of Loch Etchachan where they found the packs belonging to MacLeod and Lawrie which had lain undisturbed for two days.

Taking the rucksacks with them, they made for the summit of Ben MacDui, intending to continue from there down into the Lairig Ghru and back to Derry Lodge. They soon picked up the tracks of three men, almost certainly those of MacLeod, Lawrie and Smith on the Sunday. The path to the top of the mountain was clearly marked by cairns and these were initially visible above the snow. Surprisingly, the Sunday footprints did not follow the line of these cairns but ran some distance below it. The searchers decided to ascend by the cairns and locate the footprints at the summit but in this intention they were to be frustrated. The lead was taken by Iain Grant whose knowledge of the area was the most detailed. They followed the guiding cairns for about an hour but the snow grew deeper and deeper and eventually they lost the cairns and, with them, the line to the summit. Their difficulties were compounded by the mist which was damp and cold; it came swirling down from the mountain top and thickened to reduce visibility to no more than a few metres. When they realised that they had lost the path, they halted to check their bearings and discovered that they had veered to the south, so they changed course in the hope of relocating the cairns. They continued in this direction rather uncertainly and before long came upon a huge belt of snow into parts of which they sank up to their waists. They were concerned that they might drop over a precipice so decided that the safest course of action was to return by the way they had come. By this time it was 11.00 a.m. and they estimated, probably correctly, that they were not far from the summit, but they were far from sure of their precise position.

Retracing their footsteps, they made a return to Loch Etchachan where they mounted a second attempt on the summit by following the Sunday footprints of the young trio. In places these footprints, blown clear of the fresh snow, were quite conspicuous, but in other places they became faint and sometimes disappeared. Ultimately, after about 2km they disappeared altogether. It was about half past twelve and they felt that nothing could be

Iain Grant leading the Braemar search party.   *'The Courier', Dundee*

gained by further effort so they began their retreat from the heights and
regained Derry Lodge at four in the afternoon. So cold had they found it
that they had made only the shortest of stops for lunch and even so their
fingers had become numb. They had formed the opinion, one shared by the
searchers on the Aviemore side, that Lawrie, whose experience of the
Cairngorms was restricted and who had had only a brief sighting of the tarns
which he took for the Pools of Dee, had been mistaken and that he had, in
reality, seen not the Pools but Lochan Uaine lying south-east of the summit
of Ben MacDui. If the weather was set fair the next day, the Braemar team
would resume the search by examining this area, taking the Luibeg Burn to
give them access to the ridge, known as the Sron Riach, overlooking the
lochan. It is difficult to understand how this theory gained credence since, if
Lawrie had made his descent towards this tarn, he would most probably have
emerged on the Braemar side and not at Aviemore.

The next day, Wednesday, 9th May, the weather was much improved and
another search was mounted from the direction of Braemar. There are
conflicting points of detail in the newspaper reports of Thursday, 10th May
concerning this effort. There is some doubt as to the number who
participated: *The Courier and Advertiser* said that there were 'over a dozen',
while the *Aberdeen Press and Journal* stated that it was formed by the same six

experienced men of the hills who had been out the previous day, with the
addition of two representatives of the *Aberdeen Press and Journal* who made a
full report of the day's doings. There is similar doubt as to who went where.
The Glasgow Herald had it that the group which went through the Lairig
Ghru was led by Iain Grant and the one which went up Sron Riach was
under the command of Constable Bell. The *Aberdeen Press and Journal*
asserted that both Iain Grant and Constable Bell went with the Sron Riach
party. Since the latter newspaper had a presence among the searchers, it is
presumed that this journal is likely to be the more accurate.

On this occasion, the better weather permitted the party to be split into
two groups. The smaller one of three men was to travel by way of the
Corrour Bothy into the Lairig Ghru searching all the while for any signs of
the missing man. At some suitable point, unspecified in the press reports
but it would appear by the south-west shoulder of the mountain, they were
then to ascend towards the summit, hoping to meet the other party high on
the western slopes of the hill, perhaps somewhere close to a place where it
was thought that the accident to MacLeod and Lawrie could have happened.
The other group, five in number, including the two members of the press,
was to follow the path along the Luibeg Burn and then up the well-defined
ridge known as Sron Riach running north-westwards on to ground leading
towards the summit of Ben MacDui. This route would take the men along
high ground overlooking Lochan Uaine. If it was, indeed, this lochan that
Lawrie had seen in the brief clearance in the cloud on the Sunday, MacLeod
or evidence of his presence might be found somewhere in the area of this
line of ascent.

Both P.C. Bell and P.C. MacLean, who had the responsibility of raising
their respective search parties, seem to have preferred to rely on a small
number of experienced men. There can be little doubt that the presence of a
large number of searchers on the hill, especially if many of these are of little
experience and ill-equipped, presents difficulties and risks. However, it does
seem that the groups that searched from the Braemar side on the
Wednesday were too small for the purpose of locating the lost man and the
larger party which searched from Aviemore the next day was more likely to
meet with some success. It is to be wondered why a greater number did not
set out from the Deeside direction: even the dozen given in *The Courier and
Advertiser* was scarcely sufficient for a proper search of two different areas.

The party left Derry Lodge at 7.30 a.m. and travelled together for the first
3km at which point their routes bifurcated where the Luibeg Burn comes in
from the north. Iain Grant and his team struck northwards along the

Derry Lodge as it was in the early 1930s.   *Courtesy of John Duff*

burnside path and their adventures were recorded by the two gentlemen of the press who, to judge by their report in the following day's *Aberdeen Press and Journal*, were hill-walking tyros with a somewhat strange turn of phrase:

We started to go up the glen by a fairly respectable path, and were able to admire the game which rose with their harsh cries practically from our feet. Grouse and ptarmigan rose noisily as we walked up and up until we reached the slopes of Sron Riach. No path was there to guide us, but we followed Constable Bell in single file. The going was fairly good, and there were but little patches of snow here and there. When we came to the slopes of Ben Macdhui itself the lead was taken by that prince of mountaineers, Ian Grant. . . . Before coming on the slopes we had a difficult job crossing the Dee by stepping stones. The river was swollen by melting snow. The task of getting across was finally accomplished, but not without some slight leakages in our impromptu climbing shoes. As we breasted the slopes of the mountains [sic] the going became steadily worse. The road was one mass of boulders of assorted sizes and designs. . . . By and by the atmosphere, which had been quite warm, grew colder, and suspicious wisps of mist floated round the summit of the mighty ben. Then we reached a point about 3000 feet up, and overlooked Lochan Uaine. Here it was bitterly cold. All haste was made in donning scarves, coats, and thick gloves. A brief halt was called, and the leaders of the party held a short consultation. On account of the softness of the snow, which was breaking away, it would have meant risking lives to tackle the summit from that point. . . .

The hazardous nature of the slope prompted the decision to veer westwards to traverse the mountain south of the summit with the intention of reaching its west shoulder in the hope that they would find there a safe route to the top. This move took them across large areas of soft snow, 3 metres deep in places, into which they sometimes sank up to their waists; they had to wade through snow where even the crooks of the gamekeepers could not touch the bottom. They had found no sign of MacLeod in the area of Lochan Uaine and they met with no more success here. In the course of time, however, they reached the upper section of Coire Clach nan Taillear or Corrie of the Tailors' Stone, named after the curiously ribbed stone in the Lairig Ghru near the bottom of the corrie where, according to legend, three tailors died. [One New Year's Eve long before, three tailors had vowed to dance a reel in Rothiemurchus and another in Braemar before the night was out. They danced in Speyside but travelled no further than the stone where they died of the cold, the stone becoming their memorial.] Near the top of this corrie the Braemar party came upon some footprints. The story is continued in the words of the two reporters of the *Aberdeen Press and Journal*:

> In the snow of the Taillear Burn Corrie we discovered footprints, and we made a difficult journey downhill to investigate. The time was now half past eleven. There we got a glimpse of the other searchers far below, and when we found that the tracks continued down the burn we went down to meet them. After discussing progress and discovering that the others had drawn a blank, we told them about the footprints, and were informed that they came from the Corrour Bothy.

That the footsteps found 'came from' the Corrour bothy makes it clear that they ascended the hill and therefore could not have been made by MacLeod and Lawrie – nor by Smith for that matter. In any case, Smith had been blown well to the north of the route he had intended so they could hardly have been his. The report of the day's activities in *The Courier and Advertiser* of Thursday, 10th May confirms that these footprints were made by someone climbing but it contained a clear indication of where it was thought the body might be found. John MacHardy, a ghillie from Braemar, was a member of the search party of that day and the previous day. The account read:

> Mr M'Hardy, a veteran hillman, said that he and his companions were at the place where the missing youth was supposed to have been left. A thousand feet below they found tracks which had been made by climbers going up. Tailors' Corrie, near where the tracks were found, has a precipitous drop of about 50 yards, and it is possible that M'Leod might be buried there in the snow.

This placed the missing man in the area of Coire Clach nan Taillear or Tailors' Corrie well to the south of the Pools of Dee and, as was pointed out in the item in *The Glasgow Herald* of the same day, from that area the Pools of Dee cannot be seen. *The Glasgow Herald* gave some prominence to the discovery of the footprints and provided the following information which referred to the ascent to the top of Ben MacDui by Iain Grant, Ronald Scott and John McHardy with ice-axes and ropes from the point where the two parties met on the western slopes, estimated at a distance of 800 metres from the summit:

Shortly after starting off the party discovered the footprints in the snow of a single person coming down the mountainside beside Taylor's [sic] Burn to the Larig Gru. They followed these to the top of the burn, about 3,000 feet up the mountainside. [This is a serious underestimate of the height of the source of the stream. It starts at the 1220m level. None of the newspapers gave reliable heights above sea level, probably because the searchers themselves were none too precise. The newspapers were also generally unreliable in their estimates of the distances walked by the searchers, tending to indulge in exaggeration.]

There they discovered two sets of footprints in the deep snow and they followed them for about 50 yards only to lose them on a bare patch of rock. The footprints were leading down the mountainside. Thinking that these might be the footprints of MacLeod and Lawrie and that the accident might have happened where the double set of footprints ended, the party made a thorough search of the vicinity, but found no trace of MacLeod.

Affleck Gray (left), Iain Grant and his father, Sandy.   *A.C. Gray colln.*

Iain Grant's trio reached the summit where they carried out a fairly extensive search until the mist returned to the mountain top forcing them to abandon their work and return to the Grants' house at Luibeg. On the summit, they found the remains of a bread roll and a small whisky bottle, evidently recently left, but nothing else, not even any footprints. The remainder of the group descended into the Lairig Ghru where they searched northwards as far as the Pools of Dee, using telescopes to scan the more distant slopes. They found nothing, nor had a pair of walkers from Aberdeen whom they met at the Pools of Dee. They returned to the Grants' house at 6.00 p.m., one hour after Iain Grant's group and ten and a half hours since setting out.

It has to be asked if the footprints found and followed by Grant, Scott and MacHardy were those of MacLeod and Lawrie. If the description of two sets of footprints descending apparently from the summit and becoming one set after some distance is accurate, there must be a good prima facie case for thinking that these tracks had been made by the men as they headed downwards and that the accident had happened where the two sets terminated. However, this point was over 2km south-south-east of the high ground above the Pools of Dee which were not within sight, and to reach it MacLeod and Lawrie would have had to fight their way into the violent south-easterly wind. The press reports were quite consistent in stating that the body of the unfortunate MacLeod was found above the Pools of Dee and this itself might well resolve the matter: the footprints in the area of Coire Clach nan Taillear [Tailors' Corrie] could not have belonged to MacLeod and Lawrie.

However, there is a complicating factor: although the newspapers were agreed that MacLeod's body was discovered above the Pools of Dee, the descriptions of the area given on Friday, 11th May, while rather different from one another, were somewhat more consistent with the area of Coire Clach nan Taillear than the high ground above the Pools of Dee, and this includes *The Courier and Advertiser* whose reporter, Littlejohn, accompanied the search party which found MacLeod. *The Glasgow Herald* put the body on 'the south-west ridge of Ben MacDhui', the *Aberdeen Press and Journal* placed it on the 'west shoulder', while *The Courier and Advertiser* opted for the 'south shoulder'. These slight variations could well lead to the conclusion that the body was found on the fairly wide ridge or shoulder which descends from the summit of the mountain initially in a south-westerly direction and then veers south-south-westerly and forms the northern flank of Coire Clach nan Taillear. If the body was discovered there, the footprints found in that area on the Wednesday may well have been those of MacLeod and Lawrie. The difficulty might be insoluble if it were not for evidence from Jim Hyslop who was a member of the search party which located the body on Thursday, 10th May.

On Tuesday, 8th May, Hyslop had returned with friends from Skye to his family home in Forres by way of Fort William where he had learnt of MacLeod's misadventure. Together with Jim MacKenzie, the brother of Alistair MacKenzie who died with Duncan Ferrier in Coire Cas in January of the previous year, he had offered his assistance to P.C. MacLean as they passed through Aviemore in the early evening on their way home. The following morning they returned to Aviemore in the company of Jim MacKenzie's brother, David. Hyslop recorded the day in his diary:

> Wed. 9th May. Up 7.30. Left Forres with Jim and Dave in Cowley at 9.45. Arrived Aviemore, saw McLean and decided to go to Shelterstone. Had lunch and left car at Ryvoan bothy. Left 1.30 p.m. Reached Shelterstone by Garvault (Garbh Allt] and Saddle 5 p.m. Had tea and hunted round about but no sign of MacLeod. Left Shelterstone 6 p.m. but took ½ hour to ford river and get to head of Loch Avon. Back to car by 8.50. . . .

In the Shelter Stone Visitors' Book, they made the brief entry: 'Arrived here 5 p.m. by the Saddle returning same. All the tops misty.' They would have seen the previous entry made by five men from Aberdeen on the Sunday when MacLeod died. It read: 'Arrived here 12 noon from Derry in a terrific blizzard of snow. Climbing impossible. Returning to Derry now 1.45. Storm worse.' The five must have arrived at the Shelter Stone at about the time that MacLeod and Lawrie met with their accident little more than 2km away. A return to Hyslop's evidence will be made after describing events on Thursday, 10th May.

At 8.30 a.m. on Thursday morning a party, numbered variously at between twenty-one and twenty-eight, left Aviemore on a journey which was to find the body of Norman MacLeod; some drove to Coylumbridge and others to Whitewell where the vehicles were parked. Those selected by Constable MacLean from the large number of volunteers from a wide area were men of mountain experience and included Lawrie himself, Jim and Dave MacKenzie, Jim Hyslop and another Ian Grant, this one the son of Lieutenant-Colonel J. P. Grant of Rothiemurchus. The day started with low cloud and mist covering the mountains but as the morning progressed this was dispersed by an east wind to leave the tops clear. The party was again accompanied by Murdo MacInnes and his highland pony, Katie, whose journey on this occasion was not to be in vain.

The search began below Creag an Leth-choin, known in English as Lurcher's Crag after the dog which, according to legend, leapt over the cliff in the heat of a deer hunt. This is about 2km north of the Pools of Dee and the searchers were to advance southwards in an extended line up the steep eastern slopes of the Lairig Ghru. They started so far north of the Pools as it was considered there was a possibility that the unfortunate MacLeod would be lying there. The *Aberdeen Press and Journal* of Friday, 11th May, gave a fairly full account of the efforts of the day:

The most experienced hillmen took the top reaches, while the others spread out in lines along the lower slopes of Ben MacDhui. It was hazardous work, for although a great deal of the snow had melted, there were still deep drifts in the corries, and some of the hill streams were covered with a treacherous coating. Every step had to be tested. The most imminent danger was from boulders which, dislodged by the searchers above, came hurtling down the slopes with great velocity.... When two hours' search above the summit of the Larig Ghru had proved in vain, the leaders decided to pass on, above the Pools of Dee, to the ground which had been covered in Monday's search. James Mackenzie (Grantown), Duncan Macleod, Duncan Macdonald, and William Ironside were the foremost. They struck along the west shoulder of the Ben about 4000 feet up the mountain. The leading four had halted on a ridge near the top of a shoulder for a rest, when William Ironside, ghillie, in surveying the ground above through a telescope, saw a fluttering object on the top of a boulder. Closer examination revealed it to be the kilt worn by MacLeod, fluttering in the breeze.

The four made for the spot immediately and discovered the body of MacLeod lying across a boulder, with his face to the east and his legs doubled under him. By whistling and the waving of handkerchiefs they indicated to the party below that the search was ended. After a difficult climb the other members of the search party assembled beside the body. The spot where the body was discovered was passed on Monday, when it was covered with snow. From a close scrutiny of the position of the body, it appeared that it had been blown down from the ledge a few yards away, where Lawrie had left his companion. Lawrie had put him under a rock and built up stones on the south side to keep off the wind and snow. The fierce tempest of Sunday had blown down the stones. It is impossible that MacLeod revived and crawled down a few yards. A cairn of stones was built to mark the spot before the Herculean task was tackled of conveying the body to the valley below.

The spot at which the body was found, 4000 feet up, is one of the steepest slopes on Ben MacDhui. A stretcher was improvised by Murdo Mackenzie from crooks and staves, ropes and raincoats, and was steadied on the downward path by drag ropes. Nine men were required. Four, roped together, carried the body, and five held on to the slack of the rope to prevent the party slipping on the loose boulders and lichen. The arduous journey to the Pools of Dee occupied an hour. The party arrived there at 4.30. Before carrying their burden farther along the path, the party built another cairn underneath the spot where the body was found, to indicate the line to the other cairn, higher up. After traversing two miles of snow and rock the party, with their pathetic burden, reached the path where Katie, the Highland garron, was waiting.

With regard to the location of MacLeod's body, Jim Hyslop is quite certain that it was found high above the Pools of Dee and nowhere near Coire Clach nan Taillear. He has the following comment to make on the matter:

> We had lunch two miles short of the Pools of Dee at 12.30. We then spread out on the very steep hillside, covered in snow, and we made very slow going. We had to pick our way carefully, looking around all the time for any signs of MacLeod and watching out for loose and falling boulders and stones. We could not have made any further than the Pools by 2.45 when the body was found.

Although it is not far short of sixty years since the misadventure, Hyslop's memory is good and his recollection of the place where the body lay can be accepted as accurate. It follows that the footprints found by the Braemar searchers the previous Wednesday in the area of Coire Clach nan Taillear were not those of MacLeod and Lawrie, nor for that matter those of their friend, Charles Smith. The Friday search, then, was above the Pools of Dee when, high on the mountain, MacLeod's Gordon tartan kilt was spotted fluttering in the wind. Lawrie was one of the first of the other searchers to arrive at the spot and when he saw the body of his friend, quite understandably, he broke down.

There was debate at the time about how MacLeod had moved the short distance from where he had been left and the prevalent opinion was that he had been lifted by the storm force wind some time after his friend had departed on his quest for help. There can be little doubt that a wind of that power, if it had blown in behind MacLeod, could have rolled him from his position on the sheltered side of the boulder and this would have been made the easier if MacLeod himself had moved slightly within his protected place. Once subjected to the full force of the wind, MacLeod could have been blown some distance. However, MacLeod was a large, well-built man and he had been carefully placed in the lee of the boulder with some additional protection from the wind provided by a small wall of stones constructed by Lawrie. Although the account in the *Aberdeen Press and Journal* quoted above stated that this wall had been blown down, elsewhere it was reported that it was still in place. Moreover, MacLeod was found lying on a boulder, not against it. It is almost inconceivable that the wind, strong though it was, could have lifted MacLeod bodily and deposited him there; it could have put him on the boulder only if the top of the boulder was at the level of hard snow which had subsequently melted. Certainly much of the soft snow of the Sunday blizzard had melted, but there had been little thawing of the old, hard snow and hence the wind could not have rolled him on to the boulder.

Therefore, it is more probable that MacLeod made a temporary return to consciousness or semi-consciousness and moved away from the spot where he had been left, only to collapse so soon afterwards and die where he lay. On 11th May, MacLeod's body was dissected in Aberdeen by Professor Theodore Shennan and Dr George Duncan. MacLeod had multiple injuries and bruising of the scalp in the frontal area but the brain showed no sign of injury and the cause of death was identified as being heart failure following shock and exposure.

Whatever the truth behind MacLeod's changed position, the lowering of his body down the steep and slippery slopes to the Lairig Ghru was an arduous and slow task. Once there, it had to be carried on the improvised stretcher over rough ground to the waiting hill pony, Katie, for transportation to Coylumbridge. From there the body was taken by motor vehicle to Aviemore, which was reached shortly before 8.00 p.m., almost twelve hours since the search party set out from there and over five hours since the discovery of MacLeod's body. The body was placed in the police station for later removal to Aberdeen and interment in Allenvale cemetery.

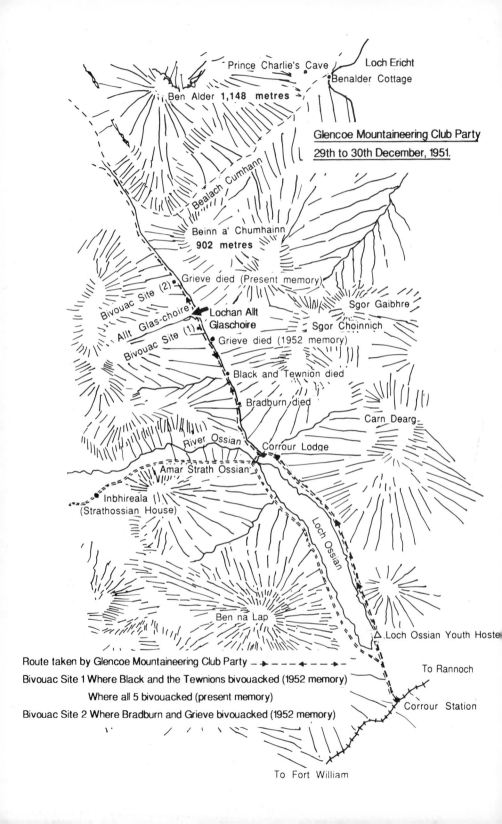

Prince Charlie's Cave

Loch Ericht

Benalder Cottage

Ben Alder 1,148 metres

Glencoe Mountaineering Club Party

29th to 30th December, 1951.

Bealach Cumhann

Beinn a' Chumhainn
902 metres

Grieve died (Present memory)

Bivouac Site (2)

Sgor Gaibhre

Allt Glas-choire

Lochan Allt
Glaschoire

Sgor Choinnich

Bivouac Site (1)

Grieve died (1952 memory)

Black and Tewnion died

Bradburn died

Carn Dearg

River Ossian

Corrour Lodge

Amar Strath Ossian

Inbhireala
(Strathossian House)

Loch Ossian

Ben na Lap

△ Loch Ossian Youth Hostel

Route taken by Glencoe Mountaineering Club Party

To Rannoch

Bivouac Site 1 Where Black and the Tewnions bivouacked (1952 memory)

Where all 5 bivouacked (present memory)

Corrour Station

Bivouac Site 2 Where Bradburn and Grieve bivouacked (1952 memory)

To Fort William

Death and Survival at Corrour. December, 1951

'Hurricane Hits Scotland' was the main headline in *The Press and Journal* of Monday, 31st December, 1951. Its effect was reinforced by other headlines: 'Many Roads Blocked by Fallen Trees', 'Scots Houses Wrecked by Crashing Chimneys' and 'Mountainous Seas Break Over Promenades'. The report on the storm then began:

> Hurricanes – winds reaching 65 knots, or more than 73 miles an hour – lashed parts of Scotland yesterday. At Turnhouse (Edinburgh) airport gusts of 101 miles an hour were recorded, the greatest gale force of the day in Britain. Last night there were gale warnings in operation all around the North . . . Towns were without light and power as electricity supplies failed. Telephone lines were torn down, isolating many communities. Trees collapsed across roads, dislocating traffic. Streets were littered with debris as chimneys, hoardings, walls and masonry crashed.

In fact, during the course of Sunday, 30th December, the whole of the United Kingdom suffered from the violence of the storm, although it was of longest duration in the north. In Dysart, Fife, one boy was killed and another gravely injured when fifty tonnes of masonry fell from a neighbouring factory on to a hut. The wind brought exceptionally high tides and in places the sea rose almost to pier level to create the impression that boats tied up alongside were sitting on the pier.

The newspapers of that last day of 1951 also carried the news that three climbers had died and one was missing near Ben Alder in southern Inverness-shire. The newspaper closest to the scene of this misadventure was the weekly journal *The Oban Times*, and it said about the storm:

> The West Coast of Argyll received the brunt of the gale and Oban suffered considerable damage through the wind and the flooding. Through the night the gale mounted in intensity and by 7 o'clock when the tide was at its highest in Oban, the wind had reached an estimated velocity of over 80 miles an hour. . . . Large pieces of concrete had been torn from the sea-wall and thrown several yards across the roadway. The whole Esplanade was covered with tons upon tons of seaweed in which could be seen the wreckage of small boats, wooden gangways, branches of trees and a

vast and varied collection of other wreckage. . . . Large pieces of the bituminous surface of the pavement in George Street were torn off by the force of the wind. The wind did not slacken after high tide, and between ten and eleven o'clock it was blowing at its full fury. . . . The wind was accompanied by torrential showers . . .

The situation was no easier in Fort William, 53km north of Oban. *The Press and Journal* of Monday, 31st December, 1951 reported that telephone communications were severed between Fort William and most of the surrounding districts, that at Kinlocheil the high tide washed away part of the railway bridge and that, with the collapse of electricity cables, power was cut off at Annat, at Inverlochy and in parts of Fort William. Loch Linnhe rose to the level of the railway platform in Fort William and the ground floor of a hotel in the town was flooded to a depth of over thirty centimetres.

The New Year meet of the S.M.C. took place at Ballachulish and, concerning Sunday, 30th December, the report of the meet in the S.M.C.J. (April 1952, Volume XXV) had the following to say:

Sunday, 30th, will long be remembered as one of the wildest days ever experienced. Winds of over 100 miles per hour, recorded at low levels, give an indication of conditions on the hills. No party succeeded in climbing a Munro, but John Wilson and Arnot Russell got very near the summit of Ben Sgulaird before valour gave way to discretion. On low ground several members were picked up and blown some distance by the wind! . . . The President's party made the bulk of the congregation at Ballachulish Church.

The 1991 yearbook of the Lochaber Mountain Rescue Team contained an article by Jimmy Ness in which he referred to the Corrour tragedy. On the Sunday of the tragedy, he was with friends on the Cobbler, near Arrochar, and his description of their attempt to reach the top well illustrates the violence of the wind at the higher levels. He wrote:

By the time we reached the steepish gully leading to the summit ridge we were down to four [in the party]. Looking upwards we could see great blocks of snow and ice hurtling from the skyline to the accompaniment of a deep thundering roar as the storm in baffled fury beat against the other side of the ridge. The whole mountain seemed to vibrate and imagination was already telling me what it might be like on that exposed edge immediately above.

During the morning and earlier part of the afternoon of that wildest of days, only 71km from Oban, 34km from Fort William, 35km from Ballachulish and 68km from Arrochar, four men and one woman struggled for survival. They were John Black, aged 24, an electrical engineer, John Bradburn, aged 24, a shipyard engineering draughtsman, James Grieve, aged 27, an engineering student in his fifth year of studies at the University of Glasgow, Sydney Tewnion, aged 29, training at Jordanhill College of Education for the teaching profession, and Anne Tewnion, aged 22, Sydney's wife of only four months, who worked as a technician with the Glasgow Blood Transfusion Service. All lived in Glasgow and were members of the Glasgow-based Glencoe Mountaineering Club, of which Sydney Tewnion was the president and John Black the secretary, and in which the other three members of the ill-starred party also held office. Black was also a member of the Junior Mountaineering Club of Scotland (J.M.C.S.). Although young, all except Grieve, who was a relative newcomer to the Club, had considerable mountaineering experience and some of them had visited the Alps. Indeed, Black and Bradburn had spent a fortnight there during the previous summer. The party also had a number of first ascents to its credit.

The five left Glasgow on Saturday, 29th December on the 3.46 p.m. train for Fort William. In those days there were only two trains a day from Glasgow to Fort William, the first leaving Queen Street station at 5.46 a.m.; if they were to travel as a party, however, it was out of the question for them to take this train as some of them had to work until lunch-time on Saturdays. They were to travel to Corrour station, a remote halt about 44km by rail from Fort William, and then journey on foot the 18km to the bothy known as Benalder Cottage, situated towards the southern end of Loch Ericht. They were to meet friends and fellow club members who had made their way to the bothy, catching the early morning train from Glasgow and alighting at Rannoch station, the stop before Corrour, some 12km south-east of it. From Rannoch they walked north-eastwards across relatively flat but rather wet ground to Benalder Cottage. This route was about 3km shorter than by Corrour but the Corrour route was easier to follow in the dark. Sadly, John Bradburn would have been with this contingent had he not been in the station lavatory when the morning train departed.

Also on the afternoon train was a joint group of S.M.C. and J.M.C.S. members, four from Glasgow and three from Edinburgh, whose plans were similar to those of the Glencoe Club party: they too would disembark at Corrour and make for Benalder Cottage where they would bring in the New Year. Among their baggage were skis which could not easily be accommodated in the compartment so they left these and the rest of their gear in the guard's van. By the time they arrived at Corrour it lay under a pile of other luggage.

Corrour station, at 410m the highest point on the old West Highland Railway, was little more than a request stop and a passing place for trains on the single-track railway line, with a signal box and the signalman's house, set down in a bleak and often hostile environment just to the north of the Rannoch Moor. It had owed its lonely existence to the presence of neighbouring shooting lodges to which access from the world beyond was provided by the permanent way and by rough metalled tracks from the station. By 1951, one of these lodges, Creaguaineach at the southern end of Loch Treig, had long ceased to be the occasional sporting residence of the wealthy and was a farmhouse. The other, Corrour, stood at the north-east end of Loch Ossian just over 7km from the station. Corrour Lodge, which had been completed at the turn of the century, was burned down in 1942, leaving only the bare walls standing. There remained some cottages, including the one occupied by the head keeper, Andrew Tait and his wife, and some other buildings. The modern lodge was not erected until the late 1950s so that, at the time of the accident, Corrour Lodge itself was in a ruinous state. The station at Corrour also gave access to Strathossian House, formerly known as Inbhireala, 4km to the north of Corrour Lodge. This was the home of the head keeper on the Strathossian Estate.

The five members of the Glencoe Mountaineering Club had travelled with their baggage in their compartment and this allowed them to alight at the station without difficulty at about 7.15 p.m. The S.M.C./J.M.C.S. party was less fortunate. Not only did they have to struggle to assemble their equipment from the pile of luggage in the guard's van, but, to make matters worse, the platform at Corrour was short and the train had come to a halt without the guard's van reaching the platform so that the men had to lower their rucksacks and skis on to the ground beside the track. Before they had completely unloaded, the train resumed its journey and had travelled just over 2km before the application of the communication cord brought it to a halt to allow those still on board and the remaining gear to be deposited in the snow beside the railway line. By the time they returned to the station almost three quarters of an hour had been lost and their only sensible course of action was to walk to the Loch Ossian Youth Hostel, 2km along the road which led to Corrour Lodge where they were joined by Donald Mill, another member of the J.M.C.S., who had spent the previous night at Benalder Cottage. There, in the comfort of the little wooden building beside the pier at the south-west end of the loch, they spent the night in the company of others also there for the New Year period. It was fortunate for them that the youth hostel had made a special opening for the festive season; else they would have had little choice other than to walk the remaining 5km to Corrour Lodge to find shelter there for the night. Since the owner of the

Loch Ossian Youth Hostel. *S.Y.H.A.*

estate, Sir John Stirling Maxwell, was honorary president of the S.M.C., there was certainly a chance that they might be provided with some kind of roof over their heads.

The Glencoe Club five had long since been driven along the lochside in a lorry from Corrour Lodge which had met the train to collect the Lodge mail. The driver had offered them a lift and had waited some time for the others but eventually set off with the lighter load. The group must have been pleased to receive the lift from the station to the Lodge: it had always been their intention to make their way to Benalder Cottage that night and the lift would reduce their long walk to the bothy from 18km to 11km. Also, their rucksacks were heavy: in addition to their usual winter mountaineering gear which included ice-axes, they carried food for four days, primus stoves and fuel and even a pressure cooker for providing culinary delights during their stay at Benalder Cottage. They had their sleeping-bags and also capes which could be used as groundsheets and covers in the event of a bivouac. Although young and fit, they were probably overburdened, especially if they were going to have to make their way through snow which might be soft and, along parts of the route, possibly quite deep.

They were deposited near the Lodge and walked over to nearby woods, not far from the white bridge which crossed the lower reaches of the Uisge Labhair, where they had a meal of soup and beans. According to the accident report in the S.M.C.J. (April 1952, Volume XXV), this seemed to be the last meal of any substance that they had before they were overwhelmed by tragedy. However, this may have been erroneous: as Mrs Tewnion remembers today, the four men, but not Mrs Tewnion herself, had a cooked meal the following morning before leaving the place where they were obliged to bivouac.

At this point, reference has to be made to the S.M.C.J. report. This report was written with the assistance of Dick Brown and Stan Stewart, two of the members of the S.M.C./J.M.C.S. party who took part in the recovery of the bodies. They were, therefore, well placed to provide details of the accident. They had direct personal experience of the weather over the weekend of the accident and subsequent recovery operations and they and other members of their party were present when the bodies and most of the abandoned gear were found and brought back to Corrour Lodge. In addition, they were able to obtain information from Anne Tewnion about what happened in the glen of the Uisge Labhair after her party set forth from Corrour Lodge on the Saturday evening. None of the S.M.C./J.M.C.S. group spoke with her while she was recovering from her ordeal in the home of Andrew Tait and his wife but some of them, including Dick Brown and Stan Stewart, had a fortuitous meeting with her in the train returning from Fort William to Glasgow on Wednesday, 2nd January when she spoke about the events in the glen. A few days later, Brown wrote to her asking a number of questions designed to clarify and expand upon what she had said in the train and she replied in considerable detail. This exchange of letters follows. The first, from Dick Brown, was dated 10th January, 1952; Mrs Tewnion's reply was dated 14th January.

My dear Anne,
I am writing a report along with Stan Stewart of the Glasgow J.M.C.S on the New Year at Corrour. This report will be published in the S.M.C. Journal and will be forwarded to the editor as soon as I hear from you. This report, Anne, must be exact and you are the only one who can supply the information. I thought of asking you when we were talking in the corridor coming down from Corrour but decided to leave it till later. Could you tell me approximately:
  (1) At what time you all reached your bivouac and had you another meal?
  (2) When did John Bradburn and James Grieve leave you at the bivouac and go on towards the bealach? [Bealach Cumhann]
  (3) After you packed up your bivouac and went up the track in the snow, at what

time did you meet John Bradburn and James Grieve coming back?

(4) You all returned – Do you remember when you reached the bivouac spot again?

(5) Was James Grieve in bad shape?

(6) Did you all have a meal before you all dumped your packs?

(7) At what time did you all leave the bivouac for the return journey? . . .

In her reply, Anne Tewnion said:

. . . Now to answer your queries. We had a drum up just before the big white bridge over the Uisge Labhair which was not long after leaving the lodge. We bivouacked about 10–10.30 p.m. John Bradburn and Jimmy Grieve continued for about another half hour before they bivouacked. On the Sunday morning, John and Jimmy started about 6 a.m. and went towards the bealach. John Black, Sid and I wakened about 8 a.m. and decided it would be easier to go on with the wind behind us than to turn back into the wind, and also, we thought the others would be worried if we didn't arrive at the cottage.

About three quarters of an hour later, we met John and Jimmy coming back. The path was impassable so we turned back with them. We were near the lochan [Lochan Allt Glaschoire] when Jimmy left his pack. He was not too bad then, just a bit slower than the rest of us. It was about here too that John Bradburn flung away his torch, complaining that it was too heavy. The rest of us dumped our packs at the bivouac site where we had left our sleeping bags as it was too cold to strap them on to our packs. The snow had fallen on the packs and frozen the straps which made it impossible to open our packs when we awoke. Also it was too cold all day to stop to eat so we just had chocolate. I would say that we averaged about 3oz chocolate and a few butterscotch each that morning. I would say that we returned to the bivouac site about ten o'clock. We took about the same time going back to there with Jimmy and John as the three of us took to the place where we met them as I was slow to start with due to sickness which fortunately cleared away. It was about here that we started to help Jimmy. We didn't put off any time at the bivvy – the wind was so strong that we would be blown backwards had we tried to stand still in one place. The hailstones were very bad then. Sid and I helped Jimmy while the two Johns walked ahead and after about 30-40 minutes we changed over. I think it was just after noon that John Black and Sydney died and I expect John Bradburn would be about the same time. I left the boys about one thirty and it took me an hour and three quarters to get to the lodge.

Mrs Tewnion had long since forgotten about this correspondence and when she saw it again she responded as follows:

My recollections of the tragedy now are after 40 years of putting the details to the back of my mind. I do not remember getting the letter from Dick Brown or replying, but obviously I did. It is fortunate that he kept the letter. I can see no reason to doubt the contents as the details were then very fresh in my mind nor do I think there was any reason for me to be evasive in my reply. Certainly I would have answered his queries to the best of my ability, but – there is this small point – I was in shock at the time and remained so for some weeks after. The unequivocal authority with which I spoke at that time should perhaps be regarded with a little caution.

In the same way that Mrs Tewnion cannot recall the exchange of letters of early 1952, she has no recollection of having ever seen the account of the tragedy as it was published in the S.M.C.J. She thinks she may not have been shown it then, 'probably out of consideration of my loss at the time'.

To return to the story, by 8.30 p.m. on the Saturday evening, the five friends were ready to set off for Benalder Cottage. When Anne Tewnion and her father, Alex Williamson, spoke to the press from their hotel in Fort William the following Tuesday, they said that the weather was good, with little if any wind, at the time when the party departed from Corrour Lodge. This is still Mrs Tewnion's recollection. Of the weather and the conditions underfoot, she says:

It was a fine night when we set off, cold and starlit. There was some snow on the ground with clumps of heather showing through, presenting difficult walking in the dark.

Donald Mill referred to this in his diary; earlier that day he had found the going 'very hummocky' by the Uisge Labhair. Members of the S.M.C. party have their recollections of the conditions when they arrived at Corrour and made their way along to the youth hostel. Charles Donaldson recalls, 'a fine, still night, clear and frosty. No moon. Snow lying, but not thick, on the road.' Professor Malcolm Slesser also remembers the night as being 'fine' and continues: 'Overnight it turned to heavy snow, then sleet.' However, Charles Donaldson does not concur with Slesser's recollection of heavy overnight snow and in this he is in agreement with Mrs Tewnion. With regard to the weather and the snow that evening, James Russell has the following comments to make:

It was a calm evening. I cannot remember if it was snowing but the amount of snow lying was very little and skis had to be carried. This I do remember as I had skis.

It is interesting to compare these memories with an analysis of the meteorological data undertaken by Marjory Roy. As the weather was to be of paramount importance in the fate awaiting the unfortunate party and as her observations do so much to describe and explain the weather of the evening and night of the 29th December and that of the next day, it is of value to present her findings here. There can be little doubt that the five friends were misled by the signs, possibly as late as the following morning when they prepared to leave their bivouac site. Marjory Roy says:

The weather charts show that a ridge of high pressure crossed Scotland during 29 December giving a mainly fine day with light to moderate winds from a westerly direction. The freezing level was around 650m, so any showers that day would have fallen as snow over ground above, say, 400m. . . . Since Loch Ossian and Corrour lie at around 400m, any showers there would have been of sleet or more likely snow.

During the evening winds backed towards the south as a depression approached the north-west of the British Isles. Away from the coast temperatures would have fallen during the late afternoon and evening when winds were still light and any cloud was thin and high, and it is under those conditions that the party would have set off. It is also very likely that it was dry with temperatures around or below freezing point when they bivouacked at around 10.30 p.m. According to the account by Anne Tewnion, written soon after the event, it would appear that she, her husband and John Black bivouacked . . . at a height of about 520m . . .

December 1951 was relatively mild for that time of year and although there had been a number of snowfalls on the mountains, particularly in the latter part of the month, none of them had been of any great intensity. Consequently it is likely that there had not been much accumulation of snow at the height of their bivouacs.

During the night the depression moved rapidly east-north-east and was close to Stornoway by 0600 G.M.T. on the 30th; it also deepened rapidly. An occluded front swept very rapidly across Scotland at a speed of around 80 k.p.h. Tiree airfield is 145 kilometres distant from Corrour and the nearest weather observing station to the west where observations were made every hour. The data recorded by the Meteorological Office staff there are particularly useful as an indication of the detailed sequence of events ahead of, at, and behind the weather front, if due allowance is made for the near sea-level site of this observing station. At Tiree the front went through at about 0530 G.M.T. which indicates that it would have passed the bivouacs around 0730. Thus, if the two who bivouacked further up the glen moved off at 6 a.m., they would have done so while the wind was still from the south and the glen would have been sheltered from the full force of the wind. The second party would have got up as the wind was swinging round into the south-west, increasing in strength, and becoming funnelled up the glen. One can understand why they thought it would be easier to go on with the wind at their backs.

Ahead of the front, winds increased rapidly and were from a southerly direction. At Tiree the mean speed had reached gale force eight by 0200 and continued at that strength until 0600, by which time it had veered to south-westerly. Behind the front winds increased further and the wind continued to veer to a more westerly direction. At Tiree the mean speed had reached storm force ten by 0900 . . . With the approaching fronts warmer air was brought temporarily over the British Isles, causing the freezing level to rise. . . . However, the hourly temperatures at Tiree suggest that the main rise in temperature at the surface occurred close to the front. . . . although at the Allt Glas-choire the temperature rose during the night as cloud increased from the west, it was still cold enough for any precipitation to have fallen initially as snow. With the continuing rise in temperature this would have become increasingly wet and sleety and the accounts by members of the S.M.C. make reference to the showers which followed being of sleet and hail which would be particularly wetting.

Taking into account the rise in temperature during the night and the likelihood that the precipitation in the morning was of very wet snow or sleet, I was puzzled by the suggestion that the straps of the rucksacks were so frozen that they could not be opened. However, it is possible that they became quite cold during the early part of the night, when the skies were still clear, and that when wet snow fell on them later on it froze on impact. . . .

On the question of the winds, although the southerly winds would have become strong during the night in areas exposed to them I think that it would have been sheltered down at the bivouac site(s). It is not possible to apply any rule of thumb relating wind speed to altitude at positions among the mountains as opposed to at the summits. It all depends on the topography, wind direction etc.

The depression continued to deepen as it moved north-east across the north of Scotland between 0600 G.M.T. and 1200 G.M.T., causing a further tightening of the pressure gradient and increase in wind speed. The Corrour/Ben Alder area lay in the region of tightest gradient and with winds veering to south-west and then west the wind would have been channelled up the glen of the Uisge Labhair. [This glen forms the first half of the route from Corrour Lodge to Benalder Cottage and it was there that the tragedy occurred.] At midday the mean wind speed at Benbecula in the Outer Hebrides was reported as . . . hurricane force 12 and the wind sweeping up the glen was probably of a similar strength or even stronger. . . . During the afternoon and evening, as the depression continued moving away north-east across the North Sea into Norway the wind continued to veer into the north-west and diminish in strength.

They [the party] may have been relatively warm and comfortable during the earlier part of the night and if initial precipitation was of reasonably dry snow that would not have been particularly wetting. The problems would have begun to set in as the temperature rose. They were getting up and packing up just at the time when conditions were deteriorating rapidly.

It is clear from this evidence and from the recollections of most of those who were present in the area that the weather was good at the time when the Glencoe Club party set off from Corrour Lodge and that it remained reasonable during the night – at least for those in the sheltered glen of the Uisge Labhair. These conditions belied the terrible storm so soon to come. Although the month of December had been relatively mild with little accumulated snow below 550m and Saturday, 29th December, had been a pleasant day, over the previous week the weather had been fairly unsettled and generally windy with gales at times and with some snow on the hills, a weather pattern which dominated the whole area of the eastern Atlantic.

The violent storm which was to strike Scotland and the rest of the British Isles during the night of 29th/30th December was forecast by the

Meteorological Office in radio weather bulletins during the 29th but not in the synoptic weather forecasts in the press of that day. It was the practice of *The Glasgow Herald* and *The Scotsman* to carry the daily forecasts provided by the Meteorological Office in London. For Saturday, 29th December for south-east, mid and north-east Scotland (the area which included Corrour), this forecast was:

Fresh or strong north-west to west winds, moderating slowly; long bright periods with the chance of scattered showers; temperatures near normal; midday temperatures 40°F–45°F [4.5°C–7°C].

As it happened, the winds on the Saturday were significantly lighter than those forecast. The further outlook, which gave the forecast for the whole country for the night of the 29th/30th and the daylight hours of the 30th, read:

Rain spreading rapidly eastwards across much of England and Wales tonight and tomorrow morning, followed by bright periods and also some showers, chiefly in the west; strong winds with gales at times.

Even if they had seen it, there was not a great deal here to warn those taking to the hills that weekend of the real violence to come – and the radio warnings would have come too late for many.

Despite the fairly clear sky, the night was dark for the expeditionists at Corrour. Cloud ahead of the approaching tempest was on its way from the south-west. Although there had been little snow on the road from Corrour station to the Lodge, there was some on the path that the party had to follow, which may have impeded progress. It was cold, but the party was fairly well-equipped, with sufficient for an overnight bivouac should that be necessary. Their clothing, to quote the accident report in the S.M.C.J.,

. . . was possibly inadequate, especially below the waist. No man wore more than one pair of trousers; two wore corduroys and one seemed to be wearing only a thin pair of wind-proof trousers: but a pair of wet flannels was subsequently found at the bivouac place.

This statement, which clearly was based on observation when the bodies were recovered, surprises Mrs Tewnion as it was unusual for the men to be clad as inadequately as this. She says:

It was the men's habit to wear two pairs of trousers – usually flanneletted pyjama trousers under ex-army windproofs which would have been treated with Mesowax.

Mrs Tewnion herself cannot now recall what leg coverings the men were wearing; that two of them were attired in corduroys she attributes to the fact that they were still wearing the clothes in which they had travelled from Glasgow. Nevertheless, she is surprised that they were not dressed in their windproofs. It is possible that the discarded flannels were left behind in simple oversight when the party departed from the bivouac place on their way to Benalder Cottage in the morning. Alternatively, it may be that they belonged to the man 'wearing only a thin pair of wind-proof trousers' and that he had removed them because they had become wet and then forgotten. Anne Tewnion thinks that they may have fallen unnoticed out of a rucksack; she is sure that none of the party undressed on the night of the bivouac. With regard to the outer clothing carried by the party, although by modern standards it was probably rather deficient, especially for the violent conditions of the Sunday, it was as good as was commonly worn by hill-walkers in those days.

There was no moon but the snow cover might provide some light and, in any case, they carried torches and knew the way to the bothy which lay about 11km from Corrour Lodge. It was at about the same altitude as the Lodge – approximately 380m – but an ascent of about 260m would be required to reach the col known as Bealach Cumhann, the high point of the route. The distance and the height to be gained was not great to people with their experience; if they maintained steady progress, they could expect to arrive at the bothy by midnight. Added to these considerations was the fact that, in accepting the lift along the loch, they had made a partial crossing of the Rubicon: they were in a situation in which they had little practicable choice other than to go forward, even if they had any reason for harbouring doubt about the weather. They were 5km from Loch Ossian Youth Hostel which was, apart from the Corrour Lodge buildings, the nearest proper shelter and to reach it they would have to walk back along the loch only to have to return the following day. In an emergency, they could seek accommodation in one of the Lodge cottages or outbuildings, but at the time there was no such emergency and there is no evidence that the Lodge lorry driver advised them of the storm forecast. Indeed, he was probably quite unaware of it. Their decision to proceed towards Benalder Cottage is quite comprehensible; in fact, it can hardly be said that they had any decision to make.

Their route followed the Uisge Labhair north-eastwards for over 5km; at this point, half way from the Lodge to their destination, they would turn south-east over the Bealach Cumhann and head for the bothy. The ground was fairly rough and, although there was a rather indistinct path up the Uisge Labhair and a somewhat better one over the Bealach Cumhann and on to the bothy, both would have a covering of snow which would increase with

Benalder Cottage by Loch Ericht, from Ben Alder's lower slopes. 2/1/52 · *Donald Bennet*

height. There was a steepish climb from the Uisge Labhair to the bealach itself, but otherwise the incline was gentle and, beyond the bealach, it was downhill or level all the way to Benalder Cottage.

Having had their meal close to Corrour Lodge, they shouldered their packs and started towards the footbridge across the Uisge Labhair which took them to its northern side. Although the ascent was gradual, their rucksacks were heavy and the snow was fairly soft and, in places, rather deep, especially in the hollows. This was exacerbated by the darkness and by the tussocky nature of the ground which caused them to stumble quite frequently. They were not long under way before their rate of progress became quite slow. Indeed, their speed was no greater than a worrying 2km per hour and at that rate they would not reach Benalder Cottage until about half past two in the morning.

After about two hours of trudging up the glen, it was decided to bivouac for the night and enjoy the rest of the walk to the bothy in the daylight. At this point, there is a major divergence between Anne Tewnion's recollections of January 1952 and her recollections of today. In 1952, she said that her party divided its forces with John Bradburn and James Grieve continuing onwards in the direction of Benalder Cottage. In the words of the S.M.C.J. report whose information derived from Mrs Tewnion:

About 2½ miles up the glen three of the party became tired, and they made a bivouac at 10.30 p.m. in the lee of a steep tributary burn. . . . Bradburn and Grieve pushed on to try and cross the bealach W.S.W. of Ben Alder; but they found the snow too soft and deep, so they, too, bivouacked half an hour later.

This is quite different from Mrs Tewnion's account today. She is quite certain – and consistently certain despite the evidence of her letter to Dick Brown in January 1952 – that the party did not split up; rather the five of them bivouacked at the same place and left together the following morning. As Mrs Tewnion describes events on the Sunday morning:

Going up the track, John Bradburn and Jimmy Grieve moved quicker than John Black, Sydney and myself and went on ahead. This was not a decision we had made – and we probably expected to catch up with them en route.

This evidential dichotomy is not concerned with a small point of detail and some effort must be made to try to decide which of the two memories is likely to be more accurate. However, there are two other important points of divergence and it is more appropriate to consider the two sets of recollections once the story of the tragedy has been told.

The party, then, had walked 4km and gained a mere 137m; it was 10.30 p.m. or thereabouts. They had reached a suitable bivouac site at the confluence of the Allt Glas-choire, which came down from their left, and the Uisge Labhair. Here, either the entire party or John Black and the Tewnions would spend the night. If John Bradburn and James Grieve did continue up the glen, they could not have travelled more than about a kilometre before themselves stopping to bivouac. The bivouac site at the meeting of the two waters was cleared of the soft snow to expose the turf on which they placed capes and on these they laid out their sleeping-bags which they covered with other capes. As Mrs Tewnion recalled at the time and still recalls today, they slept well and did not suffer from the cold. She observes:

We had a good night's sleep, huddled together in down sleeping bags between groundsheets and we were all warm throughout the night

Of the bivouac prepared by the party, the S.M.C.J. report of the accident said:

One rescue team member considered that more digging and building would have produced a better shelter in which they could have cooked.

However, this comment was based on the assumption, apparently erroneous, that there was sufficient snow at the bivouac site to allow them to do this. Anne Tewnion says that there was simply not enough snow to have made a better bivouac and it seems likely that the deeper snow which was there when the searchers arrived on the Monday had fallen after the party left. The meteorological evidence about limited December snowfall suggests that Anne Tewnion is right in what she says. In any case, during the night they were quite well protected from the increasing wind and the amount of such precipitation as there was would have been fairly small; moreover, when they prepared the bivouac, they had no reason to suspect the storm which was to come. It could be that the comment in the S.M.C.J. report was partly based on the belief that the party did no cooking after leaving the wood beside Corrour Lodge on the Saturday evening, a belief which may have been ill-founded.

The five members of the Glencoe Club had had no opportunity to make any visual check on the weather situation since arriving at Corrour station at about 7.15 p.m., well after night had enveloped the landscape; had they been able to do so, they might have had some warning of the impending change. It cannot have been long after they settled down for the night that the weather began its rapid deterioration, the most important change being a strengthening wind which made what proved to be an ominous shift into the south. By 6.00 a.m. in the area of Corrour, it would have been blowing at Storm Force Ten over the mountain tops. However, it is plain that the party was protected during the night by the high ground to the south, stretching a distance of almost 5km kilometres from Sgor Gaibhre to Beinn a' Chumhainn, almost all of it over 760m and directly south of the Uisge Labhair. The fact that those (whether three or five) bivouacking at the confluence of the two streams slept well is some confirmation of this, although it should be said that since all but James Grieve were seasoned campaigners in the hills their sleep would probably have been less easily disturbed than that of others with less experience. Although it had certainly increased in the glen by the time they awoke, they were still ignorant of the nature of the wind that was sweeping across the country and it was not until they were under way that it veered sufficiently into the west for them to experience its full ferocity. This late awareness of the strength of the wind may have contributed to the fatal outcome: had they been properly conscious of its venomous power earlier, they might well have decided to head straight back down the glen to the safety of Corrour Lodge rather than to continue towards Benalder Cottage.

The meteorological evidence suggests that the temperature in the glen was a little above freezing level at dawn, not cold enough at that time that, in the words of the S.M.C.J. report, 'It was too cold to wrap up sleeping sacks, and rucksacks were frozen.'

This statement was based on what Mrs Tewnion recalled at the time when she wrote to Dick Brown; Marjory Roy says that it is possible that precipitation during the night froze on impact when it fell on the buckles and straps and the subsequent relatively small rise in temperature was insufficient to thaw them out. This is consistent with the explanation Anne Tewnion gave in her 1952 letter. However, this is quite different from what she has to say on the matter today:

> There was no difficulty in opening or unpacking our rucksacks. We bivouacked on a fine night, had breakfast, packed away our stoves and sleeping bags and it was after that the weather deteriorated. . . . **At no time** were we unable to get things from our packs, but probably by the time the rescue teams came in the afternoon the straps could have frozen over. [Anne Tewnion's bold.]

The section of the S.M.C.J. report quoted above immediately went on to state:

> They appear to have eaten hardly any food in the morning, although the rucksacks contained a good deal of such things as chocolate, shortbread and biscuits, which would not require any cooking.

Presumably it was considered that they were denied a proper breakfast because they could not gain access to their stoves and food in their frozen packs. Mrs Tewnion is firm in her contradiction of this lack of breakfast: she is quite certain that, although she had little to eat partly because she seldom ate much for breakfast and partly because she was feeling slightly unwell owing to menstruation, the four men had a cooked breakfast and she remembers watching them eat it. In her words: 'All except myself had a good breakfast – beans, bacon and sausages. Of this I am absolutely positive.'

She is equally certain that she is not confusing the meal of the previous night in the wood beside Corrour Lodge with breakfast or that she is confusing it with a breakfast at another bivouac on another occasion with the same friends: she remembers eating at the meal close to the Lodge and she had not bivouacked before with the same group. There were two questions concerning feeding asked of Anne Tewnion by Dick Brown:

> Could you tell me approximately at what time you all reached your bivouac and had you another meal? Did you all have a meal before you all dumped your packs [at the bivouac site on the retreat down the glen]?

With regard to the first, the inference is that Brown was asking if the party had had a meal once they arrived at the bivouac site on the Saturday night and before they bedded down. Mrs Tewnion made no response to this question probably because they did not eat. In the context of Brown's letter, the second question could be taken as asking simply if the party had had a meal at the bivouac site when they discarded the remaining packs. No meal was taken on their return to the bivouac site, but this is not to say that breakfast was not eaten.

It is not possible to be precise about times during the Sunday morning. In her letter to Dick Brown, Mrs Tewnion said that Bradburn and Grieve started about 6.00 a.m. and that she, her husband and Black awoke about 8.00 a.m. Today, referring to the time when the party left in the morning, she observes: 'I am sorry I now have no idea of the time we all set off in the morning but it was darkish when we cooked breakfast.'

Bearing in mind the time of year and the cloudy conditions, this observation is consistent with the 8.00 a.m. estimate, although it may have been a little earlier when they wakened. A simple calculation based on the times given in the letter to Brown indicates that Mrs Tewnion was of the opinion that her group of three set off for Benalder Cottage at about 8.30 a.m. According to this letter, they met Bradburn and Grieve returning at 9.15 a.m. and reached the bivouac site on their retreat down the glen at about 10.00 a.m. If the party had a breakfast, cooked when 'it was darkish', their departure would have also been about 8.30 a.m. and, since it is Anne Tewnion's recollection today that it did not seem long before the three of them met Bradburn returning alone, this meeting could also have happened about 9.15 a.m., with a return to the bivouac place about 10.00 a.m.

It appears, then, that the group who had spent the night beside the Allt Glas-choire (whether three of them or all five) left about 8.30 a.m. and continued up the glen in the direction of Benalder Cottage. The glen faces west-south-west and turns west at its lower end so it is probable that when the party was preparing to leave it was still sheltered from the full strength of the wind. Anne Tewnion recalls:

There was a strong wind – maybe Force 4/5. We discussed going to Benalder Cottage or returning to the youth hostel [Loch Ossian] and decided to go on with the wind on our backs – a decision probably partly swayed by knowing our friends were expecting us. It was certainly easier to go on than to return with the strong wind against us. We all set off together towards the pass. We were in no doubt about getting to the cottage.

By the time the group set off, they had been exposed to the elements for half to three quarters of an hour since leaving the warmth of their sleeping-bags. In addition to mentioning the pair of wet flannels, the S.M.C.J. report stated that capes used as groundsheets had been left behind although Mrs Tewnion cannot recall this happening to the capes. It may be that both the

trousers and the capes were left behind inadvertently, perhaps because they
had become hidden under snow. Nevertheless, it could be a sign that they
were already suffering incipient hypothermia and were becoming careless or
were even discarding items. The fact that at least two of the men were not
wearing their windproof trousers when the weather demanded them may be
attributable to hypothermia or it could be explained by the rucksack straps
and buckles freezing and preventing the men from taking them out of the
rucksacks. It could also be that the wind had become so strong that they were
unable to control them sufficiently to put on.

It was probably shortly after this departure that the wind veered
sufficiently into the west for them to experience its full force. In fact, the
local topography caused the wind to be funnelled up the glen, thus
intensifying its power. Almost certainly it blew up the glen with speeds
reaching Hurricane Force Twelve at times. Charles Donaldson, whose
recollections are based on diary notes, describes the weather that day in
terms which reveal the awful savagery of the wind in the Loch Ossian valley.
It would have been even worse in the narrower glen of the Uisge Labhair.
He says:

> In the morning and early afternoon of the 30th a hurricane wind was blowing with
> an occasional hail shower. There was no snow. A feature was that the wind was of
> such velocity that it was ripping surface water from the loch and driving it horizontally
> like a six foot wall of rain – although in the upper air there was no rain. The wind was
> of such velocity that it carried away a shankie [an outside lavatory] when one of our
> party opened the door. Another put on skis and was blown over as soon as he left the
> shelter of the woods. The road from the hostel to the lodge was strewn with trees,
> some uprooted, some snapped across the trunk. It was that kind of wind.

There are two versions of what happened to the fated party as they made
their way up the glen in the direction of Benalder Cottage and this is the
third main divergence between Anne Tewnion's memory of 1952 and her
present one. In 1952 she said:

> On the Sunday morning, John and Jimmy started about 6 a.m. and went towards
> the bealach. John Black, Sid and I wakened about 8 a.m. and decided it would be
> easier to go on with the wind behind us . . . About three quarters of an hour later, we
> met John and Jimmy coming back. The path was impassable so we turned back with
> them. We were near the lochan [Lochan Allt Glaschoire] when Jimmy left his pack.
> He was not too bad then, just a bit slower than the rest of us. . . . The rest of us
> dumped our packs at the bivouac site . . . about ten o'clock. . . . It was about here that
> we started to help Jimmy. . . . Sid and I helped Jimmy while the two Johns walked
> ahead and after about 30-40 minutes we changed over. I think it was just after noon
> that John Black and Sydney died and I expect John Bradburn would be about the
> same time.

This is quite different from her recollection today. The five friends left the bivouac place together and then, in the words of Anne Tewnion:

Going up the track, John Bradburn and Jimmy Grieve moved quicker than John Black, Sydney and myself and went on ahead. This was not a decision we had made – and we probably expected to catch up with them en route. However, not long after that, we were surprised to find John Bradburn coming back. He told us it was too difficult up towards the pass. We asked where Jimmy was and he said, 'He was "out" so I left him.' This sounds appalling but our acceptance of this fact must indicate how we were – unbeknown to ourselves – suffering from hypothermia, a word none of us had heard of in those days.

With regard to the abandoning of the remaining packs at the bivouac place, there is another, although less significant discrepancy between the two memories. Mrs Tewnion cannot recall where the rucksacks were discarded but she is of the firm opinion that she carried hers as far as the sheep fank where her husband, Sydney, and John Black died. She observes on the matter:

I don't remember where the rucsacs were left but I did take chocolate from mine at one stage. I'm almost positive that I had mine at the fank but certainly I did not have it en route to Mr Tait's.

And, in words which so clearly reveal the dreadful state to which the men had been reduced by the elements, she says:

Certainly I know that Syd and John Black did not have their packs as I can still see them crawling on all fours – without rucsacks.

By then, the members of the S.M.C./J.M.C.S. party who had spent the night in the comfort of the Loch Ossian Youth Hostel had reached the sanctuary of a bothy beside Corrour Lodge. James Russell says:

... It was the intention of the S.M.C./J.M.C.S. party to go on to Benalder Cottage on the Sunday morning but the wind, which had started up in the early hours of the morning, was by daylight blowing with hurricane force. It was so bad that our party did not venture far. Many trees were being uprooted on Loch Ossian side.

The men made their way along the road on the south side of the loch towards Corrour Lodge. As they walked along, the raging wind blew on their backs and drove sleet into their clothing. Great volumes of spindrift were picked up from the surface of the loch and driven before the tempest coming out of the south-west. By the time they reached the north-east end of the loch, they had surrendered all intention of making for the bothy beside Loch Ericht that day and asked for shelter at the Lodge. Donaldson recalls:

On our arrival Andy Tait, the keeper, opened a bothy for us and laid and lit a fire for us to dry out, with no more than a twinkling enquiry about which asylum we had come from! A great bloke. When he came back later with Anne Tewnion's news he said he was never so glad in his life to have us there.

When Black and the Tewnions met Bradburn, with or without Grieve, on his way back, he told them that ahead the snow became deep and soft with little chance of being able to reach the Bealach Cumhann, the col which marked the high point on the way to Benalder Cottage. This offered them little alternative other than to retreat down the glen towards Corrour Lodge, a decision that entailed the most debilitating battle to make any progress into the violent wind which, by then, would have been blowing with hurricane force; they had to bend low and lean into it to make any forward movement at all and frequently they were halted and even pushed back by its intensity. To add to their misery, the wind carried with it fierce squalls of sleet and hail, the last being particularly troublesome as it struck them with painful force.

Breathing in those conditions was difficult and on occasions they had to turn away from the wind in order to breathe at all. Their clothing must have become wet, especially the trousers of those not clad in windproof leg coverings; in the conditions, however, it is doubtful if any clothing would have kept them dry – the wind driving the precipitation into the fabric of their waterproofs and through any chinks in them. Not only was the wind, aided by the damp clothing, constantly dissipating their precious body heat, but it was rapidly exhausting them as they battled down the glen: the wind was now to be the chief instrument of their fate.

The wind-chill factor was very high. The environmental temperature was just above freezing and with winds in the glen which were probably blowing consistently at 110 km/h, with frequent gusts in excess of this, the cooling effect on their bodies would have been equivalent to their being in a still air temperature of about $-23°C$ in clothes which had become wet. The wind, while maintaining its terrible temper, continued to swing towards the north as the low pressure area passed over the north of Scotland and by midday it was coming from west-north-west, the air temperature having dropped to freezing and even just below. Then, the wind-chill factor would have pushed the still air equivalent temperature down to about $-27°C$ and this is not far from the temperature at which exposed flesh will freeze. The only benefit of this changing direction of the wind was that it may have reduced its strength slightly in the glen.

Black and the Tewnions met the returning Bradburn, or Bradburn and Grieve together, at about 9.15 a.m. and it was about 10.00 a.m. when they reached the bivouac site beside the Allt Glas-choire where they abandoned three or all four of the remaining rucksacks. In an observation which implies that hypothermia struck the party quickly, Mrs Tewnion's says:

In 1951 we had never heard of hypothermia or wind chill factor, but even so I doubt if it would have made any difference as probably we were all affected at the same time – a mind-numbing experience.

Jimmy Ness, who was on the Cobbler that day, managed to reach the summit ridge with three companions, the others in his party having already retreated on account of the wind and the cold. Within seconds of being exposed to the wind on the ridge at about 800m, Ness had frozen down one side and he was of the opinion that, if he did not escape from the ridge, he would soon succumb to the cold. Michael Ward, the surgeon and authority on mountain medicine, comments:

The rate at which an individual becomes hypothermic depends on (a) his condition, (b) his clothing, (c) the weather conditions, (d) if he can move to produce heat. Usually the onset is not rapid – i.e. not immediate and sudden – but gradual over a period. However, this period can be quite short.

Physical and mental exhaustion are closely associated with hypothermia and it is quite understandable that there should be a strong temptation to discard anything tending to increase the exhaustion, however unwise and irrational the action may be. Nevertheless, in this case, if gaining the safety of Corrour Lodge was the only real chance of survival the party had, the abandonment of the rucksacks made good enough sense and may have been, at least in part, a rational decision. There can be little doubt that the packs, being relatively heavy, were a contributory factor in the increasingly fatigued condition of the party. They were only 4km from Corrour Lodge when they jettisoned the packs, most of whose contents, excepting the food and the windproof trousers which were not being worn, would be of little use to them in their struggle to safety – and food, if accessible in their rucksacks, could be carried in their pockets. They would have a better chance of reaching the Lodge if they used what remaining energy they had solely to fight their way down the glen and avoided wasting any of it bearing unnecessary loads. Furthermore, in high winds large rucksacks, even modern ones with waistbelts, can be so buffeted by the wind that they feel akin to wild animals trying to free themselves. Their movements are so unbalancing and debilitating that it can be wiser to discard them.

Corrour Lodge across Loch Ossian, 1933.   *Valentine Collection*

There was another consideration which urged them to devote all their
energies to reaching the Lodge. The party of five had set out to reach
Benalder Cottage where they would have remained until the following
Wednesday. The bothy was remote and contact with the outside world
difficult, especially in conditions such as those which had engulfed the area.
The only people who would know that something amiss had occurred would
be their friends in the bothy and they might well be able to do little about
alerting the authorities for some considerable time. By then it would almost
certainly be too late. There was the chance that the S.M.C./J.M.C.S. party
would arrive later in the day on their way to the bothy but, in such weather,
this was highly improbable. This being the situation, the members of
Glencoe Club had no choice other than to try to reach the Lodge before they
succumbed. They could have tried to shelter from the storm but, with the
wind blowing directly up the glen and insufficient snow for the digging of
snow holes, it is most unlikely that they would have found a spot well enough
protected from the elements to survive. Unfortunately, by the time the packs
were discarded, the men's condition was so weakened that the abandonment
did not make a difference sufficient to allow them to reach Corrour Lodge.

They continued their dreadful struggle towards Corrour Lodge. James Grieve, if he had not already succumbed to the conditions while in the company of Bradburn alone before the packs were abandoned at the bivouac site, collapsed in the snow about 800 metres after dumping the gear. A similar distance further down the glen, the remaining four reached a sheep fank which offered some shelter from the wind. They were 2km from Corrour Lodge and safety. Anne Tewnion recalls events as follows:

By the time we reached the fank at An t' Uisge Labhair, John Black and Sydney could only crawl and really could no longer keep moving in spite of encouragement. I stopped with them there in the lee of the fank while John Bradburn went on – and I expected him to get help. It seemed a long time I waited there – and certainly a while after I thought John and Sydney had died. I had decided there was little point in staying with them then, so took some chocolate from the pack and set off to Corrour Lodge.

When I got to the bridge [the footbridge over the Uisge Labhair, about 800 metres from the Lodge] and saw no footprints, I realised John Bradburn hadn't reached it. This upset me and, once over the bridge, I sat in the lee of a plantation. I ate some chocolate and then decided I had to get to the Lodge to let someone know where the bodies were. At the first house I came to, I was told to go to keeper Tait's. To get there I had to climb through a fallen fir tree – I really don't know if I could have walked round it or if I was just set on the most direct route to the Taits'. I do remember stopping in the middle of the tree and weeping.

It was probably about 11.45 a.m. when the group of four reached the sheep fank and it is likely that Anne Tewnion remained there for something over an hour, during which time she tried to get the two men to eat chocolate and barley sugar. However, the men were in such an extreme condition that they were unable to swallow or to assimilate any food whatsoever. As time passed, she must have drawn closer to death herself, although surprisingly she cannot recall feeling cold at any time during that awful return down the glen. Eventually, she left the fank at about 1.00 p.m. by which time she was sure both her husband and John Black were dead and that something untoward must have happened to John Bradburn. She may well have been correct in thinking that her husband and Black were dead, although it is often difficult to know when someone in the final stages of hypothermia has died since almost all vital signs, including the pulse, may be absent. However, if they did have some flicker of life, there was nothing more she could do for them at the fank.

That final stage of her dreadful journey, so short and so straightforward in good conditions, must have been a nightmare and the fact that she made it was a remarkable tribute to her strength of will and to her powers of endurance. Of her struggle after she left the fank, she remarks:

My determination to get help was increased by the thought of the difficulty a
search party would have in locating the five of us should I give up.

She did not come upon the body of Bradburn who had managed only
another 800 metres before collapsing and dying as the others had done. She
reached the plantation which afforded some protection from the wind;
perhaps it was only then that she knew she would reach safety. She arrived at
the Taits' house at 2.30 p.m. suffering seriously from hypothermia and was
put to bed after telling Andrew Tait what had happened. She was well cared
for by the Taits and by the medical practitioners who attended. Mrs
Tewnion has ever been very grateful for this attention:

I will never forget the kindness, care and support I received from Mr and Mrs Tait
and also from Dr Duff [sic. In fact it was Dr Ronald Kennedy] and young Dr Fraser
from Fort William. Dr Fraser travelled back to Glasgow with me and my parents and
paid a social visit to our home a few weeks later.

It was fortunate that the joint S.M.C./J.M.C.S. party were in residence in
the bothy at Corrour Lodge since they were able to form a rescue team to go
out at once to find the men. There was a chance, very slim though it was, that
one or two of them might still be alive, especially John Bradburn who could
not be far from the Lodge. James Russell describes events:

We were alerted by Mr Tait that Mrs Tewnion had arrived at his house and told
him that her husband and three companions had died on the hill. This was between 2
and 3 o'clock on the Sunday afternoon. Mrs Tewnion, though in poor condition and
badly shocked, was not incoherent and able to give a general picture of the situation.
The S.M.C./J.M.C.S. party with Mr Tait and two estate workers set out to search.
[Donald Mill did not accompany them: he was deputed to remain in the bothy and
prepare a hot meal and a good fire.] The wind, though still strong, was no longer
blowing with hurricane force. On the track leading to the Uisge Labhair, almost
within sight of the Lodge, the first body was found. I did not know any of the Glencoe
Mountaineering Club party but I was told that this was Bradburn. From the position
that the body was lying in it appeared that he had just fallen forward when on the
move. A short distance up the Uisge Labhair, maybe half to three quarters of a mile,
the bodies of Tewnion and Black were found in a sheep fank; they were both together
in a sitting position against one of the walls. By this time darkness was falling and the
search and the recovery of the bodies was abandoned.

Although the wind had eased somewhat, the wind-chill factor was still
very high. Long after the tragedy, one of the estate workers involved clearly
remembered that, within an hour of setting off up the Uisge Labhair, the

skin on his face had frozen and he had become deeply concerned about his survival.

The bodies were left where they were but not before they had been covered: they would be brought down to the Lodge the next day when the search for the body of James Grieve would be resumed. It was almost 6.00 p.m. before the search party returned to the Lodge. The telephone line from Corrour Lodge had been cut by falling trees which had also blocked the lochside road so two of the S.M.C./J.M.C.S. party, Robert MacLennan and Donald Mill, walked to Corrour station with a message to be telephoned from there to P.C. William Fullerton in Spean Bridge, asking him to bring a doctor to attend to Mrs Tewnion and asking also if the bodies could be brought in. The note also requested that there be no press involvement. They spent the night at the youth hostel and the following morning helped to open the road, which was done by noon. During the previous evening, Andrew Tait had constructed stretchers from birch poles and jute sacking and these, together with an estate garron, were used to carry down the bodies the next day, James Grieve being found without difficulty. The S.M.C./J.M.C.S. party, with Andrew Tait and estate workers, went out and brought down two of the bodies on the back of the garron, the other two being carried on the stretchers. They were met by a party from the youth hostel who had come to offer their help and they assisted with the stretchers. The gear was retrieved from the bivouac site but there was no sign of Grieve's rucksack which by then was probably well concealed by the snow which had fallen since the tragedy. The operation was completed not long after 2.30 p.m. An R.A.F. mountain rescue team from Kinloss which had been on a training exercise on Ben Nevis arrived at the Lodge but its assistance was not required as the recovery operation was well in hand by that time. The train which had brought the R.A.F. team also brought Fort William police constable, William Stewart, who was taken up the glen as far as the sheep fank to be shown where the bodies of three of the men had been found.

Anne Tewnion recovered slowly in the Taits' cottage. Dr George Fraser and Dr Ronald Kennedy, who were in partnership in Fort William, came on a goods train from Fort William, arriving at Corrour station at 3.30 a.m. on the Monday to attend to Mrs Tewnion. On the same train came P.C Fullerton and, apparently, a newspaper reporter: the request that there be no press publicity had proved vain. Mrs Tewnion was suffering seriously from hypothermia, but not from the frostbite to her hands and feet mentioned in several of the newspapers. Recovery from the extremely cold condition of her body inevitably and essentially took many hours and it was a long time

*From right: Andrew Tait, Bob MacLellan, an estate worker, Chas Donaldson, Jim Russell,
estate workers. Corrour, New Year, 1952*   *Courtesy of Mrs Richard Brown*

before she was able to stop shivering. However, she was able to leave the
Taits' house during the early evening of the Monday in the company of Dr
Fraser and Dr Kennedy to travel by train from Corrour to Fort William.
That train also transported the bodies of the four men and the gear which
had been recovered: it was just forty-eight hours since they had arrived at
Corrour station from Glasgow. Mrs Tewnion stayed in a Fort William hotel
with her parents who had journeyed from Glasgow.

On Wednesday, 2nd January, 1952, Sydney Rennie Tewnion and James
Russell Grieve were laid to rest in the graveyard in Glen Nevis where
Maurice Linnell had been interred almost eighteen years before. The two
men were buried side by side not far from the gate of the cemetery and the
gravestone of grey granite commemorates all four of the friends who died.
Of the other two, John Bradburn, whose father returned from the United
States for the funeral, was buried in Glasgow and John Black was cremated
in Paisley.

The loss of these four young men caused consternation both in climbing
circles and among the general public, not least because the party was
experienced and fit and they were also members of a mountaineering club;

they were not novices who had taken unthinkingly to the hills in winter with no conception of the difficulties they might have to face. If it could happen to them, it was more than likely to happen to other less experienced groups. There was also speculation on the comparative powers of endurance of men and women in such extreme conditions. It is now widely enough known that, on the whole, women are able to tolerate the effects of exposure better than men. This is due in part to better insulation provided by a thicker layer of subcutaneous fat, which helps protect the body's core from the cold, and in part also to a greater tolerance to physical stress. Perhaps also, women have a greater inherent determination to live. In Anne Tewnion's case, there was an additional factor: she was a very fit hill-walker. In a comment on her survival, Mrs Tewnion says:

> While I enjoyed rock climbing with the Club, I was also a keen hill-walker, covering quite long distances over the hills in a day – maybe 20 miles plus summits.

The Courier and Advertiser of Friday, 4th January, 1952 carried an account of one of Anne Tewnion's exploits which fully confirms how physically fit she was. It described the 1949 midsummer's day sunrise climb of Lochnagar, an ascent organised annually by the Carn Dearg Mountaineering Club. This outing involved her in making a ten hour walk alone from Glen Isla to Glen Clova where she met others with whom, after only a two hour rest, she made the ascent of Lochnagar and a return to Glen Clova. Then she hitch-hiked to Strathtummel where she spent the night and climbed Schiehallion the next day, completing the three day expedition by hitch-hiking home to Glasgow. This level of fitness, subsequently maintained, must have contributed to her survival two and a half years later.

The police were especially concerned about the loss of life in the tragedy and it does seem that they regarded the party as in some measure culpable for the fate which overcame them. J. R. Johnstone, the Chief Constable of Inverness-shire, the county in which the accident had happened, issued a widely publicised thirteen point recommendation to climbers and hill-walkers which reinforced one issued by his predecessor in 1947. In the course of his statement, as reported in the *Aberdeen Press and Journal* of Friday, 4th January, 1952, Chief Constable Johnstone said:

> However much one admires the courage and adventurous nature of all who set out to conquer our Scottish hills, admiration wanes when it is found that the bravery is not accompanied by a due regard for the elementary precautions which should at all times be taken.

The newspaper's report of the Chief Constable's statement went on to say:

It was essential to take precautions not only for the climber's personal safety but for the safety of others who so willingly went to the rescue no matter what the hazard might be. He stressed the need to learn beforehand from the weather forecasts what conditions might be in the areas in which they would be climbing. It was well-known that weather conditions on the hills could worsen almost without warning. Referring to the weekend tragedy, Mr Johnstone remarked that, on reflection, it became rather obvious that it could have been avoided had due regard been given to the very first of the thirteen points recommended to climbers in 1947 by his predecessor, Chief Constable William Fraser. It stated, 'Avoid climbing in severe weather. Snow, frost or mist are especially dangerous.

It is fairly clear that this statement was delivered as a warning to the inexperienced and it seems to reveal that the Chief Constable was lacking in much practical knowledge of climbing. Understandably, he wanted to minimise the number of accidents in the hills by discouraging relative novices from undertaking expeditions beyond their experience and capability, but to suggest that the mountaineering fraternity as a whole should avoid climbing in severe weather and that snow, frost and mist were especially dangerous was too generalised. Furthermore, the plea that those taking to the hills should learn beforehand the expected weather conditions was rather neutralised by the observation that 'weather conditions on the hills could worsen almost without warning'. It was regrettable that he should link the warning so directly with the ill-starred party which had become the centre of national attention when he was using the incident as a vehicle for a warning to the inexperienced. It is by no means inconceivable that, had events gone differently when the S.M.C./J.M.C.S. party arrived at Corrour station of the Saturday evening, they might have been given a lift to the Lodge and the next day found themselves in some similar trouble to the members of the Glencoe Mountaineering Club. It must be wondered if Mr Johnstone would have been quite so forthright in his opinion if misfortune had overtaken members of the august Scottish Mountaineering Club.

In an apparent attempt to counter public criticism of the party which had met with such misfortune, some mountaineers and some of their friends denied that the party had been blameworthy. On Friday, 4th January, 1952, *The Scotsman* contained an article on the misadventure flowing from the pen of a 'Staff Correspondent'. It started:

I have just been talking to one of the men who took part in the recovery of the bodies of the mountaineers who perished in the snow near Corrour at the week-end. He is a seasoned member of the Scottish Mountaineering Club and he was still showing the effects of his week-end ordeal. . . . My informant came to *The Scotsman* office to make the point that what happened near Corrour was not due to lack of experience or to failure to take adequate precautions. . . . The doomed party, he told me, were seasoned mountaineers. It is true that they were sedentary workers, but so are the great majority of Scottish mountaineers. They knew the country and they were well-equipped. When the bodies were found they were on a well-defined track. The dead men had hoods over their heads, they were wearing windproof clothes, and their mittens were in position. Even their electric torches were suspended round their necks. . . . The tragedy, he is convinced, was due entirely to the unparalleled ferocity of the blizzard which, he reckons, was screaming up the Uisge Labhair, at times at 100 m.p.h.

The 'informant' was Dick Brown, one of the two members of the S.M.C./J.M.C.S. party who was to be involved in preparing the report of the accident in the S.M.C.J. The article contained several references to blizzard conditions on the day of the tragedy: indeed, it had the unfortunate party 'up to their waists in snow' as they returned to the bivouac site on the Sunday morning and the lochside road blocked, not by fallen trees, but by snow. It is impossible to accept that this was said by Brown, the conclusion being that it was inserted by the staff correspondent, either to make his account the more graphic or because he could not believe that the wind alone could have killed the men. Whatever the reason, it fixed in print a misrepresentation of the truth. There was no blizzard; the angel of death rode on the wind, and the wind alone.

Hamish MacInnes, who knew three of the men and had climbed with them, says in his book, *High Drama* (Hodder and Stoughton):

The events which befell this party . . . had nothing to do with lack of equipment or lack of knowledge. . . . It was a type of accident which still happens today. The adversary is not mountain or avalanche, but the weather and that most insidious killer of the unwary, exposure.

Sydney Tewnion and John Black, in particular, were recognised as 'hard men' of their era. They had made first ascents in winter – the acme of British climbing in those days.

If the chief constable was rather unfair in his adverse criticism of the five members of the Glencoe Mountaineering Club, the counsels for the defence were probably somewhat forgiving. The truth, it seems, lies somewhere in between and rather nearer to the opinions of the latter than the former. The party did make some mistakes which, without doubt, contributed to their end and which, at least to some extent, could have been avoided. Firstly, although Saturday, 29th December had been a calm day, the weather had been quite violent over the previous few days, Thursday, 27th December being especially so with severe winds over a wide area which extended far out into the Atlantic, the following day seeing only a moderation in this windy weather. Furthermore, for several days it had been cold with some snow over high ground. It is true that the severe, devastating weather which struck Scotland during the night of 29th/30th December and continued throughout the whole of the 30th was not forecast by the Meteorological Offices until the 29th and was, therefore, not readily available to the party when they departed from Glasgow, but the sustained spell of windy and cold weather over the previous period should have alerted them to the risk of difficult conditions and perhaps also to the advisability of treating the weather forecast on Friday, 28th for the 29th/30th with some circumspection, the more particularly as they proposed to make their way to the remote Benalder Cottage in darkness. Indeed, it might have been sensible in the circumstances to have obtained the latest radio weather forecast.

However, this criticism is easily made and, at least to some extent, issues from the armchair. Sufficient has been said in the Introduction to show that weather forecasts provided in the media in those days were general and, in the Scottish Highland areas at least, too unreliable to be greatly heeded by hill-walkers and climbers; moreover, the ability of the Meteorological Offices to forecast much beyond the following twelve hours or so was quite limited. The reality was that, while the mountaineering fraternity might pay some attention to weather forecasts, their experience was that it was not altogether wise to place too much trust in them, certainly not to the extent of altering long made holiday plans which involved a rendezvous with friends who could not easily be told of any change of plan, as was the case with the Glencoe Club's arrangements. It should also be borne in mind that throughout the Saturday the weather was quite fair with no sign of the change to come. When this change came – and it did not manifest itself to them until they awoke on Sunday morning – the bivouacking party was fully committed to its expedition.

The second criticism which can be made of the party is that they were carrying loads which were probably excessively heavy, especially for carrying in the dark across rough and desolate country and through snow which might be soft and deep in places, especially on the higher levels. They were, after all, carrying food and other supplies, such as primus stoves, the fuel for these and a pressure cooker, for their four-day expedition. Exhaustion is one of the chief contributory factors in the onset and development of hypothermia and in this regard the weight of their rucksacks was of some importance and may have contributed significantly to their slow progress up the Uisge Labhair on the Saturday night. To a large extent, the amount taken was determined by the remoteness of the bothy to which they were going and the length of time for which they would be away. They had to carry with them all that they would need during this time. If they could not go to Benalder Cottage at that time of year without taking so much, perhaps they should have chosen another venue for their New Year's sojourn.

There is no doubt that the choice of Benalder Cottage was committing and, if the weather turned hostile once there, risky. It was made even more binding through the fact that, once they had alighted from the train at Corrour on the Saturday evening, there would be no trains until the Monday and after that none until the Wednesday because of the New Year holiday. The choice of venue was probably unwise because of this isolation, both in terms of the bothy's physical position and the length of time the party would be incommunicado, and because of the ever-present possibility of bad weather. In addition to these factors, the arrangement made by the party to meet their friends at Benalder Cottage did something to deny them the flexibility of making last-minute changes to their plans.

All this being said, however, the party was experienced, young and fit and, when they laid their plans for the New Year, they could hardly have been expected to anticipate the tempestuous weather they had to face. Moreover, the New Year visit to the remote bothy was part of their developing mountain experience. There are so many areas of human endeavour where, if progress is to be made, more demanding situations, quite often entailing some risk, have to be faced. If Chief Constable Johnstone's thirteen recommendations had been rigorously adopted by all those who took to the hills, quite simply there would have been no progress in the activity of mountaineering and it would have become moribund. Ideally, the risks are controlled so that, if serious difficulties are encountered, a safe retreat can be made. Desirable though this may be, it is by no means always possible and misfortunes will occur. Having decided on Benalder Cottage as their base, they had no choice other than to carry heavy loads to provide for their needs for the duration of their four-day expedition; it might even be considered sensible to take a little extra food in case of emergency. In contrast to Baird and Barrie at the end of 1927, they had quite sufficient food for their needs.

The third criticism of the party relates to their clothing. Generally, their clothing was satisfactory, certainly by the standards of the time. There is no doubt that they were aware of the need for good quality clothing and footwear and the need also to maintain them. Of this Anne Tewnion has the following observations to make:

We regularly reproofed our windproofs with Mesowax. They were good quality cotton and I used mine for many years after for hill-walking and ski-ing. The boots were well cared for with dressings of Mars Oil.

However, the S.M.C.J. accident report said that their clothing 'was possibly inadequate, especially below the waist'. Consideration has already been given to the question of how the members of the party were actually attired as they retreated down the glen and it does seem certain that at least two of the men, and probably three, were not clad in their windproof trousers, while the fourth, who was wearing his pair, apparently was not wearing trousers underneath them. That four of them died from hypothermia and the one survivor was suffering seriously from this condition when she reached Corrour Lodge undeniably indicates that their clothing was inadequate for the conditions with which they had to contend. According to the account of the interview with Dick Brown given in *The Scotsman* of Friday, 4th January, 1952: 'The dead men had hoods over their heads, they were wearing windproof clothes, and their mittens were in position.'

The hoods would have given some protection to the head and neck, additional to their balaclavas, but, with the wind blowing furiously into their faces as they struggled towards Corrour Lodge, this protection would have been fairly minimal and it would have been difficult to keep the hoods in place. Moreover, it has to be remembered that the event occurred at the end of 1951 and that what would then pass for windproof might not do so today. It is difficult to know how waterproof were their anoraks, especially in such appalling conditions with the violent wind driving sleet and hail into the fabric. Any deficiency would have allowed the precipitation to penetrate their anoraks and make their clothes underneath wet. Wet clothing, combined with the severity of the wind, would have been a constant drain on their body heat. For those not wearing their windproof trousers, even if their anoraks had been fully waterproof, the wetness in their trousers would have been drawn up into the clothing under their anoraks. With regard to precautions against the snow filling their boots, the four men had puttees and Anne Tewnion had a pair of neat-fitting elasticated gaiters and these would certainly have offered a barrier to the elements, although how effective they were in the transcendent conditions cannot be known.

In fairness, it has to be said that, with the exception of the protection they had below the waist, their clothing was undoubtedly as good as was in general use and was thought by most people to be adequate for any conditions that were likely to be encountered. They were not expecting, nor had they ever experienced, the conditions in which they were to find themselves; these conditions were extreme, the worst in the area for twenty years according to some reports. It is unlikely that there was available then any clothing which could have withstood the rigours of that storm. Stan Stewart, one of the members of the S.M.C./J.M.C.S. party which was fortunate not to find itself sharing with the Glencoe Club members the misery of the venomous storm in the glen of the Uisge Labhair, is quoted in *High Drama*, as saying of one item of clothing he was wearing that day:

> I was wearing an old Home Guard great-coat, cut to jacket length, which I had proudly thought to be my personal armour plate, proof against anything. But its hidden qualities included a large capacity for absorbing moisture and by the time we reached the far end of Loch Ossian we were only too ready to sink our pride and beg the shelter of the estate bothy.   (Hodder and Stoughton)

It has also to be remembered that the unfortunate party, in common with the vast majority of mountaineers, knew nothing of hypothermia. Their ignorance of the condition meant, of course, that they had no knowledge of the correct emergency procedures to follow in the event of its affecting any of their party. Even Donald Duff, the mountaineering surgeon in the Belford Hospital, Fort William, was only beginning to understand the condition properly at the time. He wrote a short article for the S.M.C.J. and this accompanied the Journal's report of the accident. In it he said:

> Personally I had always assumed, as did most other people, that the victims of exposure were affected by a gradually increasing lassitude and weakness, developing as the hours went by to slow, lingering exhaustion before the end came. It was often advised that affected persons be kept awake by walking them about. It is often thought that the end is painful.
>
> These assumptions are wrong where there is a complete using up of physical energy. In the case of fit men in good training, with will-power to drive them on to physical exertion in the face of cold and high wind, the end may come more or less suddenly. There is a preliminary stage when, as body heat and vitality are sapped, the faculties of co-ordination of movements, of sight and hearing deteriorate. The physical vigour of a man in good training does not give the immunity against cold that one might expect; and a woman, apparently less robust, may be the more capable of withstanding these conditions.

The members of the Glencoe Mountaineering Club were fit and in good training – even the less experienced Grieve seems to have been physically fit; they had the will-power to drive themselves on and yet, in the face of cold and high wind, the end for the four men came more or less suddenly and perhaps for Anne Tewnion it would not have been much further delayed.

The party could have had no proper appreciation of the fact that their clothing was really quite inadequate for the conditions of wet cold and hurricane force winds which they encountered; nor could they have had any proper notion of the correct measures to take when the first hypothermic signs manifested themselves: to stop immediately, find shelter, conserve energy and maintain, and if possible generate, body heat. It would have seemed quite the wrong course of action; rather, it would have appeared much wiser to continue through the storm to try to reach some safe and warm haven. Thus, their decision to fight on through the storm in the desperate hope of reaching Corrour Lodge is quite comprehensible. In fact, it may have been the correct course of action: adequate shelter would have been very difficult, if not impossible, to find and they knew that, if they did not make it back to the Lodge under their own steam, they might not be found for long enough – well after their lives had been forfeited to the all-consuming tempest. It is as well to remember that it was, in part, their fate which was to lead eventually to a better understanding of hypothermia among mountaineers and the general public.

It was probably unfortunate that during the night of the bivouac and apparently when they were preparing to leave early the following morning they were sheltered from the full intensity of the wind by the high ground to the south. It is conceivable that, if they had not been deceived about the true violence of the wind and had made directly for Corrour Lodge from the bivouac site, the end would not have been what it was. In proceeding towards Benalder Cottage, they used up much vital energy and had become seriously chilled. Admittedly, John Black and Sydney Tewnion, who certainly bivouacked at the meeting of the two streams, were further from Corrour Lodge than the wasted distance when they succumbed, but they managed to struggle 3km that morning and if they had gone straight down the glen this distance would have brought them to within about 800 metres of the Lodge. They might then have been rescued by a party from the Lodge. In all likelihood, Bradburn, wherever he spent the night, would have survived.

Anne Tewnion suggests another course of action which might have saved the lives of her husband, John Black and John Bradburn. She says:

In retrospect, had we all gone on to the pass, there we could have made a snow hole.

Such, sadly, is wisdom after the event.

There remains to be considered which of Anne Tewnion's two memories, her early 1952 memory or her present one, is likely to be the more accurate – or which parts of which are likely to be so. There is much that is common to both sets of recollections and Mrs Tewnion, who has a generally good visual memory, is still able to recall small details from the weekend of the tragedy, some of which can be verified independently. Normally, recollections of events close to the time of their happening are more reliable than those where a greater lapse of time separates memory from event. This is particularly so when the length of time is forty years as in this case. However, it is known that hypothermia can have serious effects on the memory, that accident survivors frequently have poor and distorted recall of events and that those in shock or under stress have vague or partial recollection. When Anne Tewnion replied to the questions asked by Dick Brown in his letter at the beginning of 1952, she was, in her own words, 'in shock at the time and remained so for some weeks after.' And she concluded 'The unequivocal authority with which I spoke at that time should perhaps be regarded with a little caution.'

However, she also says that, although she cannot recall the correspondence with Dick Brown, she does not 'think there was any reason for me to be evasive in my reply. Certainly, I would have answered his queries to the best of my ability.'

There are three chief points of divergence between the two memories. These are:

(1) The number of bivouac sites – one or two.

(2) Whether or not the men, be it two or four, who spent the night at the confluence of the Uisge Labhair and the Allt Glas-choire ate a cooked breakfast the morning after the bivouac. This relates to the condition of the straps and buckles of the rucksacks – frozen or unfrozen – when the party awoke.

(3) James Grieve's end. Was he abandoned when he was with Bradburn alone or when he was with the whole party?

It is not possible to be certain which of the two memories is the more reliable if for no other reason than that people respond differently to hypothermia and stressful situations and an individual may respond differently at different times. Nevertheless, there are some considerations which may provide an indication as to which one is likely to be more accurate.

Dealing first with the number of bivouac sites, the walk up the glen of the Uisge Labhair was made tiring by the darkness and the tussocky nature of the ground. This must have affected the whole party to a greater or lesser extent. By the time they reached the junction of the Uisge Labhair and the Allt Glas-choire it was probably about 10.30 p.m. and, in view of the slow progress up to that point, there was little likelihood that Bradburn and Grieve would be able to make Benalder Cottage much before morning. This would have entailed several hours finding their way in darkness in conditions that were already trying; conditions that were likely to become more difficult the higher they went. In this situation, it seems improbable that they would have seen much sense in continuing towards the Cottage and would surely only have done so if they thought they would be able to reach it without bivouacking. If they did continue, they were able to manage only another half an hour's walk up the gently rising glen and this must indicate that, when they left the others, they could not have felt fit enough to reach the bothy that night. Moreover, John Bradburn had intended to travel with the party which had caught the 5.46 a.m. train but had missed it. He must have risen that day between 4.00 a.m. and 4.30 a.m. and then, having missed the first train, he had to wait ten hours for the only other train of the day. Certainly he could have returned home for some of the time but, having had such a long and rather frustrating day, there must be some doubt as to whether he would have wanted to proceed through the night over difficult ground in order to reach the bothy when others in the party had decided to bivouac. It must be wondered also if the less experienced Grieve would have relished such a nocturnal expedition.

There is another consideration. According to Mrs Tewnion's recollections in her letter to Dick Brown, Bradburn and Grieve got under way at 6.00 a.m. on the Sunday morning. At that early hour, dawn would be two hours off and this would entail that amount of time being spent climbing up to the bealach and beyond in darkness, in deepening snow and over ground which would present considerable difficulties. It is hard to understand that they would have left at this time unless they had had a poor night and were cold so that they preferred to leave their bivouac to escape from the unpleasantness of their situation. Then, already with a lower than normal core temperature and presumably with little, if anything, for breakfast, they would have been out in the cold, further lowering their temperature, unless they were able to generate sufficient heat through physical exertion to compensate for the loss. In addition to all this, they would have been using up their reserves of energy in trying to reach the bealach. In total, they would have been exposed to heat and energy loss significantly greater than the other three whose starting core temperature was probably closer to normal.

And yet, according to Anne Tewnion's 1952 memory, this pair survived this drain on their resources to a considerably greater extent that did the other two men. In fact, Bradburn was able to reach a point closer to Corrour Lodge than all but Mrs Tewnion herself. It is also relevant to point out that, as the onset of hypothermia can be slower in those with mountain experience than in those without, it could be expected that Grieve, being relatively inexperienced, would succumb rather more quickly than the others. If Anne Tewnion's 1952 memory is correct, he withstood exposure considerably better than did John Black and Sydney Tewnion.

The balance of the evidence, therefore, is that there was one bivouac and that, on this matter, Mrs Tewnion's present memory is correct.

Whether or not the men bivouacking beside the junction of the Uisge Labhair and the Allt Glas-choire had a cooked breakfast before leaving the bivouac place is a more difficult matter. In her letter to Dick Brown, Anne Tewnion did not say that there was no cooked breakfast, although she may have already said that there had been no breakfast in her conversation with him and others in the train on the way back from Fort William to Glasgow after the accident. It should also be said that there could have been a cooked meal even if the rucksack straps froze: the primuses could have been left outside the packs overnight or, together with the food, could have been in side pockets whose straps did not freeze. However, if the primuses were available for cooking, they could surely have been used to provide heat to free the straps if they had frozen. It follows that if they cooked, they also had access to their packs. Mrs Tewnion is certain that the men had breakfast in spite of having seen again the correspondence of 1952.

On the other hand, the fact that two or three of the men were not wearing their windproof trousers during their battle down the glen when they would have been far better to have been doing so and they still had their torches around their necks when they no longer needed them could indicate that they were unable to open their rucksacks because they were frozen. If so, a cooked breakfast is very unlikely. However, it seems that they were affected by the cold and the struggle with the wind very quickly and this may have impaired their judgement with equal speed so that they did not think about the windproof trousers and the torches – or, by the time they realised that they needed their trousers, it had become simply too windy to stop and put them on.

The matter could be resolved quite simply. Anne Tewnion said in her letter to Dick Brown that her party had to leave their sleeping-bags behind because they were unable to attach them to their rucksacks and it is fairly clear from what she said about this in the letter that this was because the straps were frozen. Today, she is sure that they were able to pack the sleeping-bags: no problem was presented by frozen straps. The gear was recovered from the bivouac site on the Monday: if the sleeping-bags were found lying loose, Mrs Tewnion's 1952 memory about the condition of the straps was correct; if they were packed, her present memory is correct. Unfortunately, both Dick Brown and Stan Stewart are dead and none of the surviving members of the recovery team can remember what was found at the bivouac site or if the sleeping-bags were in, or attached to, the rucksacks, although it has to be said that generally they are of the opinion that what Anne Tewnion said immediately after the accident was an accurate account of events. This might imply that the sleeping-bags were found discarded, although this was not actually stated in the S.M.C.J. accident report, as it was in the case of the capes and the pair of flannels. Of course, the absence of sleeping-bags lying loose at the bivouac place could not be held to prove that they were taken by the party: they could have blown away in the wind. The meteorological evidence is also inconclusive: there could have been impact freezing of precipitation during the night but there is no certainty that this did happen; and, if it did happen, it might have thawed by the time the party awoke. For sure, capes and the wet pair of flannels were found on the ground, but these could have been left behind inadvertently.

Finally, there is the question of James Grieve's end. Did he succumb when he was with John Bradburn alone on the Benalder Cottage side of the bivouac, as Anne Tewnion says today, or did it happen when he was in the company of the whole party on the Corrour Lodge side of the bivouac place, as she said in 1952? There are three points which can be made on the matter. Firstly, Anne Tewnion is quite certain that her present recollection is reliable: she can remember meeting Bradburn coming back alone and even what he said when asked where Grieve was: 'He was "out" so I left him.' The coolness with which she, her husband and John Black received this news was to astonish her but she now realises that it was caused by the hypothermia from which they were all suffering. It is too striking a memory to be dismissed as imagination and, although those suffering from hypothermia commonly hallucinate, this does not have the nature of a hallucination. It does seem that there must be substance to this memory.

Why, then, should she have had a quite different recollection at the beginning of 1952? There is a possible explanation. The tragedy had only just happened and Grieve and the others had been laid to rest only a few days previously. It could have been difficult for Anne Tewnion to accept reality and reveal that they had simply abandoned Grieve, making no effort to go to his aid; after all, she, in common with almost everyone, knew nothing about hypothermia and its cerebral effects. It would have been much more comforting, both to Mrs Tewnion herself and to the relatives and friends of James Grieve, to indicate that the others had done what they could to assist Grieve at the end and, as a result, she may have unconsciously suppressed the truth and substituted a recollection more acceptable and comprehensible to her distressed state of mind. Later, when she had recovered and time had elapsed or perhaps when eventually she began to understand hypothermia and therefore also to understand their actions that day, she was able to allow the truth to return to her consciousness.

Secondly, there is the evidence in the Register of Corrected Entries. It recorded Grieve's place of death as 'about three miles east of Corrour Lodge' which is consistent with Mrs Tewnion's present recollection; if her memory of 1952 is right, the place of death should have been given as, 'about two miles east of Corrour Lodge'. Although the places of death of John Bradburn and John Black were interchanged in the Register, the distances from Corrour Lodge given for the three bodies other than Grieve were accurate and correspond with both of Anne Tewnion's memories. The interchanged places of death of Bradburn and Black could easily be explained by the fact that the men (whose names were, in any case, similar) were not known to any of those involved in recovering the bodies so the error may not be of much significance. On the other hand, it has to be said that the Register is not wholly reliable, especially when death occurs in the hills, although, since Grieve was no great distance from the readily identifiable feature of Corrour Lodge and the distances given for the other bodies were accurate, it is reasonable to posit that the Register should have been accurate with Grieve.

Death certificates were issued for none of the men. Dr Ronald Kennedy, one of the two physicians who attended Mrs Tewnion at Corrour Lodge, is named in the Register as certifying the deaths. His medical report and the police reports would have been sent to the procurator-fiscal in Fort William and he would have used these to provide New Register House with the information which was recorded in the Register. A report was submitted by P.C. William Stewart of Fort William and one would have been submitted by the policeman who arrived at Corrour station at 3.30 a.m. on the Monday morning in the company of the two doctors. Although the Northern Constabulary no longer have records extending back to the end of 1951, this policeman must have been the late P.C. William Fullerton of Spean Bridge on whose beat was Corrour and whose assistance had been requested by telephone from Corrour station the night before.

William Stewart cannot remember the presence at Corrour of P.C. Fullerton whom he knew well. However, it would have been nearing midday when Stewart and the Kinloss mountain rescue team reached Corrour Lodge and by then the lochside road was clear. It would have been sensible enough for Fullerton to return to Spean Bridge once he had carried out his police duties and, in the late morning, he may have departed from the Lodge in the Lodge lorry for Corrour station to catch a passing goods train and Stewart is now left unaware of his presence. If, as is almost certain, Fullerton arrived at Corrour Lodge before daybreak, it would be very surprising if he did not accompany the recovery team up the glen to the places where all four men were found: his duty as reporting police officer and his value as an able-bodied member of the recovery team would demand it. Certainly, later on P.C. Stewart was taken as far as the sheep fank where Black and Tewnion died. However, he went no further than this so his estimate of Grieve's place of death could be no more than an approximation. It is his recollection that this estimate was less than the 4.8km given in the Register but he acknowledges that his estimate could have been revised in the light of other evidence. The likelihood is that the places of death given in the Register came from P.C. Fullerton's report and he would have known fairly precisely how far they lay from the Lodge.

The side of the bivouac site on which Grieve died could be resolved if one of the surviving members of the recovery team present at both the finding of Grieve's body and the retrieving of the gear from the bivouac site could remember where the body lay in relation to the bivouac site but none of them can do so.

The third point which can be made about Anne Tewnion's two memories of Grieve's end is contained in the note which Robert MacLennan and Donald Mill took with them to Corrour station on the Sunday evening summoning medical and police assistance. This note, which is still in the possession of Christine Bainbridge (Donald Mill's widow), must have been written by Andrew Tait sometime after Anne Tewnion reached his cottage and is based on information which came from her at the time. It read:

Constable Fullerton, Spean Bridge
At 8.30 p.m. on Sat. a party of four men, one woman, left Corrour Lodge for Ben Alder Cottage. Apparently they were benighted. On Sunday afternoon about 2.30 p.m. the woman, Mrs Tewnion, returned alone saying two of her companions were dead and the other two missing. A search party found the bodies of three, all dead.

They are known to be: John Black, 115 Greengairs Ave., Glasgow S.W.1; John Bradburn, 151 (?) Castle St., Glasgow C1; Sydney Tewnion (husband of the woman). The fourth man, James Grieve of Greenock, is missing but it is believed he was left further up the hill exhausted.

Please do *not* inform press. Please bring a doctor to attend to Mrs Tewnion. May we bring in the bodies?

It is significant that the note reports Anne Tewnion as, 'saying two of her companions were dead and the other two missing'. She was certain that her husband and John Black were dead when she left them at the fank and, because she did not come upon the body of John Bradburn as she made her way from the fank to the Lodge, she described him as 'missing'. It is unlikely that she would also have described James Grieve as 'missing' if she had known where he lay and what had happened to him – as she would have done if her 1952 memory was true to the facts. That she described him as 'missing' suggests that she did not know where he was nor exactly what had happened to him and this is consistent with her present memory.

With reference to Grieve's end, the balance of probability points to Anne Tewnion's present memory being correct – that Grieve died when he was in the presence of Bradburn alone on the Benalder Cottage side of the bivouac site. Perhaps it can be said that, if her present memory is correct with regard to there having been a single bivouac place and to Grieve's collapsing when in the company of Bradburn alone, she may also be right in her recollection of the cooked breakfast and the rucksack straps being unfrozen. Nevertheless, there is scarcely any incontrovertible objective evidence against which to test either of the memories so that there can be no conclusive judgement.

The Loss of Five Men on Jock's Road. New Year, 1959

On New Year's Day 1959, five men set off from Braemar Youth Hostel to walk the 22km over Jock's Road to the youth hostel in Glen Doll, a small steep-sided glen at the head of Glen Clova in Angus taking its name from the Gaelic, 'dol' or 'dail' meaning 'meadow' or 'dale'. They did not reach their destination. All five came from Glasgow and were members of the Universal Hiking Club, a Roman Catholic club whose members, of whom there were about eighty in 1959, took themselves regularly into the wilder parts of the country on hiking and hill-walking expeditions. As a club it seems to have been well-organised and its members in general properly equipped. At the time of the tragedy, the Club's membership card showed that the president was Harry Duffin, an engineer with Rolls Royce in East Kilbride, the vice-president Frank Daly, an executive officer with the National Assistance Board, the secretary Robert McFaul, a teacher at Coatbridge Technical College, the hiking convener Joseph Devlin, a plasterer from Clydebank whose wife, Louise, was social convener, while one of the committee members was seventeen-year-old James Boyle, an apprentice marine fitter from Dennistoun in Glasgow who had been a member of the Club for two years.

These five men were the central figures in the drama which occupied the attentions of the press and the efforts of over a hundred searchers at the beginning of 1959. All the men, with the exception of young James Boyle, were experienced hikers and hill-walkers. Daly, who was in his mid-forties and the oldest of the group, had been an active hillman for about thirty years, with experience both in Scotland and on the continent. Devlin, Duffin and McFaul were in their mid-thirties. Devlin and his wife, Louise, often went hiking together with other members of the Club and in 1958 had enjoyed a hiking holiday in Switzerland and Italy; Duffin was a big man, over six feet tall, whose initial motive for joining the Club apparently was to reduce his weight and he became one of its most regular attenders; McFaul was one of the most experienced in the Club and was much trusted by the mother of

James Boyle. She said of him and the others in the *Scottish Daily Express* of
Monday, 5th January, 1959:

I have never worried about Jimmy. I would let him go anywhere with Robert
McFaul and the others. They were very cautious and would never do anything
foolhardy. . . .

The Universal Hiking Club had organised a large meet for the New Year
period. In total twenty-five members would be dispersed between Deeside
and the area of Glen Clova. On Saturday, 27th December, 1958, McFaul,
Devlin and Daly left Glasgow by the Perth train bound for upper Deeside.
They spent the next five days basing themselves in different youth hostels in
the area, the final two nights being spent in the Braemar hostel run by Marie
Ewan, the warden, with assistance from her husband, Robert, a bus driver,
and Edward O'Hara. The days were spent walking and exploring and it
seems that they made their way to the Braemar Youth Hostel by following
the old bridle path through Glen Tilt, part of which follows an old drove
road. Duffin and Boyle travelled from Glasgow to Braemar the following
Wednesday, the last day of the year, in readiness for the walk the next day to
Glendoll Youth Hostel where they would meet up with other members of the
Club who were to travel there on New Year's Day; these included Louise
Devlin. It was intended to finish the holiday with the combined group
walking over Capel Mount and the path across the hills to Ballater where
they would attend mass and meet the remaining members of the Club who
had spent the time in Deeside before the return journey to Glasgow.

Like Jock's Road, the Capel Mount (or Mounth) path is part of the old
Highland system of drove roads along which cattle were driven at a leisurely
pace to the great cattle fairs or trysts at Crieff and Falkirk. Along the Capel
Mount road came cattle from the gathering areas of Cabrach and Huntly
while Jock's Road served cattle collected from Speyside and places like
Deeside along the route. These two roads joined at the head of Glen Clova
from where the cattle travelled by way of Kirriemuir to their destinations.
Jock's Road is thought to have been named after a John Winters who, taking
the side of Lord Invercauld, challenged Lord Aberdeen over his claim to
possession of the road, with the eventual result for Winters that he had to
take refuge from the attentions of Lord Aberdeen at the top of Glen Doll.

Today, there is confusion about the time when the five men departed on
their fateful expedition. It is known that before leaving they attended mass
and received holy communion in St Andrew's Roman Catholic church in the
village but the time of the service is not certain. Mario Conti, bishop of
Aberdeen, says:

My Secretary has ex-
amined the appropriate
Directories and can give
the assurance that, at the
time of the accident, Mass
was said at St Andrew's,
Braemar, at 8 a.m. and 11
a.m. on Sundays and at 10
a.m. on holidays of obligation. The 1st of January
would be regarded as a
holiday of obligation and
therefore it would be
reasonable to assume Mass
was 10 a.m. It is just possible that, with it being a
public holiday, the Mass
times were as on a Sunday
even though the 1st of
January was a weekday.

On 1st January, 1959
mass was celebrated by
the Very Reverend
Canon Alexander Kerr:
he died in 1962. He was
succeeded by the late
Right Reverend Edward
Douglas, the retired
bishop of Motherwell,
and then by Father John
Copland in 1964. It is
very likely that, until
Canon Kerr's death,
New Year's Day con-
tinued to be regarded as
it had been in 1959 and
that this practice was
followed by the Right

Universal Hiking Club Party:
Jock's Road, 1st January, 1959

Reverend Douglas during his short incumbency of the parish. In Father
Copland's time in St Andrew's, 1st January, if it fell on a weekday, was

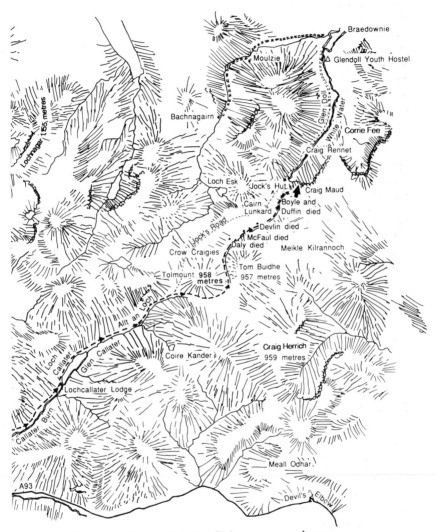

Route taken by the Universal Hiking Club party – – – – ▶ – – –

regarded as a holiday of obligation and mass was at 10.00 a.m. so it is reasonable to postulate that this was the time of mass on 1st January, 1959.

Nevertheless, Robert Ewan is sure that mass began at 8.00 a.m. and that the men returned to the hostel after the service for some breakfast. On the matter, he says:

> Early morning Mass and Holy Communion in the R.C. Church, Braemar, was at 08.00 hours and still is; the next service was not until 11.00 hours. I remember my wife and I wishing them luck on their way outside the hostel, never dreaming of the tragedy that lay ahead. Others who were acquainted with them through being frequent users of the hostel watched them leave on the road to Auchallater from the food lockers window. Sadly, these have all passed on.

Apparently, Robert Ewan saw the men turn left as they set off on their way; this direction would have taken them along the main A93 Braemar to Spittal of Glenshee road towards Auchallater, the home of Charles Smith, a sheep farmer, and his wife, where they would have left the main road and headed into Glen Callater. As Ewan remembers, the men departed at 9.00 a.m. or soon after. However, it is possible that Ewan, who is not Roman Catholic, is remembering the times of mass on Sundays – and 1st January, 1959 was a Thursday.

There were two references in the national daily press to the time when the men left Braemar: *The Courier and Advertiser* of Monday, 5th January, 1959 gave the time as 'about 9.30 a.m.', while *The Glasgow Herald* of the same day stated 'between 9.00 a.m. and 10.00 a.m.' The reporting in both newspapers was normally fairly reliable and therefore attention should be paid to them. There is, however, no indication of the source or sources of this information although it is likely that it was obtained from the youth hostel in Braemar, from either staff or hostellers. In addition to these two daily newspapers, the weekly journal, the *Glasgow Observer and Scottish Catholic Herald* of Friday, 9th January, 1959 in an article, rather defensive of the men, said that the party left 'about ten o'clock'. The reporter who wrote the article had been present at a meeting in Robert McFaul's house a few days after the accident, a meeting attended by thirty members of the Universal Hiking Club and by Father Patrick O'Donohoe, a priest from Forfar, who had comforted the men's relatives and friends who were present in Glen Doll at the time of the search. It is not stated who provided the 10.00 a.m. departure time but the inference is that it was Father O'Donohoe.

The R.A.F. Leuchars Search and Rescue dispatch to the Air Ministry gave 0900 hours. Flight Lieutenant (now Squadron Leader) Bill Brankin has the following to say about how this time was obtained:

All I can recollect from memory is that I interviewed the wives/girlfriends/friends of the missing party before any search plan took place. They informed me the men left Braemar Youth Hostel at 0900 hours on New Year's Day. If they [the men] were delayed or diverted, there was no evidence to that effect in my inquiries at the time. The support party of wives etc. was to drive round the mountains and meet the walkers at Glendoll Youth Hostel for the evening meal. I cannot with any conviction confirm where the group came from that I questioned but they certainly implied that some had travelled round the mountain by road. In fact, I understand they were principally responsible for raising the alarm.

Gwen Moffat, in her book, *Two Star Red*, published in 1964, says that there was a group from the Universal Hiking Club who were staying in Braemar Youth Hostel at the same time as the five men and who motored round to Glendoll Youth Hostel on New Year's Day to meet the men when they arrived. It is certain in Glendoll hostel a party from the Club, having travelled from Glasgow that day, were awaiting the arrival of the men: three men and eight women, one of these being Mrs Louise Devlin. However, there are several reasons for doubting the existence of a motoring group from the Club who had been staying at the youth hostel in Braemar and travelled to Glen Doll on the day of the tragedy, one of these being a statement from Robert Ewan:

I can confirm that there were most certainly no other members of the Universal Hiking Club at the Braemar Hostel who would have been travelling by road to Glen Doll. In those days, motor cars were taboo at youth hostels. Confusion may have arisen from the fact that the other part of the Club were already waiting at Glen Doll for the ill-fated lads whom they were intending to join prior to crossing over to Ballater.

There were other members of the Club staying elsewhere in the Deeside area and some of them may have travelled by road to Glen Doll on the day of the accident, perhaps calling at the Braemar Youth Hostel en route and being told that the five expeditionists had left at 9.00 a.m. If so, it seems that the members of the Club revised this time within a few days: otherwise it is difficult to account for the time of 'about ten o'clock' given to the reporter from the *Glasgow Observer and Scottish Catholic Herald* at the meeting in McFaul's house.

The Universal Hiking Club's report of the accident, also somewhat defensive of the men, was written some time after the event by James Reid, James Boyle's brother-in-law. It stated that the men had left Braemar Youth Hostel at 9.00 a.m. on the morning of 1st January and that they had attended

Braemar Youth Hostel.   *S.Y.H.A.*

mass and received holy communion in the church of St Andrew's. In addition, it said that Canon Kerr was the last person known to have seen them alive.

Although the time of departure from the youth hostel given in this report coincides with that from Robert Ewan, the inference to be made is that the men went to the church service after, and not before, leaving the hostel: if so, the Universal Hiking Club's report suggested a departure time from the village considerably after 9.00 a.m. Indeed, if mass was at 10.00 a.m., the men could not have left Braemar until much closer to 11.00 a.m. However, there is the possibility that the report said that Canon Kerr, rather than Robert Ewan and his wife, was the last person known to have seen the men alive because Reid was concerned for the sensibilities of the relatives and friends of the dead men.

Colin McIntosh, a Roman Catholic and long time resident of Braemar, was one of those involved in the search for the men. His brother-in-law, Alec Walker, was barman in the Invercauld Arms Hotel in the village. McIntosh has made an investigation which has provided the following information. He says.

There was only one Mass on New Year's Day [1959] and that was at 10 a.m. This the men attended. Mass ended at approximately 10.20-10.30. Canon Kerr spoke to them after Mass and advised them against carrying out their intended hike. They were present in the Public Bar of the Invercauld Arms Hotel at opening time – approximately 10.30 a.m. – and they left at about 11 a.m.

Colin McIntosh is quite specific in his details of what the men did and there is independent evidence that Canon Kerr tried to dissuade the men from undertaking their expedition because of the weather. Father (now Monsignor) John Copland, who moved to the parish in May 1964, has made a reconstruction of events on the morning of New Year's Day based on what people in Braemar told him. He says:

When they [the men] left the hostel, they would have taken their packs with them and gone on to the ten o'clock Mass at St Andrew's. On leaving the church approximately at 10.45 a.m. they looked in at the bar of the Invercauld where Mr Alec Walker, the barman at that time, remembers them. Some time after eleven they would have set off.

Both Monsignor Copland and Deacon Futers of the Diocesan Office in St Mary's Cathedral, Aberdeen, are of the opinion that the service would have been of a somewhat longer duration than the twenty to thirty minutes estimated by McIntosh and may have lasted for about forty-five minutes. If so, the men could not have arrived at the hotel much before 11.00 a.m. nor left much before 11.30 a.m.

Charles Smith, the sheep farmer at Auchallater, was working with his sheep that day bringing them down from the hillsides to the lower ground. He started at 8.30 a.m. and worked more or less continuously until about 3.30 p.m., all the time in the general area of his house. He could see the main road and the track to Lochcallater Lodge which meets the main road beside Auchallater. At about 12.15 p.m., he saw five men with rucksacks making their way past his house and wondered where they were going in the deteriorating weather. He is quite sure that it was the party who were later to be reported missing; they were the only party he saw going along the track to the Lodge and it is unlikely that he would have failed to notice another group. This fits well with the evidence coming from Colin McIntosh, the more especially if it is accepted that the church service lasted longer than McIntosh indicates. It would have taken the men about forty minutes to walk the 3km from Braemar to Auchallater. If they left the village at about 11.30 a.m., they would have been at Auchallater at approximately 12.15 p.m., the time when, as he recollects, Charles Smith saw the five passing his house.

The best sense that can be made of the confusing picture is that the party

Auchallater Farmhouse.   *Charles Smith*

did leave the youth hostel in Braemar at 9.00 a.m. or soon after but, in spite
of what Robert Ewan says, without attending mass. It does seem that mass
was at 10.00 a.m. It was traditional for members of the Universal Hiking
Club to attend mass whenever they could when they were away and the men
may have been somewhat uneasy at missing the service, particularly since it
was New Year's Day, but, owing to the weather and to the length of their
route which was across relatively remote terrain, they decided to leave
without attending the service. However, a short time after getting under way,
they reconsidered the position and, unknown to Robert Ewan and the others
in the youth hostel, decided to return to the village and go to 10.00 a.m. mass
where, of course, they were seen by others and, later, by Alec Walker in the
Invercauld Arms Hotel which they left probably about 11.30 a.m.

   They had before them a walk of 22km, the first 3km of which were along
the main A93 Braemar to Spittal of Glenshee road. At Auchallater
farmhouse they turned off into Glen Callater. There was, and is, a private
road going to Lochcallater Lodge, standing at the west end of Loch Callater,
and this they followed with the Callater Burn, the wide outflow of the loch,
on their right. At the Lodge, which was unoccupied in winter, they would
have taken the footpath along the north side of the loch and proceeded up

Glen Callater, following the line of the stream called Allt an Loch. This took them past the attractive Coire Kander on the west side of the glen and eventually brought them to the head of the glen which is a steep sided corrie named Coire Breac, dominated by the bulk of Tolmount standing at a height of 958m.

To understand the situation that day, it is necessary to provide some heights and distances. By the time the men had reached the headwall of the corrie they had travelled almost 13km and ascended gradually to a height of 530m from their starting height at Braemar of about 335m, a modest increase of 195m. At this point, however, they had to ascend the headwall of the corrie, a steep climb of about 230m in a distance of 800 metres and from there make a gradual ascent across the plateau beyond to the summit of the path at about 915m, 2km further on. They would then be just over 15km from Braemar and about 7km from Glendoll Youth Hostel, the former Glendoll Lodge, which lay mainly downhill from the summit of the path.

Because it was an old drove road, the path from Loch Callater to the youth hostel in Glen Doll was fairly well-defined in most places and generally visible in good conditions when the ground was free from snow. However, the section over the summit of the route was indistinct and, although marked by some rusted iron strainer posts at irregular intervals, care had to be taken, even in the summer, in bad weather and poor visibility not to lose line of the track after it climbed out of Coire Breac on to the plateau. It was not uncommon for walkers to take the wrong direction and head for Glen Isla to the south instead of south-east towards Glen Doll. Almost three years before, in late March 1956, a nineteen-year-old student from Newcastle, Malcolm Bruce, journeying alone from Braemar to Glen Doll, had reached the plateau safely but had taken this wrong turning and become lost. His body was found a month later, about 8km from Tulchan Lodge in Glen Isla, on a cliff face high on the 959m Craig Herrich which overlooks Caenlochan Glen. Jim MacGregor, the Tulchan stalker, saw several crows working on something on the crags and, on going to investigate, he found the body of the unfortunate young man. As a measure of the navigational dangers of the Jock's Road route in winter, it is worth quoting from the accident report on the loss of the five members of the Universal Hiking Club in the S.M.C.J. (Volume XXVI, May 1959):

> The existence of an old drove road does not imply a continuous path, even in summer. In a blizzard there is a stretch of 2 or 3 miles with no landmarks at all, and every chance of failing to hit off the descent into Glen Doll.

The five friends seem to have been fairly well equipped. This was stated both by the Ewans and Edward O'Hara, and by the searchers who, three days later, were to find the body of James Boyle. It is known that they had waterproof clothing, proper walking boots, gloves, sleeping-bags, primus stoves, paraffin, dixies, compasses and food. Louise Devlin was of the opinion that they would not have been carring much food, presumably because there would be ample food for them when they arrived at Glendoll Youth Hostel and they would need to carry only sufficient for their day's walk. However, Edward O'Hara said that the men left with plenty of provisions and this was given some confirmation by part of the report on the accident in the *Glasgow Observer and Scottish Catholic Herald* of Friday, 9th January, 1959.

The men may not have been as well equipped as they might have been, however. While they had waterproof jackets (which Robert Ewan referred to as 'plastic overjackets' and which included a rather longer plastic Pac-o-mac type of raincoat) and capes (which also seem to have been made of a plastic material), Robert Ewan recalls that, as the men made ready to leave the youth hostel in weather that had turned raw, cold and wet, he noticed an absence of waterproof leg coverings. Boyle's only protection for his legs were trousers of a thick worsted material; these may have been adequate for dry conditions but in the wet they would probably have absorbed a lot of moisture. The men were to be confronted by rain and heavy sleet in Glen Callater and driving wet snow at higher levels; in these conditions waterproof overtrousers would have been indispensable. Not only must their trousers have become saturated but the dampness would have been drawn up into the rest of their clothing no matter how waterproof their anoraks may have been. Once this happened, their clothes would have been a constant drain on their body heat, engaged as it would be in the unequal battle of drying them out.

Furthermore, it is not known how windproof were their outer garments, but, judging from the descriptions given of them, they were certainly inadequate for the extreme conditions which overtook them on the plateau. If so, the men must have suffered severely from the biting wind which would have cut through their clothing causing even greater loss of heat. There is also doubt about how much protection the men had for their heads. During the extensive search, a pack which contained a beret was found buried in the snow. When McFaul was found buried under the snow two months after he died, the first sign the searchers had of his presence was his hair and when Devlin was found his hair was detached from his head. Neither was wearing any kind of head covering. Certainly, a glove, which must have belonged to one of the party, was found lying in the snow near the spot where Boyle was discovered. But it is not clear how well supplied with gloves was the party as a whole. They did not have ice-axes, even though there was a good deal of old snow on their route and these might be needed.

It is to be presumed that they carried maps as well as compasses. However, according to Edward O'Hara in *The Scotsman* of Tuesday, 6th January, their compasses were of a German prismatic type. Prismatic compasses give bearings precise to a degree but are much more difficult to use accurately in the field, especially in bad conditions, than the Silva type of compass in general use today. Silva compasses, which incorporate a protractor and ruler into their design for ease of operation, were introduced into the United Kingdom about 1938 and were widely used by 1959 so it would be surprising if the party was not equipped with at least one Silva compass. However, if the men were dependent solely on prismatic compasses, unless they had calculated all the bearings they would require before leaving Braemar Youth Hostel, it is highly unlikely that, in the conditions they faced, their compasses could have been used to provide accurate directions, especially once they had deviated from their intended route. In these circumstances, their compasses could have given them no more than an approximate direction to follow and it would have been quite easy to have taken a wrong course. In view of the fact that they did not foresee any serious problem in reaching Glendoll Youth Hostel, it is fairly certain that they departed from Braemar without having calculated any compass bearings they were going to need.

They carried with them items of equipment which could have served them well in the event of an enforced bivouac. It is known that they had sleeping-bags, primus stoves, paraffin and dixies as well as capes. The sleeping-bags were carried because they were using them in the youth hostels and the primus stoves, paraffin and dixies were taken perhaps for a 'drum up' during their walks and perhaps also for use in the youth hostels since these might be busy and the men may have preferred not to queue for cooking. These items provided them with the necessaries for a reasonable bivouac if they could find shelter from the weather. In spite of their late departure from Braemar, it is quite evident that they had no thought of spending the night in the open and it is equally evident that, when faced with a possible bivouac, the prospect of enduring a night in the storm that was to engulf them would have been thoroughly unpleasant. But the four older men were seasoned campaigners in the hills and could be expected to be willing to sit out the storm in as protected a place as they could find.

Two other matters are deserving of comment. The first is the time of their departure from Braemar. The men had a long route of 22km with a total ascent of at least 610m ahead of them across wild country, quite uninhabited after they had left the main road at Auchallater. It was a route which demanded commitment and which offered no safe escape routes once they had attained the plateau above the headwall of Coire Breac. Even in good conditions, six and a half hours would be required to make the journey to the Glendoll Youth Hostel so that, if they left Braemar at 11.30 a.m., they could not expect to arrive at their destination until 6.00 p.m., an hour after night had fallen. If conditions became poor, they would need correspondingly more time. It can only be concluded that they were of the opinion that the route would provide no particular problems and that there would be little difficulty in following the final section of the Jock's Road path in the dark. Even if they left at 9.00 a.m., as Robert Ewan thinks, they would not arrive at the Glendoll hostel much before the light was beginning to fail. Although in summer the route from Braemar to Glen Doll over Jock's Road may be no more than an easy, if long, walk, in winter it can call for a good standard of mountaincraft and a knowledge of winter conditions, among which is a recognition of the many factors which can lead to unexpected, and sometimes lengthy, delays.

The second matter deserving comment concerns the loads they were bearing. They may have been fairly well equipped, but some of what they carried was heavy and superfluous to their needs in making the actual crossing, while some of the items were cumbersome and awkward to carry. It has already been said that the sleeping-bags, and perhaps the primus stoves, paraffin and dixies, were taken chiefly for their needs and comforts at the youth hostels. It is quite possible that their packs contained other youth hostel extras, such as cutlery, cups and plates. Certainly McFaul was found still holding a cup and a small bottle of milk and this confirms not only that some crockery was carried but also such commodities as milk, an additional weight hardly essential to the journey. The primus stoves and paraffin would be especially cumbersome and there is some evidence that these were carried in small knapsacks, separate from the men's main rucksacks. This would increase the discomfort of the men's loads. The carrying of excessive equipment and its consequent weight into the hills can be as dangerous as not taking sufficient; the skill is to take enough but not too much. Although it is understandable that there might be a need for extra items to be taken for their stays in the youth hostels, this expedition was not the best to choose if it could not be undertaken without them.

Substantial amounts of snow already lay on the higher ground. Malcolm Douglas, warden of the Cairngorms National Nature Reserve, was one of the large party of searchers who went out from Braemar on Sunday, 4th January. Five of this group, including Douglas, went as far as Tolmount, following footprints which were quite visible in the snow. It is almost certain that these belonged to the missing men. In an account of their adventures, given in *The Scotsman* on Monday, 5th January, Douglas said:

> There were drifts five to six feet deep of compressed snow and drifts of fresh snow three feet deep in places.

The compressed snow was old and its depth indicates that the higher levels, at least, had a good covering of snow. Both Robert and Marie Ewan were to some extent unhappy about the men's intentions and advised them to reconsider their plans, but not to the extent reported in the press. Ewan has the following to say:

> I had to contradict, at the fiscal's enquiry in Aberdeen [at which the Ewans and P.C. William Low, the local Braemar policeman, were interviewed], exaggerated press reports about me giving them warning of blizzard conditions in the weather forecasts. This just was not quite true. In those days weather forecasts were more of a general pattern and were normally taken with a pinch of salt. To explain how the misunderstanding arose was when the boys were preparing to leave it had turned into a miserable wet morning, and noting the absence of waterproof leg coverings I did say maybe it would be more comfortable to wait another day in the hope that the weather might dry up a bit. This little conversation was overheard by one hosteller and completely misinterpreted to the press.

Care has to be exercised in handling the meteorological data for 1st January if a proper understanding of the weather which faced the five men is to be had. Marjory Roy has examined the data and she has the following observations to make:

> There is no major problem in understanding what is likely to have happened if one interpolates between the weather maps for 12.00 G.M.T. and 18.00 G.M.T. on 1st January. At 06.00 G.M.T. the weather map shows that a frontal system was crossing the British Isles with an occluded front clearing the Braemar area about this time and a wave was beginning to develop on the cold front which was trailing out to the west. By 12.00 G.M.T. this wave had developed into a small depression which deepened as it approached northwest Scotland. It continued to deepen as it crossed northern Scotland, with its centre close to Wick by 18.00 G.M.T., and it then continued eastwards across the North Sea towards Norway. As the centre passed to the north of the Eastern Grampians the pressure gradient over the area would have tightened and the winds increased rapidly from the southwest, though there may have been a short

period during the morning after the passage of the occlusion when it was dry with relatively light winds. It is likely that the Tolmount area was briefly within the warm sector during the afternoon with temperatures on the plateau rising to around or even above freezing point. Cloud would have covered all high ground and there would have been whiteout conditions. Precipitation on the plateau was probably of wet snow or sleet until after the cold front went through in the early evening. Behind the cold front there would have been squally showers of snow and hail with winds veering into the west and then northwest and gradually moderating overnight. . . . Winds were likely to have been of violent storm force 11 over the plateau. . . .

Unfortunately the storm was at its most severe just when the party were at the most difficult part of the route, where good navigation was essential. I doubt very much if any advance warning would have been issued to skiers since the wave developed so quickly and it was only probably by mid-day that it was obvious that it was going to be so stormy. There might have been one issued about that time or during the afternoon. The radiosonde ascents at mid-day at Aldergrove and Leuchars recorded freezing levels of around 1,000m and 950m respectively, which is slightly above the highest point on the Tolmount route. Consequently although temperatures on the plateau at that time would have been close to freezing point I am pretty sure that down in Glen Callater at about 550m temperatures would have been significantly above freezing and any precipitation would have been of rain or at worst sleet. The scenario that I envisage is that they would have been well sheltered from the wind and would not have been aware that it had increased until they climbed out on to the plateau. Also they would not have encountered falling snow until they were well up on the climb. . . . Once the cold front went through in the early evening temperatures fell rapidly. . . .

The temperature on the plateau would have been at freezing level at midday and about −1.5°C by 6.00 p.m. Clearly, with the wind reaching Violent Storm Force Eleven, the wind-chill factor was very high and this would have made the equivalent still air temperature on the plateau about −25°C when the men were at that altitude – and the misery of their journey was compounded by the blizzard with which they had to contend.

Other contemporary evidence shows how strong was the wind and, over the higher ground, how unpleasant were the conditions. For instance, *The Courier and Advertiser* of Friday, 2nd January reported that the wind had taken the roof off the stand at Forfar Athletic's football ground. More relevant to the conditions which were to confront the Universal Hiking Club party was the account given by the newspaper of the situation on the slopes of Meall Odhar, near the Devil's Elbow on the Braemar to Spittal of Glenshee road. Meall Odhar, which was a popular ski-ing venue, stands at a similar height to the plateau crossed by Jock's Road from which it is only 8km distant to the south-west. There, members of Dundee Ski Club faced winds blowing with an estimated speed of between 80 and 100km/h and carrying a mixture of snow, sleet and rain which blocked the road. The following day's issue of the same newspaper reported that cars had been trapped at the Devil's Elbow by a blizzard which had raged for two days since early on 1st January, with the snow being blown back across the road as soon as the snowploughs had passed.

The men, or at least some of them, had made the crossing from the youth hostel at Braemar to the one in Glen Doll the previous September and this may have convinced them that they could accomplish the journey safely in spite of the weather as it was when they left Braemar and the amount of snow on the heights: they were, as they thought, well enough equipped. Indeed, had the weather been more normal almost certainly they would have done so. The storm to come was the worst for many years in the opinion of the people of Braemar. The storm, which brought large accumulations of snow, lasted more or less continuously for two days during which time the winds on the plateau probably reached 110km/h at times; on the Beaufort scale this is almost Hurricane Force Twelve.

If the men left Braemar at about 11.30 a.m., they could not have been much beyond the east end of Loch Callater, 10km from Braemar Youth Hostel, by 2.00 p.m. by which time the weather had deteriorated considerably. Charles Smith, who saw the men pass Auchallater at about 12.15 p.m., says that by 2.00 p.m. heavy sleet was falling. It is even possible that the party were no further than Lochcallater Lodge at the west end of the loch by 2.00 p.m. because a large number of footprints were found by searchers at the stables of the Lodge, indicating that the men had spent some time there. The men's clothing must have been already quite wet by the time of the onset of the heavy sleet and the weather prospects were becoming more depressing. Their resolution to continue on the proposed route to Glen Doll was a most serious error of judgement. Had they retreated down Glen Callater, there can be no doubt that they would have lived. If the men did consider the matter, why did they elect to continue? The following reasons can be advanced.

(1) They had arranged to meet Louise Devlin and their friends at Glendoll Youth Hostel in the evening. If they returned to Braemar, it would be difficult to communicate this decision to those in Glen Doll because the youth hostel there had no telephone and it was in a remote area. This would cause Mrs Devlin and the others unnecessary worry and it might be some time before their minds could be put at ease. There was also a possibility that their friends would mount a needless search for them, perhaps at some personal risk. However, if they returned to Braemar, the men could have

contacted the Kirriemuir police who would probably have been able to notify the youth hostel of the change of plan. It may be that the men were unsure if the police would be willing or able to do so or perhaps they were disinclined to involve the police.

(2) They were almost certainly misled by the relatively calm weather in the glen into thinking that conditions higher up would present no particular problems. They do not seem to have been properly alert to the difficulties of accurate navigation over the plateau which was cloud covered and where, as they should have realised, it would be snowing. Throughout the sad story of the loss of these five men there does appear to be a fairly constant theme of lack of winter mountain experience and awareness of the perils of that season. It is true that development of skills requires new and more testing situations but these have to be controlled. It is inconceivable that the men deliberately made this journey into the wildest of weather to extend their experience: they simply did not understand how dreadful was the challenge they were taking up.

(3) Having set off on an expedition, it can be difficult to make the decision to abandon it. Not only does it entail a change of plan which may cause problems, but it also creates a sense of failure: one has been defeated, perhaps allowed oneself to be defeated, by nature or by the elements when a little courage might be rewarded with success. The temptation is to continue. The greater the delay in making a decision to retreat, the more difficult it can be to make that decision and the point can be reached when it has become too late.

The party continued along Glen Callater and reached Coire Breac at the head of the glen. By then it must have been about 3.00 p.m. and there would be no more than, at most, two hours of daylight left. They had been following a south-easterly course as they walked along the glen but they had to turn east to follow Jock's Road up the steep ascent out of Coire Breac. They did not do this; rather they continued in a south-easterly direction and began climbing the slope leading to the summit of Tolmount. When they reached the craggy ground about 150m from the top they veered to the south-west, thus skirting the summit, and then turned south-east again to bring them down into the glen of the White Water.

Why did the men turn off Jock's Road? As the newspapers said and as people thought at the time, they may have taken 'a wrong turning' and lost the line of Jock's Road. This is, indeed, the most likely explanation. The weather was continuing to deteriorate and much of the ground above was concealed in cloud, sleet and snow. Accurate navigation would demand constant compass work. Not only were the weather and the time against them, but they must have been finding themselves growing very cold and any delays would exacerbate this. When the men reached Coire Breac, it is more than likely that they took only an approximate bearing of the direction in which they should go and then wandered away from it. Once they reached the higher ground, the severe buffeting from the wind would have added to the men's confusion and disorientation.

However, there is an alternative explanation of the men's action in deviating from Jock's Road. It is possible that it was calculated and intentional. The men who had covered the route the previous September would have known from that visit that, once they reached the plateau above, the next 3km of Jock's Road traversed the exposed high ground before descending fairly steeply at and beyond Cairn Lunkard towards upper Glen Doll. When they deviated from Jock's Road they were still in the shelter of Coire Breac and probably still ignorant of the true violence of the storm above. However, they may have appreciated that, in the very poor visibility, navigation along Jock's Road, whose topography over this section was so ill-defined, might be difficult and that it would be safer to go over the summit area of Tolmount and down into the glen of the White Water which could be followed towards Glen Doll. When they reached the craggy terrain below the top of Tolmount they were forced to contour round the summit. That they chose the southern side which forced them to struggle into the fierce wind may indicate that they found they had more control over their progress going into the wind than they would have had with it behind them.

The route would be navigationally simpler than continuing along Jock's Road since the men would follow down the fairly well-defined glen with its stream which would take them in the direction of Glen Doll. Although the visibility would not be much better than it was on the higher ground, so long as the men ensured that they journeyed on approximately correct bearings – and this they could certainly achieve with prismatic compasses – and maintained a constantly downward path, they had a good chance of navigating successfully towards Glen Doll and its youth hostel. In distance there was little to choose between the two routes and, by skirting the summit of Tolmount, there was little difference in the height which had to be climbed. There was one main danger in taking this route and great care would have to be exercised in the blizzard and darkness to avoid it. The glen down which the White Water flows lies parallel to Jock's Road which is a short distance to the north. After 3km, the glen drops steeply beside the precipices of Craig Maud into upper Glen Doll and the stream plunges down the White Water waterfall. Charles Oswald, one of the men sent by the earl of Airlie to assist in the later search, was quoted in *The Courier and Advertiser* of Tuesday, 6th January as saying of the steep gully used by the White Water waterfall: 'That is an awful gully at the best of times. It is a terrible gorge just now filled with snow.'

Even in clear weather this descent has to be made with care; it would be an extremely hazardous undertaking in a blizzard where visibility would be little more than several metres. It would be much worse in the dark. However, it was not necessary to take this line down into Glen Doll because, for almost 1km before reaching the point of danger, Jock's Road, albeit under snow, would be within 250 metres to the north. This could then be followed down Glen Doll to the youth hostel. It cannot be known if the men knew where they were nor, if they did, if they were aware of the danger that lurked in wait at Craig Maud. If they realised that they had found the glen of the White Water, it is likely that they knew of the danger and that they intended to regain Jock's Road before reaching it. Their main problems would be estimating when to make for the track and knowing when they had found it. However, since it would have been very difficult to follow Jock's Road down from high on the plateau, this second problem was perhaps not of great moment to the men. There might be one other problem to confront them once they reached the point where they should endeavour to regain the track: would they have enough energy and strength of will to climb through the lying snow the 30m or so to reach the track?

As they climbed Tolmount out of Coire Breac they would have become increasingly subjected to the wind and the sleet would have been changing to wet snow. The conditions, combined with the steepness of the ground and the weight and probable discomfort of their packs, must have made for hard going. As they moved out of the shelter of Glen Callater, they would have faced the full intensity of the storm, the driving precipitation reducing visibility to only a few metres and they may have had to contend with white-out. The snow would discover any chinks in their clothing; in addition, it seems that they were not equipped with gaiters so that, before long, their boots would fill with snow. The wind was the chief enemy: it would have made progress extremely difficult and exhausting and may well have further disoriented them; it would chill them more quickly than the blizzard itself ever could; and, combined with the snow, it would obstruct breathing and obscure the way ahead.

They could still have turned back when they realised how appalling were the conditions separating them from their destination; if they had, they might have survived, although there must have been an increasing risk of some of the party becoming hypothermic as they made their way back along Glen Callater. However, they would escape from the violent wind and the worst of the blizzard and, in the event of an emergency, they should be able to find some shelter at the unoccupied Lochcallater Lodge; they would certainly find shelter at Auchallater with Charles Smith and his wife. However, even if they did consider a retreat once they were faced with the full fury of the storm, they would probably have decided against it. They would have been influenced by the fact that they were almost 14km from Braemar and only about 8km from the Glendoll hostel where Mrs Devlin and their friends would become worried if they did not arrive. In addition, apart from the greater distance to Braemar, a retreat in that direction would entail a longer time spent navigating in the dark. Also, in view of their experience of the weather in Glen Callater, they may have thought that they would escape from the extreme conditions once they lost some height on the other side of the plateau.

By the time they began their descent from Tolmount towards the glen of the White Water it must have been close to 4.00 p.m. This gave them little more than an hour of daylight, in the most atrocious of weather, to cover the remaining distance of 8km to the safety of Glendoll Youth Hostel, not just their destination but, apart from the old wooden refuge known as Jock's Hut which would be difficult to find in a blizzard, also the nearest habitation. If the wind was their chief enemy, time was its close ally. When they began their ascent out of Glen Callater they must have known that they would not reach Glendoll Youth Hostel before nightfall; when they began their descent into the glen of the White Water the awful fear that they might not reach it at all may have entered their minds.

While this drama was being played out, the Glen Doll contingent of the Universal Hiking Club, including Louise Devlin, were travelling from Glasgow to reach the youth hostel during the afternoon in readiness for the arrival of their five companions. Time passed, the storm continued and the temperature began falling as the wind veered through west into the north-west. As the cold front passed through in the early evening, the sleet and wet snow in the area of Glendoll Youth Hostel changed to dry snow. Still the men did not arrive and worries increased. Had they not set out from Braemar after all? Or had they turned back and were spending another night in the youth hostel on the other side of the Mounth? Or were they out there in the blizzard somewhere along Jock's Road? Neither the youth hostel in Braemar, nor the one in Glen Doll had a telephone. There was one near the

Glendoll Youth Hostel.   *S.Y.H.A.*

Glendoll Youth Hostel in the home of George Thow, the Glen Doll head forester, and his wife, Margeret. Indeed, it was the only telephone in the area, the next one being in a hotel 6km distant down Glen Clova. No attempt was made to reach Braemar by telephone on the Thursday night and by the time Mrs Devlin tried to do so on the Friday morning, the telephone lines were out of order because of the blizzard which had also blocked the road out of Glen Clova. Eventually, she was able to contact Braemar on Saturday morning when her worst fears were confirmed and she communicated with the police in Kirriemuir.

No search was made for the men on the Friday. At that time there was no certainty that they were in the white wilderness between Glen Doll and Braemar: assuming that a motoring group from the Universal Hiking Club *had* brought the news that the men had left Braemar at 9.00 a.m., there was the possibility that they had turned back in the face of the deteriorating weather. Moreover, the blizzard continued unrelentingly for the whole of the day and, even if it were known that the men were out in the storm, there would be few people with sufficient competence and knowledge of the area available to mount a search. Added to this, the Glen Clova road was blocked by snow. On Saturday afternoon, however, once it had been ascertained that the men were seriously overdue, a party of local gamekeepers, stalkers and shepherds with dogs, together with some hostellers, made a limited search which took them as far as Jock's Hut, but without finding any trace of the missing men whose chances of survival were by then extremely small, unless they had been able to find shelter somewhere. Meanwhile, the police in conjunction with R.A.F. mountain rescue units were preparing for a major sweep of the whole area from Glen Doll to Braemar the following day. P.C. (now ex-Inspector) Thomas Deas, who played an active part in the extended search for the men, recalls being dispatched on his motor-cycle to contact all local gamekeepers and stalkers so as to have as many as possible on the search on the Sunday.

The operation was under the overall control of Superintendent Alexander Knight of Angus County Police with assistance from Inspector Walter Hutcheon. The R.A.F. team from Leuchars arrived in Glen Clova on Saturday night and made camp about 1km from Glendoll Youth Hostel, alongside the road leading to Moulzie farm. A radio signals van was put in position beside the hostel which itself became the headquarters of the search operation. The warden, Mrs Baxter, went to great efforts to cater for the large number of searchers involved. Full co-operation was given by the Thows who allowed their telephone to be used by the police. The radio van would, it was hoped, provide communication between search headquarters and the individual teams in the field, all of whom were equipped with walkie-talkie sets, as these radios were then popularly called. In the event, this radio contact was of limited use since the area was notorious for poor communications and this was made worse by the extreme weather which existed during much of the period. Indeed, on occasions a man had to be sent to one of the nearby hilltops to relay messages – a most unenviable task in the conditions. The radio van, however, did perform well in maintaining links with the R.A.F. Northern Rescue Centre at Pitreavie Castle in Fife and this helped co-ordinate the efforts being made by the helicopters with those being made by the teams on the ground. As with radio communications in the area, the cruel weather limited the effective contribution that the helicopters could make.

In the three days from Sunday to Tuesday when the search was abandoned, over a hundred searchers took part, the main contingents being mountain rescue teams from the R.A.F. bases at Leuchars and Kinloss and one from the naval base at Arbroath, H.M.S. Condor, together with men from the Angus police. In addition, help was rendered by members of the Glasgow Ski and Outdoor Club who were staying at the hostel, members of the Carn Dearg Mountaineering Club whose members came largely from the Dundee and Angus areas, local gamekeepers, stalkers and estate workers. Among this large band of willing helpers was the well-known hillman, Davie Glen, who was close to fifty and lived in an old railway carriage at Tealing, near Dundee, and who knew the hills of the area better than anyone. It was his efforts in the subsequent weeks which were to be paramount in finding three of the bodies. While the R.A.F. contingents camped in the neighbourhood in conditions that must have tested the stoutest heart, other searchers were accommodated overnight in the youth hostel. In this way the search parties could be ready to set out at first light and not have the worry of facing blocked roads.

The search on Sunday started at 9.00 a.m. The omens were unfavourable: the gale force wind, which had eased on Saturday, had returned to create again the blizzard conditions which had dominated the weather during the first two days of the year. The weather prevented much use of the helicopter which took off from Leuchars: it hovered over the search area for a short time before being forced back to base where it remained grounded for the rest of the day. Five search parties were involved, one of these following the men's route from Braemar.

The Braemar party numbered about thirty and included police, stalkers, workers from the Invercauld estate, skiers and climbers, and hostellers from Braemar Youth Hostel. They followed the men's route along Glen Callater and were able to pick out in the snow footsteps which they were sure were those of the men. The footprints had been made in soft, wet snow, partly formed from the sleet which had fallen during the time when the missing party had made its way up the glen and partly from previous snowfall. To some extent because of the north-westerly wind which blew down the glen, these footprints had not completely filled with the snow which subsequently fell and they remained as shallow saucer-shaped depressions. These had been made the more permanent through having frozen in the colder weather. When the search party reached Coire Breac, five men, including Charles Smith, Colin McIntosh and Malcolm Douglas, left the main group and followed the footprints towards the top of Tolmount. They traced them over the summit area and on beyond the Aberdeenshire/Angus boundary but had to abandon any attempt to follow the footprints any further because of the intensifying storm. However, the efforts of this search party had made it clear that the missing men had gone down the glen of the White Water. It had been planned that the Braemar party would meet up with the other search parties but the weather precluded this. In any case, if they had been able to continue onwards, they would have followed the glen of the White

Water and this would have taken them in a direction different from that intended.

One of the other four parties was a mixed R.A.F. and civilian team under the direction of an R.A.F. corporal. The bearded Davie Glen was a member of this large search party. They went north, following the glen down which flow the upper waters of the River South Esk. This took them past the R.A.F. camp and on beyond Moulzie; then they bore eastwards to the ruined shooting lodge of Bachnagairn, 2km further on, after which they turned southwards towards Loch Esk and onwards to reach Jock's Road. There they would rendezvous at Jock's Hut with the team searching Glen Doll itself. This hut was not to remain standing much longer; it collapsed, probably as a result of old age and the attentions of the deer. Davie Glen was himself instrumental in having another hut erected and he did much of the building himself. This new refuge was a stone structure with a sod roof and it stands about 500 metres to the north-west of the old wooden hut; it is affectionately known as 'Davie's Bourach'. The area covered by this mixed search party may seem rather far to the north of where the men were likely to be. However, it was considered that there was a good chance in the conditions prevailing on 1st January that the men, when they reached the plateau, would have continued on an easterly course, instead of veering to the south-south-east, the more especially with the wind tending to drive them in that direction. In this way the men would have descended the wide and shallow glen which contains Loch Esk and from there they may have worked their way in the same general direction along the upper waters of the River South Esk and past Bachnagairn. The distance travelled by this team to reach the hut was fully 11km but nothing was found of the men. Thomas Deas was one of the party and he well remembers the weather:

The wind returned on the Sunday. It was, without doubt, the worst day I ever spent on the hills. The whole of the right side of my face became clogged solid with snow and ice particles within a very short time. The better kitted R.A.F. lads were even finding it very hard going.

A second team set out from Glendoll Youth Hostel to ascend the high ground immediately to the south of Glen Doll. They traversed the ground above Corrie Fee, the large southern corrie of Glen Doll, with its waterfalls and long stretches of crags and, in summer, its green meadows which were, no doubt, grazed by the cattle in the days of droving. Then they travelled further north-westwards to Meikle Kilrannoch from where they dropped down to join Jock's Road for the return to base. However, as with the R.A.F. and civilian team, they found no evidence of the missing men.

Tulchan Lodge lies near the head of Glen Isla some distance to the south of the main search area and belonged to the earl of Airlie. From there, a party under Jim MacGregor, the earl's stalker, proceeded northwards to the head of Glen Isla and then eastwards across the hills in the direction of Glen Clova. In this way they would cover ground the men might have taken if they had turned south from their intended route in the way that the nineteen-year-old Newcastle student, Malcolm Bruce, had done three years before. It was believed that the five men, or some of them, could have made this mistake and wandered towards either Glen Isla or Glen Prosen and MacGregor's task was to investigate this possibility. The discovery of the footprints across Tolmount by the Braemar search party later that day made it almost certain that none of the men had strayed in that direction and there was some confirmation of this when a body was found at the head of Glen Doll the same day.

The fourth team, under the control of Sergeant Sykes of the R.A.F., left the youth hostel in Glen Doll to follow Jock's Road north-westwards. The weather was so severe, with the fierce wind whipping the snow into a turbulent blizzard, that the searchers could make progress at times only by bending low and turning their sides or backs into the storm to gain some respite from its fury. At the moment when the body was discovered three men were in the lead as the party made its way up the glen. They were Peter McKinlay of the Glasgow Ski and Outdoor Club, Dick Gowers of the Creagh Dhu Mountaineering Club and Jack Reid, of the Carn Dearg Mountaineering Club. It was about midday and they had worked their way up the path, invisible under the snow, to just beyond the top of Glen Doll and were near to Jock's Hut when footprints were spotted quite close to the path. As with the ones found by the Braemar searchers, although there had been large accumulations of snow since the men had passed by, the wind had blown much of it off the footprints. They veered downwards away from the path, along the line of the stream, also concealed under the snow, and headed for the precipitous drop into upper Glen Doll where the stream descends as the White Water waterfall. *The Scotsman* of Monday, 5th January contained the following quotation from Dick Gowers, who actually first sighted the body:

We had followed Jock's Road for quite a distance and then we found traces of footprints leading back towards Glen Doll. The track led us round a buttress away from the path. About four miles from the hostel, I spotted the man's body lying beside a big boulder near a waterfall. He was properly dressed for hillwalking with thick trousers, boots, anarak and a knapsack. We saw other footprints beside the body and followed them without success. We searched the area for about an hour but conditions were terrible. We could scarcely see through the gale force winds.

The *Scottish Daily Mail* of the same day carried an account, given by Peter McKinlay, of the finding of the body, He said:

> The prints just missed the track by a few feet and then swerved right away from it. We followed them for 400 yards over rough ground with deep snow drifts. First we found a glove and then at the edge of a gully a man lay face downwards in the snow. He had obviously collapsed with exhaustion.

Other newspapers of the same day, including *The Courier and Advertiser* and the *Scottish Daily Express*, mentioned that a handprint was clearly visible at the top of the gully where the body was located, suggesting that someone had fallen or stumbled.

It is almost certain that the footprints had been made by two of the missing men. The whole area was under deep snow and it is not possible to be sure how close to the path the footprints were, but they seem to have been fairly close. This would show that the men had returned to the line of Jock's Road but had then, most unfortunately, turned sharply away from it. It may be that they had simply wandered from the route they were following along the White Water and then, realising they had done so, had suddenly returned to it. On the other hand, in view of the fact that in reaching the path they had to climb through soft snow a height of about 30m from the White Water, it is possible that they had remembered the need to avoid the dangerous drop into upper Glen Doll and had been trying to find the path. If so, it is difficult to understand why they turned away from it, but the most likely explanation is that they were disoriented by the blizzard and the darkness.

McKinlay, Gowers and Reid had found the body of seventeen-year-old James Boyle some distance down the gully. His rucksack, which was not particularly heavy, was still on his back and he lay, his face frozen into the snow, curled over a drop of about 25m into the stream below. According to a report in the *Scottish Daily Express* of Monday 5th January, 'Police said, "He was badly injured and had obviously fallen a considerable distance".'

Other newspapers did not provide this information which appears to be misleading. Thomas Deas says:

> I never saw any sign of serious physical injury on any of the bodies I viewed nor did I hear of any being found other than on Boyle, and his were consistent with coming into contact with rock or ice. He also had a slight spinal deformity which gave him a hunched appearance and may have led to a supposition by some of the media who saw him that he was badly injured.

It is likely that these injuries had already happened before Boyle reached the gully in which he was found, perhaps through a fall of some kind or the wind blowing him against boulders. Certainly, they did not kill him. His cause of death was given as 'heart failure due to exposure to inclement weather'. He was in a gully on Craig Maud near the point where the stream enters upper Glen Doll from the glen above and close to the White Water waterfall. He was about 6km walking distance from Glen Doll Youth Hostel.

The snow in the gully had drifted to a depth of 3m or so and the body lay at the bottom of the easier-angled upper section of the gully, just before it plunged steeply downwards. It seemed that the young man had realised at the last moment that if he descended any further he would fall into the stream far below and had stopped himself on the edge, but that he simply did not have the strength or the will to drag himself back up and find another way into Glen Doll. Later, after the body of Harry Duffin had been found in the White Water at the foot of the gully, it was considered that Duffin had been attempting to help the younger man down and had himself fallen to the bottom. Boyle had then tried to go to his assistance, but had become stuck and died where he was. Tragically, he and Duffin had just passed Jock's Hut which lay no more than 200 metres away. Nevertheless, their deviation from the path and their failure to find the hut may not be of great importance: they may have been so close to the end that nothing would have saved their lives.

McKinlay told *The Scotsman* that when they found the body they tried to make radio contact with the R.A.F. signals truck at the youth hostel where the officer-in-charge, Flight Lieutenant T. J. Belson, was standing by with men ready to bring out stretchers. They were unable to do so and McKinlay, Reid and a few others made haste back to the hostel to summon help. Sledge stretchers and additional ropes were brought to the spot, sufficient for the finding of other bodies, and an R.A.F. field ambulance journeyed as far as it could along the rough track. Twice it was blown off the track and had to be manhandled back. It managed to travel about 3km before having to give up the unequal struggle. There it waited for the rescuers to return.

There were risks attending the recovery of Boyle's body because the fresh, soft snow might avalanche into the stream, taking the rescuers with it. Steps were cut down to the body which was strapped into a stretcher and, with some difficulty, dragged up the slope from where it was hauled down Glen Doll with an escort of forty men. It was exhausting work and required a passage to be cleared through the snow for the sledge stretcher. The body was taken to the youth hostel and then to the police mortuary in Forfar where it was identified by James Boyle's father the following day.

Efforts to locate other bodies in the area that day were without success and worsening weather and the approach of darkness forced Superintendent Knight to call off the search until first light the next day. Other members of the Universal Hiking Club had arrived at Glendoll Youth Hostel to offer help in the search and on the Sunday night most of them returned to Glasgow, some in the Glasgow Ski and Outdoor Club's bus. Mrs Devlin and a friend went to Forfar where they joined those relatives of the five men who were staying there while the search proceeded.

The search parties assembled just before daybreak on Monday morning. A few hours earlier, at 2.00 a.m., the mountain rescue team from Kinloss had arrived to supplement the efforts of the Leuchars team which had played a major part in the previous day's action. The two teams camped together beside the Moulzie road and they provided a combined total of about fifty men. To these were added a further twenty or so coming from the ranks of the police, climbers and local gamekeepers, stalkers and shepherds. Some of the local contingent brought dogs with them. One of the local men was Sandy MacDonald from Braedownie, a farm at the head of Glen Clova and close to the youth hostel. He was sixty and had done much over the years to save people in trouble in the neighbouring hills for which he had received the B.E.M. in 1952. He made his tractor and trailer available to the rescue effort and a Weasel snow vehicle was brought in on the Monday, although not much use of this appears to have been made as it was left half way along the track to Craig Maud. No further operation was mounted from the Braemar side: the finding of Boyle's body at Craig Maud led to the belief that the remaining bodies were likely to be found also on the Glen Doll side of the route.

The area to be searched was extensive. Although it concentrated on the area of Craig Maud where the body had been found the day before, it covered ground 2km wide along the line of Jock's Road as far as Cairn Lunkard and continued on a narrower front as far north-west as Tom Buidhe and Tolmount, with the top of Meikle Kilrannoch and the area of Loch Esk being revisited. The weather was much better: there was still a wind, and it was strong and keen, but the sky was clear and it was soon sunny. The weather remained bright all day and the night which followed was to be bitterly cold. In parts of the north-east, indeed, it was the coldest night of the winter with the temperature at Strathdon in Aberdeenshire plunging to −19.5°C.

A helicopter took off from R.A.F. Leuchars at 9.15 a.m. and spent most of the morning sweeping Glen Doll and the area beyond as far as Tolmount.

Much of the time it was at an altitude of 30m and sometimes even lower. Below, the crew could see the searchers spread out in two groups line abreast as they moved up the glen and along Jock's Road and they were able to maintain links with the search parties through Pitreavie Castle and the radio communications van at the hostel. Footprints were observed but, with so much activity in the area over the last two days, the crew were of the opinion that these would have been made by the searchers, not by the missing men, and nothing was seen from the air which would lead to the men. This was not surprising because the snow which had fallen in such large amounts since the men had left Braemar would have covered most, if not all, traces of the men which might have been visible from the air.

There was more success on the ground. The press reports on the progress made there were rather confusing, particularly with regard to the sets of footprints that were found and to the location of two discarded pieces of equipment. The press generally stated or implied that the searchers managed to follow four sets of tracks from close to Tolmount to near the gully in which the body of Boyle had been found. There they petered out. This was not the case – or, if it was, they were not made by the unfortunate men since only two of them reached that point. To judge from later developments, it does seem that they were the men's footprints and other contemporary evidence confirms that there were no longer four sets by the time they approached Craig Maud. Certainly, Thomas Deas is fairly sure that there were only two sets in the area of the White Water waterfall. The tracks were fairly indistinct and disappeared from time to time and an error may have been made by some of the searchers. However, it is equally possible that the representatives of the press misunderstood or misinterpreted the situation. If the footprints were not made by the men, the ones discovered followed a course remarkably similar to the one that the men were later known to have taken.

The footprints started almost 3km north-west of Jock's Hut and were traced down the glen of the White Water, past the places where the bodies of three of the missing men were eventually found. Along this route a cape and a dixie were found, although there was some conflict in the newspapers as to exactly where this happened. However, it is Thomas Deas's recollection that they were discovered about 2km from the place where Boyle's body was located and this estimate is confirmed by accounts in the press following the discovery of the body of Robert McFaul in early March. This being the case, they were found very close to where McFaul lay entombed in the snow. Neither the cape nor the dixie could be identified by the relative to whom they were shown; however, since they were near the surface of the snow – 'lying half buried in the snow' as the *Scottish Daily Express* of Tuesday, 6th January put it – they must have been lost or abandoned not long before so it is almost certain that they did belong to the men.

Much of the activity on the Monday centred on the vicinity of the gully where Boyle was found, with members of the R.A.F. teams descending the gully on ropes to investigate its lower reaches and men with spades digging in the area for any signs of the men. But the snow was too deep and in places the cold weather had made it quite hard. The gully had snow to a depth of 3m and more, while in other areas it had drifted as much as three times that depth and some gullies were almost obliterated. As Sandy MacDonald of Braedownie pointed out: the searchers could be standing on top of the bodies and they would not know. Shortly after 3.00 p.m., the men began to make their way back down Glen Doll to the youth hostel.

Tuesday dawned cold and clear and the intense overnight frost had put a hard crust on the snow. The two R.A.F. teams were reinforced by a contingent of thirty servicemen from the Royal Navy base, H.M.S. Condor, at Arbroath from where they had been brought by a naval bus. The helicopter from R.A.F. Leuchars made its third appearance in three days. Altogether about eighty men set forth up Jock's Road. Stretchers were left at the base and shovels were carried for excavating in the area of Craig Maud, in the area where the cape and the dixie had been discovered and in any other place where evidence of the men's whereabouts might be found. The depth and the increasing hardness of the snow made this an arduous task. Davie Glen was again one of the searchers. Thomas Deas recalls:

Davie was like a walrus. He crawled upstream below the ice and kept coming up for air every time there was a hole in the ice. A very remarkable man. In fact he must have passed the very spot where Devlin's body was found but at that time it would have been encased in snow and ice.

With the Leuchars helicopter making low-level sorties over the area during the morning, the searchers directed their steps towards the Craig Maud area. They formed a 500 metre line with the men 5 metres apart. From time to time flares were fired to keep the line straight. They made a sweep up Glen Doll and then continued for 2km north-westwards from the gully where Boyle's body had been found. Digging was started where the dixie had been discovered the previous day and, after much effort, a primus stove (or at least parts of one) emerged from the snow in what the newspapers called variously a 'satchel', a 'knapsack' and a 'haversack'. This was probably of the type that is slung diagonally across the shoulder. The relatives who were staying in Forfar and had come that day to Glen Doll in the company of Father Patrick O'Donohoe were unable to recognise it but there is no particular reason why they should. Boyle lived with his parents and Devlin was married, but the other three were single and they may well have had gear that their relatives had never seen. Such items are not normally discarded by those who go into the hills. Moreover, the cape, the dixie and now the haversack were on the line of the footprints discovered the previous day. It is more than likely that they did belong to the men and were abandoned, the men, by then, becoming thoroughly exhausted and desperate, and succumbing to the hypothermia which was to kill them.

Apart from the haversack, nothing was found in spite of a search lasting six hours and covering an area of about 8km^2, this including a sweep of Corrie Fee by the team from H.M.S. Condor. Considerable efforts were made in digging and probing areas where it was thought there might be some trace of the men. However, it was clear by the end of the day that there was no chance at all that the men would be found alive. The whole area between Braemar and Glen Doll had been thoroughly searched, both on the ground and from the air, and it was quite reasonably concluded that the remaining four men would not be discovered until the coming of a sustained thaw. The conditions for the search parties were difficult and there was always the risk of harm befalling some of them. There was also little, if any, financial justification in continuing to engage so many men in a search operation which, at best, would locate only corpses. Superintendent Knight consulted with those in charge of the service units and it was agreed to call off the search until the conditions improved and made success more likely. The public was advised of the danger of mounting individual and unorganised searches for the missing men and asked not to attempt to do so.

Certainly no one seems to have come to any harm in the area in the few weeks that elapsed before the remaining bodies were found, but the area was a popular one with hill-walkers and climbers and it may well be that some chose to go there rather than elsewhere in the hope of finding the missing men. One man, however, went out most weekends in the hope that he would find the men: this was Davie Glen. His motive was not gruesome curiosity, but a wish to find them as quickly as possible so that they could be buried before they had suffered too much from natural decay and the attentions of predators. There were the feelings of the relatives to consider. Also, it was an area he loved, knew well and visited often. Not only did he see to the replacement of the old Jock's Hut when it went the way of all huts, but he

Davie Glen   *'The Courier', Dundee*

spent much time improving and reconstructing footpaths to help reduce the erosion caused by the boots of so many walkers. So fond was he of the area that he named his home after that most beautiful of places, Bachnagairn, with its ruined lodge, its larches and green meadows and its nearby broken crags. Davie Glen could himself hardly rest while the men lay undiscovered somewhere in his favourite countryside. They would have to be found before it would resume its old beauty.

If Davie Glen and others were out along Jock's Road in the weeks that followed the abandonment of the search, no trace was found during the rest of January and the whole of February. However, the end of February saw the onset of much milder weather which produced a rapid thaw of the lying snow with the streams filling and tumbling down the mountain-sides; the White Water would well have deserved its name and its waterfall at the head of Glen Doll must have presented a fine sight. With this change in the weather, there was a good chance that an organised search might locate one or more of the bodies and Glen put together a team which went out to search over the weekend that straddled the end of February and the beginning of March. *The Courier and Advertiser* of Monday, 2nd March contained a fairly full report of the finding of the body and it takes up the story:

> Davie Glen, Bachnagairn, Tealing, who has taken part in many rescues in the area, made the discovery at noon on Sunday. He was at the head of a team of six climbers [which the *Press and Journal* and *The Scotsman* numbered at thirty] who had been searching all weekend. They followed the river and had just reached the point where Boyle was found when one of the party saw clothing in the stream. Wading knee deep, Davie Glen came upon the body fifty yards from where Boyle was found and only a hundred yards from a hill hut and safety.

Young James Low from Forfar descended Jock's Road to telephone the police and he returned with three policemen, led by Chief Inspector John Duncan. The body was lying in the water, in a pool at the bottom of the White Water waterfall and below the 30m gully towards the top of which James Boyle had been found on 4th January. The body had to be brought up this gully. It was a difficult and strenuous task. A stretcher was lowered by rope and the body strapped into it. The body was heavy, the gully was steep and there were not many places where the stretcher could be rested on its way to the top. Scree was constantly dislodged on to those escorting the stretcher as it was manhandled up the gully with assistance from the men hauling from the top. It was the worst job of its type that Glen had done and there was considerable relief when, after much expenditure of energy and time, the stretcher and its load arrived at the top.

It was then carried down the rough track towards the youth hostel as the light of the late afternoon began to fail. Members of the Glasgow Ski and Outdoor Club were again at the hostel as their base for the weekend and they came up the path to assist the stretcher bearers. Sandy MacDonald of Braedownie had been notified by the police and he had driven his tractor and trailer as far up the track as he was able and he was there to take the body the remaining distance to the hostel from where it was transferred to the mortuary at Forfar police station. It had taken three hours to transport the body from the top of the gully to the youth hostel. The following day the body was identified as that of Harry Duffin.

The discovery of Duffin's body and the continuing thaw which cleared much of the snow from all but the higher levels encouraged the thought that the remaining bodies might well be located without too much difficulty and it was decided to mount a major operation the following weekend. There was still some snow in the glens and especially in the hollows and gullies which had received less sunshine. This snow, being old, was hard and icy. The Angus police were able to enlist the assistance of members of the Carn Dearg and Grampian Mountaineering Clubs and they were joined by service teams, policemen and, as it transpired again, members of the Glasgow Ski and Outdoor Club. Inevitably, stalwart Davie Glen was present. The operation was under the control of Chief Inspector Duncan of the Angus County Police. In the event, about eighty searchers set out to cover a wide area, although the main efforts would be made in the vicinity of the places where the bodies and the discarded belongings had been found.

This search for the remaining three men was most fully covered in *The Courier and Advertiser* and its issue of Monday, 9th March gave a quite detailed account of the discoveries made during that weekend. Its headline was, 'Missing Climbers' Packs Found in Glen Doll. Snow Threat Ends Weekend Search. Searchers Combing Torrent-Filled Gorges.' Then it continued:

. . . On Saturday forenoon, in the cover of a huge rock where he had apparently crept to shelter from the gale, searchers found the body of Robert McFaul. Yesterday only a few yards from where McFaul was found, searchers saw what appeared to be clothing in ice-topped snow about five feet deep. Using R.A.F. ice picks and shovels, they brought to the surface a rucksack full of climber's equipment. The search was intensified between the spot and the place where, about a mile down the glen, were found the bodies of Boyle and Duffin. A thorough search was made of the gullies and rock-strewn heights. Damage was done to the axes and shovels so energetic was the search over a stretch of about a mile around Meikle Kilrannoch and this side of Tom Buidhe. Wearing waders, Davie Glen walked in the raging White Water looking into corners screened by overhanging rocks. R.A.F. men picked holes in snow and ice bulges over the river. They held each other by the heels so that they could examine minutely the pools underneath. Every possible snow-filled corrie was picked and dug as far as possible with the deep snow. About a hundred yards down the glen the men retrieved from a hole in the snow a pack containing a beret. Shortly after, the White Water yielded up another case containing an expensive camera believed to belong to one of the missing men, Joseph Devlin.

The R.A.F. men's theory is that the men were together where McFaul was found on Saturday. Further north at the beginning of the year searchers found footsteps leading south and dug up a primus stove and a cape. Indicative of the weather conditions over the period was the comment of an R.A.F. man yesterday: 'Just where we found McFaul we dug up a mess tin at New Year. It appeared to have been left on the top of the rock where McFaul was sheltering. At that time the rock looked about two feet high. Yesterday, when the snow had gone, I was surprised to see the rock was about twelve feet high.'

Thomas Deas recalls the finding of McFaul's body:

McFaul was in a sitting position and so far as I can recall he was not in a sleeping bag, unless it was around his feet. He had obviously been having something to drink as he had a cup in one hand and a small bottle, which I am sure contained milk, in the other. The opinion at the time was that he had been making tea and fallen asleep during the time he was awaiting the primus to boil the water.

McFaul was found on the east side of the White Water about 2km north-west of Jock's Hut which itself was almost 5km from the youth hostel in Glen Doll. Unless he had become separated from his friends and had found the rock on his own, he was left there by his companions and this would not have happened if he had been sufficiently fit to continue. It is likely, therefore, that he was seriously hypothermic when he was making the drink and once he fell asleep death would come quickly. The discovery of the cape, the dixie (or mess tin) and the haversack at the beginning of the year, all close to the rock where McFaul was found, suggests that the men were beginning to abandon gear by the time they reached the boulder and the existence of the rucksack full of climber's equipment a few metres distant from this boulder may indicate that it, too, had been jettisoned, although it is possible that it was blown there from the boulder by the wind. The discarding of equipment continued a short distance down the glen from the rock as was revealed by the finding of the pack containing the beret and the case containing the camera. The abandonment of this gear is a clear indication of how exhausted and hypothermic the men had become, no more than 3km after they had crossed the summit area of Tolmount and when they were still 7km from Glendoll Youth Hostel.

The next Sunday, 15th March, the fourth body, that of Joseph Devlin was found, almost inevitably, by Davie Glen who, on this occasion, was in the company of two students from Queen's College, Dundee, one of these being Dugald Kippen, son of a Kirriemuir policeman who had played an active part in the search in January. The two young men had spent Saturday night at Glendoll Youth Hostel and had departed the following morning for Braemar where they had arranged to meet a friend for a week in the Cairngorms. As they travelled up Jock's Road on a sunny and calm day, they met Davie Glen with whom they continued their walk. At a quarter past ten they saw a body lying in the stream and one of the students, Nicholas Gardiner, descended the track and telephoned the police in Kirriemuir. Sergeant Kippen himself came with a party of police and the body was strapped to a stretcher and carried back along the path where, as before, Sandy MacDonald was waiting with his tractor and trailer to transport the body the final leg to the youth hostel from where it was taken to the Forfar mortuary and identified the next day. His body had laid only about 400 metres from where McFaul had been found.

The last body was not discovered for a further five weeks. Although the thaw had continued, snow still lay on the ground and, in places, quite deeply. On Sunday 19th April, members of the Carn Dearg Mountaineering Club came upon the body of Frank Daly, the smallest member of the party, lying on a metre of snow on the south side of Crow Craigies about 90 metres from the upper reaches of the White Water and 400 metres from Jock's Road. Of the five, Daly was found furthest from Glen Doll: he was about 400 metres to the north of where McFaul had been discovered and his body must have been well buried under the snow when the main search was being undertaken. One of the searchers was reported in *The Courier and Advertiser* of Monday, 20th April as saying:

We saw haversacks in the snow, then we came upon the body. It was obvious that he had succumbed first. There were two haversacks round his head and capes had been laid over them.

There may be an error here in that the reading should have been, 'capes had been laid over him' rather than 'capes had been laid over them' for there were plastic capes on the ground and over the lower part of Daly's body. It is quite likely that the upper part of his body had also been wrapped in a cape but subsequently it had blown off. He was found lying as he had been left by his friends, with the packs placed to protect his head, and his arms folded across his chest in the posture of death. Like the others, he had died from hypothermia and clearly his companions were sure he was dead before they left him.

One member of the Carn Dearg team descended to Glen Doll to telephone the police and a party of policemen under Chief Inspector John Duncan of Forfar made the journey up the glen for the last time. The body was brought down on a stretcher by a team of thirty and was taken to Forfar where it was identified. The finding of Daly's body brought to an end the tragic adventure which began on New Year's Day. There is sufficient evidence to produce a reasonable account of what happened, although as with any evidence of this type, it is capable of different interpretations. Within limits, it seems possible to deduce the train of events.

The men left Braemar at about 11.30 a.m. on Thursday, 1st January, 1959. They walked just over 3km along the main A93 Braemar to Spittal of Glenshee road and turned off at Auchallater to take the track to Lochcallater Lodge. It was about 12.15 p.m. when they left the main road and by 2.00 p.m. – by which time it was sleeting heavily in Glen Callater – they were probably not much beyond the east end of Loch Callater. By this time their clothes must have been quite wet. They continued to the headwall of Coire Breac and then left the line of Jock's Road to ascend Tolmount. Bearing in mind the unpleasant conditions and the weight they were carrying, it is unlikely that they could have reached the summit area of Tolmount before 3.30 p.m.

Thus far one can argue with some confidence. From that point onwards events and timings become more conjectural. Daly died about 2km from the start of the descent of Tolmount and it must have taken the party half an hour at the very least to cover this distance. It is impossible to know how long the party was delayed by the death of their friend and much would depend upon how quickly he died or at least had given all the signs of having died. The delay can scarcely have been much less than half an hour. Certainly, at least one of the men and probably all four remained with him until they were sure he was dead because he was laid out and wrapped in the capes. In that time they must have become badly chilled themselves. It is not without significance that they went to this trouble for Daly because it indicates that the four remaining men were unaware of their own condition; perhaps Boyle and Duffin were surviving fairly well, but it is difficult to say the same of McFaul and Devlin who did not get much further. There can be no doubt of their loyalty to their dying friend. By the time the four men were ready to resume their battle through the storm, if it was not already dark, night was close to hand.

Plaque by Jock's Road.   *Courtesy of Alfie Ingram of Carn Dearg M.C.*

It was believed at the time that Daly had died and then the remaining four had gone the short distance to the boulder where McFaul was left either to await the arrival of assistance summoned by the others to take Daly down the glen, McFaul being able to mark the spot where Daly lay, or because McFaul was himself in a serious condition. The other three had then pushed on down the watercourse in an unsuccessful effort to reach Glendoll Youth Hostel and had died in the attempt. It is improbable that the men would have seen much sense in leaving McFaul behind to await the arrival of a party to retrieve Daly when McFaul himself might well succumb to the conditions. In any case, it must have been obvious that such a party would be unlikely to set out in the prevailing weather and in the darkness simply to retrieve a dead body. It is much more probable that McFaul was left at the boulder, which they must have come upon by chance, because he could go no further than the 400 metres from the place where Daly perished. All the gear found in the area of the boulder may have belonged to McFaul or some of it may have been left there by the others. Whatever the truth, James Boyle, Joseph Devlin and Harry Duffin left Robert McFaul at the rock and disappeared into the blizzard and darkness. Not long after his friends departed, McFaul, whose judgement was by then probably weakened by hypothermia, began to make a cup of tea. Before the water was ready he fell asleep or lapsed into unconsciousness and before long he was dead.

Devlin, whose condition must have been very serious, was able to go only a further 400 metres before he fell through the snow into the White Water and could not rise again, having already shed some of his equipment, possibly all of it. If he was still in the company of Boyle and Duffin, they had to abandon him. These two managed to struggle about another 2km, possibly aware of the danger ahead of them at Craig Maud. They almost found the line of Jock's Road but, perhaps disoriented by the blizzard and darkness, perhaps because they were simply lost, they turned away from it and soon after found themselves trying to descend the gully beside the White Water waterfall. Duffin, who was leading, lost his footing and fell down the gully into the stream below and Boyle, exhausted, hypothermic and demoralised by the loss of all his companions, could find no further energy or the will to fight on and died where he was.

There is another course of events that could have followed the abandonment of Daly and this should be given some consideration. It is fairly clear that it must have been dark or close to darkness when the men left Daly in the snow and they were still 7km from Glendoll Youth Hostel. Three of the remaining four were seasoned hill-walkers and may have appreciated the wisdom of a bivouac for which they had sufficient equipment. In view of the time and the conditions, it is very unlikely that they came upon the boulder where McFaul was found as the result of any kind of systematic search but, when it emerged before them, they may have decided that they should avail themselves of its protection until the morning by which time the storm might well have blown itself out.

However, when morning came the storm continued with unabated fury and there was no sign that it was going to end. During the night, it is unlikely that hunger could have been warded off by much of a meal and their wet clothes would have made them progressively colder so that by morning Devlin was close to the end and possibly also McFaul. Morale would be low and their opinion may well have been that, if they did not make a dash for it then, they would simply die where they were – and in this, almost certainly, they would have been correct. In the blizzard, the more especially as they had deviated from their intended route, there was little, if any, chance they would be found by searchers, should a search operation even be undertaken. So the decision was made to set out down the glen, McFaul remaining behind either because he was unable to continue or because he preferred to wait longer in the hope that the weather would moderate. But it was too late and the difficulties were insurmountable. Devlin was able to struggle only

400 metres before he collapsed into the White Water and the other two managed only another 2km before they succumbed.

If the men did sit out the storm on the night of 1st/2nd January, there is somewhat less substance in the charge made in the report of the accident in the S.M.C.J. (art. cit.) that they 'tried to force their way through the pass in the teeth of the blizzard.' However, it did not strike the search party which found McFaul that they had bivouacked and, although there was at the boulder some equipment that could have been used in a bivouac, there was little of this and what there was could have belonged to McFaul. Surely Devlin, Duffin and Boyle would have left behind their own bivouac equipment – indeed all their equipment – and travelled the more lightly towards Glen Doll. The conclusion, therefore, is that there was no bivouac.

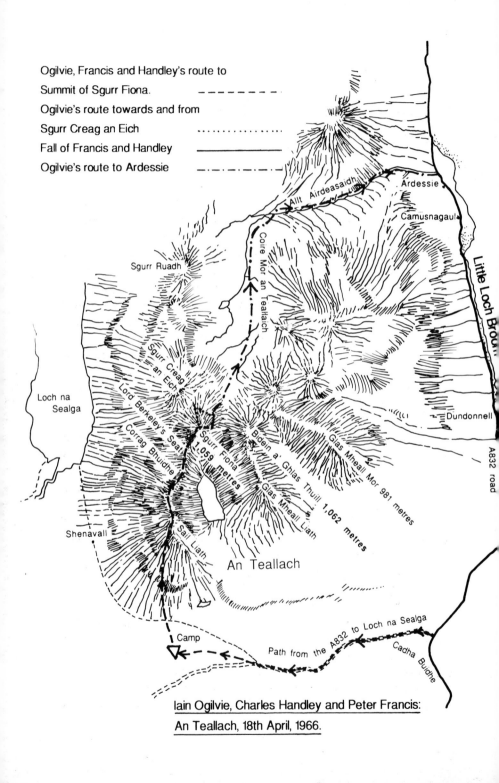

Ogilvie, Francis and Handley's route to
Summit of Sgurr Fiona. — — — — —

Ogilvie's route towards and from
Sgurr Creag an Eich ....

Fall of Francis and Handley ————————

Ogilvie's route to Ardessie —·—·—·—·—

Ardessie

Camusnagaul

Little Loch Broom

Allt Airdeasaidh

Coire Mor an Teallach

Sgurr Ruadh

Sgurr Creag an Eich

Loch na Sealga

Lord Berkeley's Seat

Corrag Bhuidhe

Sgurr Fiona 1,059 metres

Bidein a Ghlas Thuill 1,062 metres

Glas Mheall Liath

Glas Mheall Mor 981 metres

Dundonnell

A832 road

Shenavall

Sail Liath

An Teallach

Camp

Path from the A832 to Loch na Sealga

Cadha Budhe

Iain Ogilvie, Charles Handley and Peter Francis:
An Teallach, 18th April, 1966.

Accident on An Teallach.
April, 1966

An Teallach is a grand mountain. It lies in Wester Ross and dominates the skyline above Dundonnell and the head of Little Loch Broom from which it rises to a height of 1062m. It is an ancient mountain, 700 million years old, hewn out of banded Torridonian sandstone and in a state of continuous decay as is witnessed by the masses of scree which lie on its ledges, fill its gullies and litter the base of its precipitous slopes, the result of an aeon of wind, rain, snow and frost. It was, therefore, once an even grander mountain. There is no single peak named An Teallach; it is the name given to the massif itself, the highest point being called Bidein a' Ghlas Thuill. An Teallach is Gaelic for The Forge, so named presumably because it can be reminiscent of a blacksmith's forge when viewed from the east, looking directly towards the large corrie known as Coire Toll an Lochain. On days when the cloud and mist swirl in the steep-sided corrie, the resemblance to the smoke and the steam from a forge can be quite close. In the case of An Teallach, it is not inappropriate that the Gaelic word 'coire', whose anglicised form is, of course, 'corrie', means 'cauldron' in English. The corrie is dominated by the jagged silhouette of Corrag Bhuidhe and its adjacent buttress and by the smoother shape of Sgurr Fiona. In some books the name of this peak is translated as Peak of the Wine, after the Gaelic word for wine, although the Dionysian connection is not immediately clear; nor, for that matter, is any connection with a lady called Fiona. It may be that the original name was not Sgurr Fiona but Sgurr Fionn, meaning Fionn's Peak, after Fionn Mac Cumhail or Mac Coul (Ossian's Fingal).

The ridge of An Teallach is one of the finest in the country and can be rivalled only by the Cuillin ridge in Skye and the Aonach Eagach in Glen Coe. It curves and twists its way in a crescent shape around and beyond Loch Toll an Lochain far below for a distance of about 5km. The main ridge has two outlying branches, one being the eastern ridge which leads from Bidein a' Ghlas Thuill to Ghlas Meall Liath. The other, which has a part to play in the events described in this chapter, strikes westwards from the

245

summit of Sgurr Fiona, which is only marginally lower than Bidein a' Ghlas
Thuill, and after 1km reaches the point known as Sgurr Creag an Eich at
about 1017m; then the ridge descends gradually for a further 2km in a
north-westerly direction before reaching its final top, Sgurr Ruadh. The
ridge of An Teallach offers a route of high quality with variety and challenge.
Even in the summer, parts of the ridge have to be respected; in the winter,
the traverse of the ridge is a serious expedition, requiring some technical
competence.

On Friday 15th April, 1966 five friends, three from the south of England,
forgathered in Wester Ross for a week's climbing. Iain Ogilvie, a native of
Perthshire, was a civil engineer who lived in Surrey and Charles Handley,
who was known to his friends as Tommy, was a Norfolk farmer. Both Ogilvie
and Handley were very experienced mountaineers who had climbed
extensively both in Britain and the Alps and had been to the Himalaya.
Ogilvie was a member of the S.M.C. of which he had been a committee
member, of the Alpine Club and of the Swiss Alpine Club; Handley was a
member of the Climbers' Club and the Alpine Club and he was a former
president of the Alpine Ski Club. Both these men were in their fifties,
Handley being the older by six years; in contrast, Peter Francis, an insurance
inspector from Harlow New Town, was only thirty and had no experience of
winter climbing. The visit to the north-west Highlands was to be his
introduction to the sport. He was, however, an experienced rock-climber.

Ogilvie and Francis had journeyed together. Handley had made his way by
train to Inverness where he was met by Charles Gorrie, a teacher of
mathematics at Mackie Academy, Stonehaven. On the way to Wester Ross,
they picked up Jim Clark who was hitch-hiking to Dundonnell to work on
the old smithy which he was converting into a climbers' hut for the
Edinburgh section of the Junior Mountaineering Club of Scotland
(J.M.C.S.) and which was to be named the Clarkson Memorial Hut in
memory of Jim Clarkson who died while abseiling from the Carn Mor Dearg
arête into Coire Leis on Ben Nevis. It was believed that he may have
suffered a heart attack which caused his fall. In the events that were soon to
unfold on An Teallach, there was later to be a suspicion that a similar hand
may have been laid upon one of the men present.

Camp was made beside the old smithy at Dundonnell on the Friday night
and the next day the five men climbed Sgurr Breac and A' Chailleach in the
Fannichs, not far from An Teallach. On the Sunday, Clark parted company
from the others, remaining at the smithy to attend to the work for which he
had come. Ogilvie and Gorrie ascended a further three Fannich peaks,

Sgurr nan Each, Sgurr nan Clach Geala and Meall a' Chrasgaidh, all five hills being over 915m. Instead of climbing, Handley and Francis had been deposited at the point on the A832 road, some 4km east of the village of Dundonnell, where the track from Achneigie reaches the main road. Handley and Francis transported half the camping gear the 10km from the road to their chosen campsite beside a small lochan to the north of the footpath to the bothy of Shenavall and below the Sail Liath shoulder of An Teallach. Later, Ogilvie and Gorrie carried up the rest of the gear, Gorrie himself returning to his Dormobile van for the night as he had no camping equipment of his own. It was his intention to return early the following morning, Monday, 18th April, to make the traverse of An Teallach; the men agreed that Handley and Francis would do only the tops on the main ridge but that Ogilvie and Gorrie would include also the outlying tops.

After completing the traverse of An Teallach, Gorrie would return home as he had to start work the next day after his Easter holiday. Ogilvie, Handley and Francis would spend the Monday night in their tents beside the lochan and then proceed the following morning further into the remote fastness of Wester Ross, moving camp to Larachantivore, a locked cottage to the south of the east end of Loch na Sealga. From this tented base, they would spend three days or so scaling a number of worthy peaks to the south: Beinn Dearg Mor, Ruadh Stac Mor, A'Mhaighdean, Beinn Tarsuinn, Mullach Coire Mhic Fhearchair, Sgurr Ban and Beinn a' Chlaidheimh. This would bring their climbing holiday to an end. The weather signs were promising. The winter snowfall had been heavy and much of the considerable quantity of snow which still lay on the hills of the north-west was old and firm. The temperatures had been low since the beginning of the month and the settled cold spell was forecast to continue.

Monday dawned cold and clear. With clear skies overnight, the air temperature at the base of An Teallach would have fallen close to or below freezing point but it would have risen quite quickly after sunrise. On the higher slopes, the temperature would have been below freezing all day, being in the region of $-4°C$ on the ridge of the mountain, although the sunlight reflected off the snow would have made it feel warmer. With hopes high for an excellent day's climbing, the three men prepared for a departure at 8.00 a.m. Gorrie, however, did not arrive: he had overslept. The others waited a short time but they were obliged to depart without him. Nonetheless, they took a spare rope in case he should be following; as events were to conspire, this rope was to be pressed into a service rather different from what would have been expected. There was fairly general snow cover as low as 650m.

Peter Francis and Charles Handley on Sail Liath.   *Iain Ogilvie*

Iain Ogilvie throughout his mountaineering life kept a diary in which he described his climbing adventures. For the An Teallach outing he recorded:

The snow conditions were quite exceptional. I have never experienced it so hard. At the high levels, you couldn't leave a footprint. You had to stamp hard to get a grip with crampons. The weather was perfect.

The party was well equipped. Ogilvie and Handley had nailed boots over which Ogilvie could strap the ten-point crampons which he carried; Handley had no crampons. Peter Francis wore vibram-soled boots to which he attached a pair of ten-point crampons when the snow became hard. All three had wooden-shafted ice-axes and Ogilvie carried a piton hammer which was actually a slater's hammer with a good pick on it. They carried two 37 metre hawser-laid nylon ropes; one was a full weight No. 4 and the other a light weight No. 2 line, the latter being the one taken in case Gorrie eventually arrived. In addition, Ogilvie carried two rock pitons, one ice-screw, two rope slings and some karabiners but, as the route was not a difficult one for men of the experience of Ogilvie and Handley, there was no need to burden themselves with an excess of ironmongery. Ogilvie also carried a penknife which was to be as valuable to him as one had been to Kirkus on Ben Nevis 32 years before.

The ascent of Sail Liath went without difficulty. As they gained height the views expanded and their eyes were drawn constantly to their left in the direction of Beinn Dearg Mor which stood, bold and imposing, across the flat ground of the Strath na Sealga. As they gazed, they searched out interesting routes for their intended ascent of it the following day. Beyond it lay the other peaks on their itinerary and beyond them the many hills of Torridon and of Skye. Ahead and slightly to the north, the scene was dominated by the great headwall of Coire Toll an Lochain and the rocky battlements of An Teallach set against the blue of the cold spring sky. Ogilvie referred to this in his diary:

> After we had walked up the snow to the top [of Sail Liath], we couldn't keep our eyes off the ridge ahead of us. It must be the finest we have apart from Skye. Today it was plastered with snow. The conditions couldn't have been better.

The party then followed the twisting, undulating ridge which took them to Cadha Gobhlach, a small, subsidiary peak which lies close to the narrow, forked pass which gives access to Loch Toll an Lochain down what is a stone shoot in summer and a narrow, steep snow-filled gully in winter. The ground began to ascend more steeply towards the Corrag Bhuidhe Buttress where Ogilvie cut steps up the steeper sections for the others to use. The higher they climbed the harder became the snow. Beyond the Corrag Bhuidhe Buttress, the ridge becomes narrow and, after a short drop in height, the men reached the bottom of a long snow slope which led to Corrag Bhuidhe itself. Translated from Gaelic, the name means literally Yellow Finger and is named after one of its four prominent sandstone pinnacles which to some extent impede progress along the ridge. Ogilvie's diary takes up the story again:

> Corrag Bhuidhe, capped with a crown of rock, looked difficult but probably could have been climbed direct, but we went round to the south-west side and after traversing the heads of some shallow gullies, for which we roped up, we turned right and up and after a few easy pitches on hard snow and ice and snow-covered rock, we came out again on to the narrow ridge with a great drop below, down to Loch Toll an Lochain. This is the best of the ridge and for some way it rises and falls over a number of rocky tops, all much the same height and far more like an Alpine ridge than a British one. The last of these, a little separated from the others, is Lord Berkeley's Seat. It has a steep, short face and we took it direct. It was easier than it looked. There is a big drop beyond and then an easier snow slope towards Sgurr Fiona. Sgurr Fiona also has a crown of rock and again we traversed on to the south-west side to avoid the steep edge of the ridge [overlooking Loch Toll an Lochain]. Turning right again, we reached the top and sat down for lunch.

Sgurr Fiona, Corrag Bhuidhe and Corrag Bhuidhe Buttress from Sail Liath. 18/4/66
Courtesy of Mrs Francis-Johnston

They had travelled something over 4km and had climbed from their camp at 390m to a height of 1059m. With the undulations on the ridge, the actual amount of climbing was rather greater than the 669m height difference. When they reached the summit of Sgurr Fiona it was about 12.30 p.m. As the three friends ate their lunch, they looked out over an almost endless array of snow-capped peaks to north, to south and to east. North lay such magical peaks as Stac Pollaidh, Cul Mor, Suilven, Canisp, Quinag and Ben More Assynt; east lay Beinn Dearg and Ben Wyvis; while to the south, beyond Beinn Dearg Mor, were Slioch, Beinn Eighe and Liathach, one behind the other, and beyond them the mountains of Skye; in the distance to the south-east, the snow covered Cairngorms were plainly visible. To the west the scene was different. There lay the sea with, close to hand, the Summer Isles and neighbouring little islands in scattered array beyond Little Loch Broom down below; while further away lay the islands of the Outer Hebrides with the hills of Harris conspicuous. All three men were exhilarated by the experience. Peter Francis had never seen anything like it and, as Ogilvie recorded, 'he was beyond himself'.

Then there was the ridge itself, much closer than the rest. They looked back along the route they had taken, to Lord Berkeley's Seat, poised precariously over the precipitous 500m drop to Loch Toll an Lochain, to Corrag Bhuidhe, to Cadha Gobhlach and to Sail Liath at the foot of which, unseen from the top of Sgurr Fiona, lay their tents. Ahead of them 1km to the north was the highest point on An Teallach, Bidein a' Ghlas Thuill, almost at their level but separated from them by a col, the descent to which was steep in places. To the west about the same distance away but slightly lower lay the outlying peak of Sgurr Creag an Eich along a curving ridge.

There was plenty of daylight left for the remainder of the route which, in any case, should not offer any difficulties and Ogilvie was keen to take in this outlier as had been intended when they set out. He felt fit and was going well and he could be there and back within forty minutes. The others did not wish to accompany him, but were quite content that he should go. They might wait for him to return to the top of Sgurr Fiona or they might begin making their way towards Bidein a' Ghlas Thuill. It was agreed that if they did move on and came to any ground that required a rope they would wait there for Ogilvie to arrive, not just for their own safety but also because Ogilvie might need the security of the rope. Although the main difficulties of the route had been surmounted, the snow conditions demanded constant vigilance. Iain Ogilvie's diary reveals the ensuing events:

I left at once and ran down easy snow which got steeper lower down. I was glad of my crampons. Soon I reached a col and set out along a long ridge over a small hump. I looked back and saw them starting. They were roped but hadn't waited for me but they were moving together fast. It looked easy. As I went over the hump, I couldn't see them. As I came up the slope beyond a small gap, I looked back again and to my horror I saw them falling down the west side of the ridge. I didn't see the start of the fall and I don't know how it started. They had already slid down 50 feet of snow and then shot over a rock band and now there was no hope for them stopping. I think they crossed another rock band and then on the snow again. All of a sudden they stopped. Their rope had caught. Neither of them moved. They had fallen at least 300 feet. [The following year Ogilvie returned to An Teallach and made some measurements. Then, he estimated that the men fell 115 metres].

By coincidence, their fall was of a not dissimilar length to that of Kirkus and Linnell on Easter Saturday 1934 and it was brought to a halt in a similar manner. The col between Sgurr Fiona and Sgurr Creag an Eich was about 350 metres from the summit of Sgurr Fiona and it involved some 140m of descent. The hump mentioned in the diary was only a short distance up the long snow slope leading to the top of Sgurr Creag an Eich and, since Ogilvie ran down some of the way, he must have reached the hump within ten minutes or so and it was at that point that Handley and Francis were moving off. They were not long in deciding to make their way towards the next peak.

Sgurr Fiona.   *Donald Bennet*

It is likely that, in spite of their initial speed, they proposed to take their time to give Ogilvie a chance to make up the ground before they attained the summit of Bidein a' Ghlas Thuill. That neither man had chosen to accompany Ogilvie need not be ascribed to fatigue. It had not been planned that they should do the outlying ridges and, in any case, Ogilvie has no memory of either man showing signs of tiredness. Of Handley, who was nearing sixty, Ogilvie says, 'I have no recollection of Handley feeling tired at the top of Sgurr Fiona; in fact he was going rather well.'

Their early departure from the summit of Sgurr Fiona may have been the result of the simple consideration that it would make good sense to get a start on their friend so that they could move at a leisurely pace and perhaps take some photographs. More probable as an explanation is that they were beginning to feel cold and preferred to proceed in order to generate some heat. This problem commonly faces those who take to the hills, even in summer. The person's body perspires freely on the ascent, making the clothes next to the skin damp. This is of little consequence so long as the person continues producing heat from the physical effort of the ascent, but when a stop is made the damp clothes chill the body, a condition exacerbated by any wind. If it is unpleasant enough in summer, it is significantly worse in winter.

They were, however, using the rope in spite of the agreement that they would await Ogilvie's arrival if they needed to use it. The ridge travelling north from Sgurr Fiona down to the col between Sgurr Fiona and Bidein a' Ghlas Thuill is gradual at first but then there is a steep step. The summer path leaves the crest of the ridge to avoid this step and goes down the face to the west, rejoining the ridge below the step. Handley and Francis evidently took approximately the same line: as Ogilvie watched them descend from the summit, he saw them moving slightly towards him as they avoided the rocky step and then they stopped as if debating the best line to follow down to the col below. Ogilvie had then continued on his way, however, and he did not see what happened next. When he looked back again about five minutes later, Handley and Francis were falling down the west face of Sgurr Fiona. Iain Ogilvie, who has spent a great deal of time thinking about the accident, says of the men's departure from the summit of Sgurr Fiona:

The whole of this is a bit perplexing. I can understand them going down the gradual part of the ridge without waiting for me but not descending the face, unless it is not nearly as steep as it looked from where I saw them. But then, why were they roped anyway, even for the easy bit?

There may be a straightforward and reasonable explanation for the men's action. Handley was very experienced and the initial snow slope down which they had to move would present no risk to him. Francis, however, was a novice in winter mountaineering and there was always the chance that he would make some simple mistake. It may well have seemed to Handley that it would be wiser to put Francis on a rope as they left the summit. It seems that the fall occurred not very long after the men had turned off the ridge to descend the west face in order to avoid the rocky step on the ridge and it may well be that they felt confident enough to continue down, knowing that they could stop if they came upon any difficulties. To wait where they were would have entailed getting cold again. Sadly, some misfortune struck them without warning.

Handley and Francis had met with their mishap high on the west face of Sgurr Fiona at an altitude of about 970m and their fall had taken them down towards the twisting Coire Mor an Teallaich which, as its name indicates, is the largest of the several corries of the An Teallach massif. They had fallen down a straight slope angled at about 45 degrees and had come to a halt at about 890m, having slid 115 metres down the slope. The ground below this point descended with an unrelenting steepness of about 50 degrees to 750m, a vertical distance of 140m. The angle then flattens out considerably for a walking distance of about 400 metres before steepening somewhat for a further 600 metres down to an altitude of just over 600m which was at that time below the snow-line. It was down this slope that Handley and Francis were to be lowered.

In his diary, Iain Ogilvie described the place and, in so doing, indicated some of the difficulties that were going to confront him as he tried to save the lives of his companions:

The upper half of the face is composed of rock bands, sometimes not quite continuous, of Torridonian sandstone, separated by narrow bands of very steep snow. Sometimes tongues of snow cut through the rock bands. The lower band is rather higher. Below this the lower half of the slope is an almost continuous snow slope at about 45 degrees from the foot of the lowest cliff but easing off at the foot to the gently sloping head of the valley.

Immediately he saw his friends careering downwards, Ogilvie turned round and ran back to the col about 300 metres down the slope up which he had just come. At the col, his friends were somewhat below him in height and 275 metres away across the hard snow of the face. He could see them and there was still no movement nor any sound. There were no other people anywhere within sight upon whom he could call for help and the nearest house was 8km away down the trackless Coire Mor an Teallaich. If his friends were still alive, they were clearly badly injured and were unlikely to survive unless he could provide some assistance. In emergencies, those involved do not stop to consider their own safety; their only concern is the welfare of the person or persons in distress. This was certainly the case with Ogilvie, but he dismissed it as of no consequence in his diary:

Looking back on events, there were two things I could do: go straight for help or get across to them. Actually, I can't remember even considering the first alternative at the time. . . . Using one of the bands of steep snow, I cramped straight across to them. By picking the less steep bits, it was fairly easy but there must have been bits where I would have thought twice under different circumstances.

I reached them on very steep snow. The rope between them had caught on an incredibly small rock spike above. I was afraid to touch it in case the rope came off. Francis was about 20 feet below Handley and the snow was red with blood. I looked at them both. They were unconscious but alive. I didn't think a lot of their chances but there *was* a chance if I could get them off the cliff on to the snow below and then go for help. There would have been no chance at all if I left them where they were hanging and I could do nothing for them where they were so I set to work.

On that day in mid April 1966, several jagged rocks protruded from the snow and the one on which the rope had snagged was very small. Later, in summer, Ogilvie recrossed the route from the col to the place where his friends had been hanging. On this visit, he made the following observations:

It was then a good ledge with a deer track on it and easy to walk along. There was a cliff [about 30m high] below it and a rock band of lesser height above it. On the day of the accident this was banked up with snow, from the top of the cliff to near the top of the rock band, forming a snow slope at about 45 degrees. The snow was very hard. At the place where they were hanging, both the cliff and the rock band were much higher and the snow slope was higher and steeper. The rock spike from which they were hanging was high above the ledge in summer but easy to reach from the snow on the day of the accident.

The position for Ogilvie was very awkward, if not desperate. The men were seriously injured, especially about the head, and both were un-conscious; they would be heavy unmanageable weights which he would have to move on steep and difficult ground. Moreover, he had no way of knowing what other injuries, some perhaps serious, they had suffered and it could be that, in moving one or both of them, he would make the injuries worse. However, moved they had to be. For one thing it was already after 1.00 p.m. and the night was evidently going to be cold. They would have no chance of survival unless he could get them lower down where there might be some shelter. Equally, and more urgently, the men's weight was being taken to some extent on their waists; if they were left in that position for very long there was a risk that they would die from asphyxia. Although Handley had been wearing a rope harness earlier in the day, it seems that both men were tied directly on to the rope at the time of the accident.

There was also a serious danger that, if one of the men regained a measure of consciousness, he would move and the rope would slip off its precarious hold on the sandstone spike, plunging the men all the way to the bottom. The risk of the rope slipping from its tenuous anchor would also be present when Ogilvie was working to secure the men; and the fact that the two men were counterbalancing each other's weight would create a considerable problem when one of the men had to be detached from his end of the rope in order to be lowered down the mountain. There was also the problem of suitable equipment. Ogilvie did have the spare 37 metre rope in his rucksack, and without it his task would have been made so much more difficult, but he did not have a great deal else and reliable belays would be scarce. The steepness of the face on which he had to work, the hardness of the snow and the patches of ice would make the task highly demanding and very dangerous, all the more so since his crampons did not have front points. It would not be difficult to have a slip which could quickly become a headlong fall. Ogilvie would require great powers of concentration and steadiness of nerve. He would also need considerable reserves of energy, both physical and mental. Lonely was the struggle which now must ensue.

Ogilvie's first task was to do something to secure the rope at the rock spike. He used his ice-axe to clear the snow just above the spike and exposed a rock bollard over which he placed a rope sling which reached sufficiently close to the spike to allow for the use of a karabiner to link the sling with the rope. Now, if the rope came off the spike, it would be held by the sling. The bollard, once cleared of the snow, proved to be a good belay and Ogilvie could have used it to lower the bodies, one at a time, down the mountain: the bollard was solid, a suitable size and, with Ogilvie working from below it, there was little chance that the sling would come off as the weight of the body being lowered would exert a downward pull keeping the sling firmly in place. But An Teallach was not going to be so obliging because there was the 30m cliff immediately below. However, about 9 metres away to the left as Ogilvie looked down the slope, the rock band was cut by a shallow snow gully down which the snow ran almost continuously and on which the bodies could be gently lowered. It was not possible to see what lay beyond the end of this gully but it offered the beginnings of a descent and there was nothing else as promising.

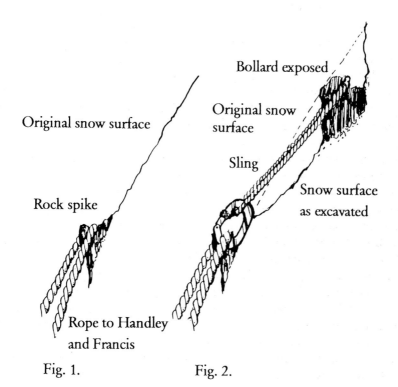

Bollard exposed

Original snow surface

Original snow surface

Sling

Rock spike

Snow surface as excavated

Rope to Handley and Francis

Fig. 1.   Fig. 2.

Ogilvie would need a suitable belay above the gully and in line with it. He moved over and searched for one. He wanted something quite secure, such as another spike over which to place a sling or a crack in which to drive a piton, but he could find none; nor was there anywhere for him to fix an ice-screw. His difficulties were made no easier by the relatively thin snow cover in that area of the slope. After searching for a little, however, he found a deeper patch of snow and was able to drive the shaft of his axe into it a distance of about half a metre. This was not as secure a belay as he would have liked, but it would probably be sufficient. On the other hand, it would deprive him of the use of his ice-axe in going up and down the steep, hard snow as he must in his efforts to lower the bodies; he would have to rely on his piton hammer which would be much less effective. He took the spare 37 metre light weight rope from his rucksack, uncoiled it and looped it around the shaft of the ice-axe. Then he returned to the two unconscious men.

Handley was lying about 14 metres below the rock spike and Francis about 20 metres so Ogilvie tied Handley, who was nearer to the ice-axe belay, on to one end of the line and took in the slack to minimise any movement from Handley's body when he carried out the next stage of the operation.

This stage was fraught with danger. Handley was now attached to two ropes: the one looped round the ice-axe above the shallow snow gully and the one that linked him, via the rock spike, to Francis. Ogilvie had to free Handley from the latter rope but because Handley was counterbalancing Francis, Ogilvie would have to act with speed to prevent Francis hurtling off down the slope. There was a risk that, when Handley was released from Francis, Handley would swing out across the slope towards the ice-axe to which he was belayed. To avoid this, Ogilvie took both ropes attached to Handley in his left hand and, with his penknife in his other hand, cut the rope joining Handley to Francis a little way below his left hand. Then, still holding both ropes in his left hand, with his right hand he quickly tied the cut end of the rope on to itself with a stopper hitch. This knot was just over 8 metres above the unconscious body of Francis. In this way, Francis was secured to the spike by making his rope form a large loop around it.

Then Ogilvie carefully swung Handley across the slope until he lay below the ice-axe and was in position to be lowered. During this process, Ogilvie had kept an eye on the axe and was relieved to see that it held firm. He climbed up to the axe, began slowly feeding the rope round the shaft and Handley slid down the shallow gully, over a lip of iced rock and out of sight. Ogilvie had hoped that he might reach a ledge before the rope ran out as this might enable him to remove the belay and use the axe to descend to Handley for the next lower. However, this did not happen and once the full length of the rope had been paid out and Handley's weight was still being taken on the ice-axe, Ogilvie had to tie the end of the rope to the ice-axe. He would have to make the descent with the aid of only the piton hammer; to make matters more difficult, he felt unable to use Handley's rope for any assistance as he doubted if the ice-axe belay would take much additional weight. He started down the slope, knowing that this time he would have to find a rock bollard or a belay for a piton or an ice-screw.

If the rescue had gone quite smoothly up to this point, Ogilvie was now to receive a bad jolt. It is best told in the words of his diary:

The snow got very steep, to about the limit where my crampons would bite and all at once they didn't. I shot over a small rock face some 10 feet high and landed on more snow below, face down. I got the spike of my hammer in and put my weight on it. I stopped. But I had dropped both my pitons and though I don't think I had hurt myself, I had had a nasty bang and felt exhausted. After that it was all much more of an effort.

He was approximately 110m from the bottom of the steep section of the corrie, the snow was very hard, his piton hammer was not the best tool with which to stop himself, and there was no one who would be able to help him if he came to harm. If he had not arrested his fall, he would have continued onwards well beyond the steep section and probably would not have come to rest until he had travelled a total distance of 220 metres or so and this would have represented a vertical height loss of 165m. Fortunate he was that he landed face down and feet first since this made braking easier. He managed to get the pick of the piton hammer with his weight over it into the snow quickly before he gained too much speed and he was able to retain hold of the hammer. If he had not responded so swiftly to the crisis, he might well have lost control and accelerated all the way to the bottom. However, if he had begun his rescue attempt with rather little in the way of belaying aids, with the loss of his pitons he now had even fewer. The incident revealed clearly how tenuous was his hold on the mountain and it must have seemed then a hostile and a lonely place.

Ogilvie, bruised and rather shaken, made his way down the remaining distance to Handley whom he found suspended against a small rock face. It was clear that Handley would have to be lowered a further rope's length and that first he would have to be anchored to the rock while Ogilvie climbed up and freed the rope from the ice-axe above. The pitons had gone but he still had the ice-screw. However, there was no ice suitable for its placement and he had some trouble in finding any kind of adequate belay. After some searching, he found a small crack and into it he was able to insert the ice-screw, partly by driving it and partly by screwing it. It would penetrate only two-thirds of its length and seemed quite insecure, but there was nothing else available. Handley still had a length of the cut rope attached to him and Ogilvie used this to secure him to the belay. Then Ogilvie ascended to the ice-axe and, because Handley's weight had been transferred to the ice-screw, he was able to use the rope as a handrail; he released the rope and descended again to Handley, this time with the aid of his ice-axe.

Handley was lowered a further rope's length from the ice-screw belay which, in spite of Ogilvie's worries, held firm. When the rope was fully extended, Handley was just below the lowest band of rock. Ogilvie climbed down to him without incident and noticed for the first time that Handley's ice-axe was still attached to his wrist by a loop. It is surprising that Ogilvie had not noticed it earlier since it must have been quite conspicuous. When he saw the axe, Ogilvie regretted having failed to notice it as it would have been most useful and might have prevented his having the fall. The snow slope at the point where Handley had come to a stop was steep and Ogilvie had to spend a good deal of time cutting out a ledge on which to place his friend. When he had done so, he used Handley's ice-axe and the short length of the cut rope still attached to Handley to anchor him to the ledge and covered him with most of his spare clothing. Ogilvie then untied the 37 metre length of line from Handley and, taking it with him, began to climb back up the slope towards Francis who was now about 59 metres above.

He reached the ice-screw belay and, as he was detaching the rope from it, the ice-screw fell out of the crack and bounced off down the slope, a clear sign of how insecure it had been. Now even it would not be available for lowering Francis. By then Ogilvie was suffering from the physical effort that he had made and probably also from the shock of his fall and he found the climb to Francis quite exhausting, even though it was not continuously steep. After all, since starting to lower Handley, he had descended 101 metres and ascended about 93 metres in conditions of great stress without relief or respite – and all this in addition to the energy he had expended excavating the ledge for Handley (over and above climbing to the summit of Sgurr Fiona during the morning which at that moment, if he had stopped to consider it, would have seemed a lifetime away).

When he examined Francis, who lay as motionless as he had after he came to rest, Ogilvie thought that he was dead, but decided to lower him to join Handley. In this respect, too, Ogilvie faced a situation similar to that which had confronted Kirkus in 1934: he should make every effort to save a companion whom he suspected was dead. The task of lowering Francis was made slightly easier than it had been with Handley in so far as he now had more rope at his disposal: the 37 metre line with which he had lowered Handley and the full weight No. 4 rope that held Francis to the sandstone spike. In separating Handley from this rope, Ogilvie had cut off almost 3 metres so that there remained about 34 metres, giving a total joined length of 71 metres. This length would have been quite sufficient to allow Ogilvie to lower Francis directly to the point where Handley was lying, but he could not do so because of the 30m cliff below. It would have been enough also, using an ice-axe belay in the patch of snow from where the first lower of Handley was made, to lower Francis on one combined rope's length to join Handley, but a belay there was none too secure so Ogilvie went higher and found a frozen rock, about a metre above the rock spike on which the rope had snagged and 3 metres to its left looking down the slope.

Iain Ogilvie.

He cut round this frozen rock, in the way that he had prepared the earlier rock bollard, and placed another rope sling with karabiner over it. This was the most secure anchor point which Ogilvie had found. He passed the line through the karabiner, descended to Francis whom he made fast to one end of the line, took in the slack by pulling on the other end and dragged Francis across the slope until he was almost under the belay. Keeping the line tight, he climbed up to the stopper hitch in the Number 4 rope, whose other end was still attached to Francis, and untied it. Remarkably this rope had remained in place on the small spike on which it had originally snagged and Ogilvie flicked it off this tenuous anchor and then pulled it through the belay he had set up using the rock bollard just above the spike to hold the rope if it had slipped from the spike. Abandoning the sling and the karabiner still attached to the rock bollard, he ascended to his new belay with the free end of the Number 4 which he passed through the karabiner and returned to Francis where, having taken in the slack in the Number 4, he attached its free end to the free end of the line and untied Francis from the line which he pulled back through the belay above. In this way Francis, still attached at the waist to the Number 4, was hanging free from the new belay about 21 metres above. As Ogilvie puts it 'It was a complicated process, but swinging him across was made easier as my new belay was a bit higher up.'

Ogilvie began to lower Francis using the doubled joined rope running from the rock belay and this allowed him to descend with Francis, steering him over the rocky bits. Ironically, soon after he had started the descent, Ogilvie saw Francis's ice-axe sticking out of the snow about 15 metres above where Francis had come to rest after the fall had been stopped. However, by that time Ogilvie was committed to the operation and it was too late to retrieve the axe. The first lower was brought to a halt after 10 metres when the knot linking the two ropes reached the karabiner at the belay and, of course, would not pass through it. There was no secure belay to be found close to Francis and Ogilvie had already lost his ice-screw and his pitons so he drove his ice-axe into some deep snow and belayed Francis to the axe. He was too far below the belay to flick the sling off it so he pulled the rope back through the karabiner which, along with the sling, he abandoned. Then, working from the ice-axe, he gently lowered Francis the remaining 49 metres to where Handley was belayed. He could not see Handley from his position at the ice-axe but he was able to locate the bottom of the rock band where Handley lay and the lower was stopped when Francis was beside Handley but still hanging on the rope. Ogilvie secured the rope at the ice-axe and descended with the aid again of the piton hammer. His diary says:

The last bit of snow, passing through the rock band, was extremely steep and icy and again, just before I reached Francis, my crampons failed to hold. I slipped a few feet, almost recovered my balance, but came against Francis's body, tripped and pitched over him head first down the slope. I had stopped with the piton hammer before but I had not been going head first. I might have pulled out of the fall with my axe but it was at the top of the rope. I tried with the hammer and it swung me round the right way up. I tried again but now I was going very fast and it was wrenched out of my hand. I was now helpless. I remember seeing two rocks sticking out of the snow on about my line. I waited for them. I hit them both and then seemed to go even faster. I wondered if the slope would ease off before reaching the patches of bare scree below. It seemed to take a long time and then at last I slowed down and stopped, head first, face down on the snow. I picked myself up and found I was still able to move about a bit but I was bleeding in a good many places and had clearly done myself a fair amount of damage (including a slipped disc in my neck, as I discovered later). I looked up to the cliff. It was a long way above me. (Tom Patey told me later that it was two lengths of his 300 foot rope. That is 600 feet on the slope. Perhaps 400 feet vertically.) I doubted if I could climb up to them. I certainly couldn't have helped them if I had.

In fact, the vertical distance of the fall was about 140m. Ogilvie was fortunate to emerge from the fall without even more serious injury. However, he was badly bruised and bleeding and soon other injuries were to manifest themselves. He must also have suffered from shock. Handley was safely belayed to the ledge and was protected as well as possible with Ogilvie's spare clothes. Francis, on the other hand, was still suspended on the rope; however, he was almost certainly dead and there was still a possibility that, if Ogilvie could reach some habitation and summon assistance quickly, Handley's life could be saved. If he was to give a rescue party a chance to save life, it must be able to reach the men before nightfall; otherwise the men might be hard to find and it was evidently going to be a cold night which neither man, even if still alive, could reasonably be expected to survive. Furthermore, Ogilvie knew that it would take some time for a rescue team to be put together, so scattered and sparse the local population. He was also aware that, in his condition and with so little warm clothing left, his own chances of surviving a night in the open were minimal. For their sake as well as his own, he must make all the speed he could to find help. However, this itself would be a major struggle. He was about 7km from the nearest houses – at Ardessie, a small group of crofts on the main A832 road. To reach them, he would have to descend about 700m by following, first in a north-westerly direction, the stream draining Coire Mor an Teallaich and then, half way to Ardessie and still following the Allt

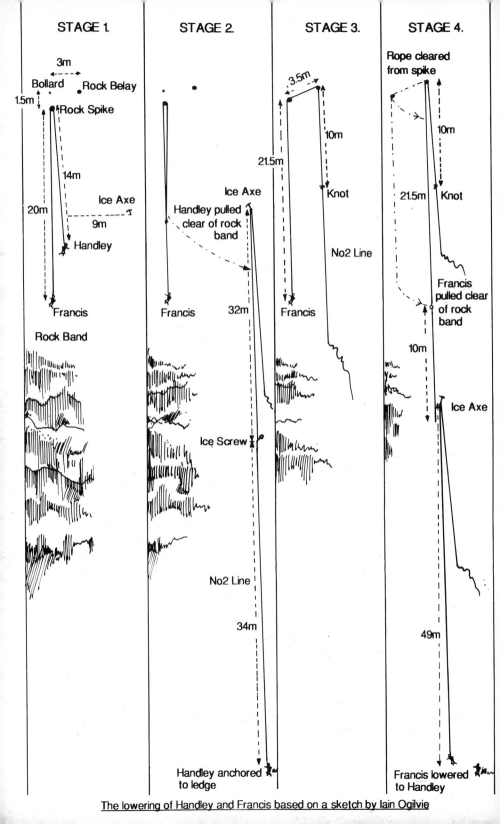

The lowering of Handley and Francis based on a sketch by Iain Ogilvie

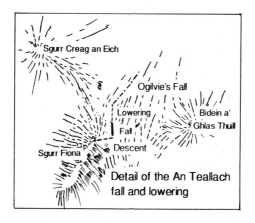

Detail of the An Teallach
fall and lowering

Airdeasaidh, turning northwards for the remaining distance. The ground
was rough and intersected by many peat hags. Except for the last 2km, there
was no path and Ogilvie was very tired, injured and shocked. To return to
the description of events given in the diary:

I set off, fairly easily at first but soon I started to go lame in my left leg. This slowed
me down and gradually got worse. Soon I was off the snow. Then I got to where the
valley turned north and got very rough, with lots of peat hags. I could step up on to
them but I had to sit down and slide down as I couldn't step down. I was getting a bit
exhausted. . . . I had reached a burn running down a bit of a ravine and thought I
could see a path on the other side so I climbed down to cross over.

This descent, which he made by sliding rather than by walking, must have
been painful, bruised and battered as he was, but he had to climb up the
other side and he was close to exhaustion.

I was just wondering how on earth I could summon up enough energy to cross and
climb up the other side, when I remembered the lump sugar in my rucksack. Sugar
has lots of energy. I sat down by the burn and ate handfuls of sugar. It all seemed very
quiet and peaceful and it was hard to realise what had happened in the last few hours.
After about ten minutes I forced myself to go on. It was surprising how quickly the

sugar had worked and I crossed fairly easily and got up the other side. . . . The path was only a deer track and gave out almost at once.

Characteristically, Ogilvie dismisses the matter briefly and without comment, but it must have been a demoralising disappointment. He stayed on the west side of the Allt Airdeasaidh for 2km and then he saw what he thought was another path on the other side, the side on which he had been originally descending. The terrain had become very rough on the west side so he decided to cross the stream again and, as previously, took some of the lump sugar before he made the attempt. It worked again. The diary takes up the last part of the journey to Ardessie:

A vague path came to the top of the 1,000 foot slope down to Little Loch Broom. I could see the road and some crofts below and this was encouraging but the path deteriorated into a steep-sided water course, full of boulders, and I left it and took to the grass. Sometimes there were steep little bands of rock and I had to sit down and slide but I could see the end now and I knew I could make it. I think I had known all the time. The doubt had been whether I could get down in time to get help in daylight. I crossed the road to Mrs MacKenzie's croft at Ardessie. I was down. . . .

It was 5.30 p.m. He had descended the 7km in two and a half hours, a most commendable achievement considering his injuries, his state of fatigue and the nature of the terrain. He must have been greatly relieved to be down and able to summon help. His two friends, however, were still high on An Teallach at an altitude of about 840m and the cold night would not be long in laying its hand on the mountain. Iain Ogilvie knew Dr Tom Patey who, besides being a world famous mountaineer, was in general practice in Ullapool, about 45km away and the nearest place of any size. He needed to telephone him to raise the alarm.

Unfortunately, Mrs MacKenzie did not have a telephone but she sent her young son to the main road to stop a car to take Ogilvie to the home of Mrs Ross who lived in the neighbouring hamlet of Camusnagaul, 1km to the east, and who did have a telephone. A car drew up but when the driver learnt that the man he was being asked to take was injured and bleeding he refused to help and drove off. Mrs MacKenzie told her son to cycle along to Mrs Ross and a few minutes later Mrs Ross's son arrived in his car to take Ogilvie to Camusnagaul. Ogilvie telephoned Tom Patey who arrived forty-five minutes later, having already notified the local rescue team, R.A.F. Mountain Rescue at Kinloss and the Ross and Cromarty police at their headquarters in Dingwall. He listened to Ogilvie's description of what had happened and the injuries sustained by Handley and Francis and took the map on which Ogilvie had marked the spot where the two men would be found. He did not treat Ogilvie's injuries, saying: 'Well, if you could get down from there by yourself, the district nurse can deal with you. I must get up in daylight.'

It was 6.45 p.m. and darkness would be falling within 2 hours. Patey set off, wearing an old pair of trousers and with his anorak tied around his waist, in the company of two others; he had his ice-axe and a 91 metre rope. They were followed by a team of eleven, composed of local people and police. Patey travelled with remarkable speed, aided partly by the traces of blood which Ogilvie had left as he struggled down, and moved ahead of his two companions. He reached the bottom of the face, 750m above his starting point, in about an hour, a measure of his fitness and concern for the plight of the two mountaineers. It took him a little time to find the men in the failing light but when he did they were dead from a combination of their injuries and the cold. By this time it was about 8.30 p.m. and he saw the rescue party approaching below. Darkness was close to hand and he preferred that the rescuers remained below as the conditions were potentially dangerous, so he worked the bodies to the bottom of the face in two lowers apiece with his 91 metre rope and the body of Peter Francis was taken down the mountain that night, arriving at the road at 3.00 a.m. Soon after the local team had begun its descent with the body, it was met by an eighteen-strong R.A.F. Mountain Rescue team from Kinloss who were on a training exercise in the area. Four of this team assisted in taking the body down while the rest bivouacked close to the point where the two teams had met. At 5.30 a.m., this group set forth to recover Handley's body which was reached an hour and a quarter later and brought down to arrive at the road at 9.00 a.m. Both bodies were then taken to Dingwall for formal identification. Iain Ogilvie spent three days being cared for by Mrs Ross and then his brother came to Camusnagaul and drove him home in Iain Ogilvie's own car. The tents and camping gear were brought down by a party of police.

Iain Ogilvie's effort to save the lives of his friends was described as heroic by the police and the rescue personnel, the local police regarding it as the most courageous piece of mountain rescue work of which they had heard. Dr Tom Patey, in his report on the accident for the Ross-shire procurator-fiscal, described Ogilvie's attempt as superhuman. Later, both Ogilvie and Patey were to have their respective efforts recognised: Patey received the Queen's Commendation for Brave Conduct and Ogilvie received both the M.B.E., in the days when it was awarded for gallantry, and the Royal Humane Society's Bronze Medal.

It remains to ask, and try to answer, the question, 'How did the accident happen?' The person best placed to offer an opinion on the cause is Iain

Ogilvie himself and he has the following to say:

As nobody saw the start of the fall, it is impossible to tell how the accident happened but we have some meagre evidence from which it is possible to speculate about a possible sequence of events. The evidence is as follows. Tom Patey reported that Handley's hands were unhurt as if he had made no effort to stop the fall. He wondered if he had had a black-out. Francis's hands were skinned and bleeding which showed that he had tried to stop the fall. After the accident, Handley's ice-axe was hanging on his wrist in such a way as to have prevented him from belaying on his axe shaft. Francis was seen by me to put his exposure meter into his rucksack on the top of Sgurr Fiona. It was not in his sack after the fall. After the accident, his axe was seen sticking in the snow on the line of the fall.

The possible sequence of events is as follows. As the initial slope was not steep, it is probable that they were moving together. This is supported by the way Handley's axe was slung. Francis may have stopped to take a photograph. At this point, Handley may have had a black-out and fallen. Francis could not get a belay on his axe shaft in the very hard snow in the time available, but he could and did try to get the pick of his axe into the snow with the rope over it and with his weight on the axe. Possibly because he was taking a photograph, he was caught unawares and acted too late. He continued to try to get the pick into the snow as he was dragged down, hence the state of his hands. Where they got their head injuries we have no evidence but it was probably when they crossed one of the rock bands. Francis could have lost his axe at the same time. Handley may have been held up for a moment on one of these bands so that Francis came past him and so was hung up below him when the rope caught.

This is one of a number of possible explanations of the accident. It is rather fruitless to consider all of them since each is conjectural. Ogilvie's suggested explanation attributes the fall to Handley's being rendered unconscious by the sudden onset of some unexpected physical condition. Handley was fifty-nine and it is certainly within the realms of possibility that something of this nature happened, particularly if, in spite of appearances given earlier in the day, he was suffering from his exertions. When Ogilvie saw them not long before the fall, they were moving together and, although they could have had a belayed descent operational in the five minutes that elapsed between then and the point when he saw them sliding down the slope, it is unlikely that the experienced Handley would have continued downwards with the tyro, Francis, if there was a need for this use of the rope: it is probable that he would have waited for Ogilvie who, in any case, might require belaying himself. Ogilvie is certain that they were moving together when the accident occurred, one reason for his certainty being that he does not consider the slope was sufficiently difficult to require a belayed descent. Also, as Ogilvie says, that Handley was found with his ice-axe attached to his wrist indicates that he was not belaying Francis at the time of the fall.

That the two men were probably moving downwards unbelayed has some bearing on whether Handley suffered a black-out. The experienced Handley would have been occupying the responsible position at the rear and it is to be expected that he would have been keeping a careful watch on his young friend for any sign of a slip – if for no reason other than that, if Francis fell, Handley, being roped to him, would go with him. This would apply also if Francis stopped for some reason, such as to take a photograph. Handley would have carried much of the rope in coils with little slack between the two men and so he should have had sufficient time to drive his ice-axe into the snow on the first sign of trouble and hold Francis. If he had doubts about being able to do so, it is probable that he would have used a belayed descent. With so many years of mountaineering in different parts of the world behind him, it is more than likely that he would have held a slip by Francis – and, for that matter, one by himself: that he did not could well indicate that he made no attempt to do so and that he had suffered a black-out as surmised by Patey. In the Register of Corrections Etc. the cause of death of both Handley and Francis is given as 'Intracranial haemorrhage resulting from fracture of the skull': they died as a direct result of the head injuries they received in the fall. However, although this was the actual cause of Handley's death, the fall itself may have been initiated by a black-out. There is, indeed, the possibility that the two men had left the summit of Sgurr Fiona in a hurry because Handley had become unwell. However, it is unlikely that they would have moved without trying to obtain help from Iain Ogilvie who would still have been within earshot and no attempt seems to have been made to attract his attention.

All this being said, there is still the possibility that the fall was started by Francis, a fall that Handley was unable to hold. There are two main ways in which the accident may have been started by Francis. The first is that, as the two men were descending, Francis caught the points of one of his crampons on the stocking or trousers on the other leg. This is easily done, especially by beginners, and would cause Francis to stumble forwards and, the slope being steep, he would be unable to recover his balance. In falling he would begin to slide head first down the slope on his front, accelerating rapidly, and in this situation his ice-axe, tending as it would to poke its spike into him, would be of little service to him. With his almost complete lack of experience in handling an ice-axe, he would find it very difficult to use the axe properly to turn himself feet first down the slope in order to use the axe to stop himself – as Ogilvie was later to do with his piton hammer when he fell for the second time.

The second possibility is that Francis found himself suddenly and unexpectedly on a patch of ice and that his crampons slipped. Ogilvie said in his diary that the snow on the higher levels was so solid that it would not take a footprint and it was necessary to stamp hard with the crampons to get a grip. It is probable that, on the slope down which the two men were moving, there were some sections of ice for which Francis may well not have been alert. Indeed, it may have been such a consideration that prompted Handley to use the rope for safety from the summit of Sgurr Fiona. The sudden slip of the crampons need not have been in any way serious and, if Francis had managed to remain calm, the crampon points may well have held. However, it would be so easy for him to panic and fall. In this case he would be more likely to fall on his back, feet first down the slope. He would almost certainly be able to turn over on to his front but by then he could have been gathering considerable momentum and have been unable to use his ice-axe to any effect. If any of the points of his ten point crampons caught in the snow, in all likelihood it would result in his somersaulting downwards and quite probably losing his ice-axe – indeed, he would be better to get rid of it in case it caused him serious injury. It is certainly possible that Handley, who was wearing nailed boots without crampons, may have had a slip but, with his experience, he should have been able to stop himself with his axe.

However, all this is speculation and the truth may be quite different. What is certain is that two men lost their lives and that one of these died because he was on a rope.

Index

(p) = passim